Education for Democracy: Contexts, Curricula, Assessments

Edited by
Walter C. Parker
University of Washington, Seattle

INFORMATION AGE
PUBLISHING

80 Mason Street • Greenwich, Connecticut 06830 • www.infoagepub.com

Library of Congress Cataloging-in-Publication Data

Education for democracy : contexts, curricula, assessments / edited by Walter C. Parker.
    p. cm. – (Research in social education ; v. 2)
Includes bibliographical references and index.
   ISBN 1-931576-25-4 – ISBN 1-931576-24-6 (pbk.)
  1. Citizenship–Study and teaching–United States. 2. Democracy–Study and teaching–United States. 3. Multicultural education–United States. I. Parker, Walter. II. Series.
   LC1091 .E3845 2002
   370.11'5–dc21

                                             2002007462

Copyright © 2002 Information Age Publishing Inc.

All rights reserved. No part of this publication may be reproduced, stored in a retrieval system, or transmitted, in any form or by any means, electronic, mechanical, photocopying, microfilming, recording or otherwise, without written permission from the publisher.

ISBN: 1-931576-24-6 (paper); 1-931576-25-4 (cloth)

Printed in the United States of America

CONTENTS

Introduction
    Walter C. Parker   *vii*

Acknowledgments   *xv*

PART I. CONTEXTS

1. Democratic Education and the American Dream:
   One, Some, and All
   Jennifer Hochschild and Nathan Scovronick   *3*

2. Citizenship Education: Anti-political Culture and Political
   Education in Britain
   Elizabeth Frazer   *27*

3. The Irony of Exclusion: Citizenship Education in Seattle
   During the Japanese American Incarceration
   Yoon K. Pak   *43*

PART II. CURRICULA

4. Education for Democratic Citizenship: One Nation's Story
   Carole L. Hahn   *63*

5. Issue-Centered Education for Democracy through *Project Citizen*
   John J. Patrick, Thomas S. Vontz, and William A. Nixon   *93*

6. Political Tolerance, Democracy, and Adolescents
   Patricia G. Avery   *113*

7. Teaching for Diversity and Unity in a Democratic
   Multicultural Society
   James A. Banks   *131*

8. Educating "World Citizens": Toward Multinational
   Curriculum Development
   Walter C. Parker, Akira Ninomiya, and John J. Cogan   *151*

PART III. ASSESSMENTS

9. An Assessment of What 14-year-olds Know and Believe about
   Democracy in 28 Countries
   Judith Torney-Purta and Wendy Klandl Richardson   *185*

10. Classroom Assessment of Civic Discourse
    David E. Harris   *211*

Contributors   *233*

Index   *237*

INTRODUCTION

Walter C. Parker

Liberal democracies depend on the knowledge, character, and imagination of their citizens. Some would add love. Martin Luther King, Jr., did so when accepting the Nobel Peace Prize in Oslo on December 10, 1964. He asked why the prize had been awarded to a movement that had "not yet won the very peace and brotherhood which is the essence of the Nobel Prize." He answered,

> I conclude that this award, which I receive on behalf of that movement, is a profound recognition that nonviolence is the answer to the crucial political and moral questions of our time: the need for man to overcome oppression and violence without resorting to violence and oppression. . . . The foundation of such a method is love. (1964, p. 1)

Short of love, many members of religious and other ethnic and racial minorities will gladly settle for tolerance. Tolerance assumes not love or even affection, but disapproval or dislike. In a democracy, citizens try to tolerate beliefs and lifestyles they reject and protect the right of people to express them. They might not go as far as suggested in the aphorism attributed to Voltaire: "I disapprove of what you say, but I will defend to the death your right to say it." Yet, the phrase expresses well the concept of tolerance, and it suggests that tolerance is, in a diverse society that is trying to be democratic, a virtue. Tolerance, as we learn from Patricia Avery in this volume, is an acknowledgment of everyone's right to basic civil liberties in a democracy, whether we love them or not.

Three assumptions underlie this volume. First, democracy is morally superior to autocracy, whether religious or secular, utopian or mundane. I mean liberal democracy generally, leaving aside the debate between capitalist and social variations.[1] Among actually-attainable ways of living together and making decisions about common problems and projects, liberal democracy[2] is simply better than the alternatives; or as Winston Churchill said, it is the worst form of government except all the others (Gutmann, 1996). It is better than the alternatives because it aspires to and, to varying degrees, is held accountable for securing civil liberties, equality before the law, limited government, competitive elections that are procedurally fair, and solidarity around a common project (a civic *unum*) that exists alongside individual and cultural manyness (*pluribus*).

That democracies fall short of these aspirations is a plain fact and the chief motive behind social movements that seek to close the gap between the actual and the ideal. Thus, Dr. King demanded in his 1963 March on Washington address not an alternative to democracy but its *fulfillment*:

> (W)e have come to our nation's capital to cash a check. When the architects of our republic wrote the magnificent words of the Constitution and the Declaration of Independence, they were signing a promissory note to which every American was to fall heir.... We have come to cash this check, a check that will give us upon demand the riches of freedom and the security of justice." (1963a, p. 1)

The purpose of the Civil Rights Movement was not to alter the American Dream but to realize it. *"Now is the time to make real the promises of democracy,"* King said. When a democracy excludes its own members for whatever reason (slavery, patriarchy, and the Jim Crow apartheid system being the U.S.'s most egregious examples to date), it is "actively and purposefully false to its own vaunted principles," wrote Judith Shklar (1991, p. 12). Here is democracy's built-in progressive impulse: to live up to itself. Typically, it is the unjustly treated members who are democracy's vanguard, pushing it toward its principles. "We know through painful experience that freedom is never voluntarily given by the oppressor; it must be demanded by the oppressed" (King, 1963b, p. 80). The Framers of the U. S. Constitution may have been the birth parents of democracy, American style, but those who were excluded, then and now, became the adoptive, nurturing parents (Parker, 2002).

Second, democracies are rare historically and inherently fragile. "To ask why democracy does not exist at a particular time or in a particular country is on the face of it a distorting question," writes historian Robert Wiebe (1995, pp. 9–10). "Its absences does not compel explanation. Nor does any nation have a special claim on its future." Appreciating this, actually coming to grips with democracy's contingency, allows us to recognize how remarkable was its arrival in the stream of time and place, how shaky the ground beneath it, and how uncertain its future.

The third assumption, related closely to the first and second, is that there can be no democracy without democrats. Democratic modes of association are not given; they are created, and much of the creative work is undertaken by citizens who share some understanding of what it is they are trying to build and sustain together. These citizens are not given either. They are not "natural"—born already grasping principles of democracy such as toleration, equality and impartial justice, or the need for limits on majority power. They are not born already inclined toward or capable of deliberating public policy issues with other citizens whose beliefs and cultures may be sharply different. These things are not, as is everywhere too apparent, born into our genes. They are social, moral, and intellectual attainments, and they are hard won. On this third assumption, we can appreciate the formidable challenge of educating democrats.

On the three assumptions taken together, educators are justified in shaping curriculum and instruction toward the formation of democratic citizens, and they are expected to do so. This has been the case for a very long time. Aristotle argued that "the constitution of a state will suffer if education is neglected" (1958, p. 332). A state's constitution was, for Aristotle, both its organization of government and its way of life. "The citizens of a state should always be educated to suit the constitution of their state," he continued, because "the type of character appropriate to a constitution is the power which continues to sustain it, as it is also the force which originally creates it." Two millennia later, Thomas Jefferson stated the expectation this way: "The influence over government must be shared among all the people," and for this reason "their minds must be improved to a certain degree" (1787/1954, p. 148). He argued vehemently but unsuccessfully for an amendment to the Constitution that would aid public education. Benjamin Barber (1993) compared Jefferson's idea of the role of education in a democracy to James Madison's:

> For Jefferson, the difference between the democratic temperance he admired in agrarian America and the rule of the rabble he condemned when viewing the social unrest of Europe's teeming cities was quite simply education. Madison had hoped to "filter" out popular passion through the device of representation. Jefferson saw in education a filter that could be installed within each individual, giving to each the capacity to rule prudently. Education creates a ruling aristocracy constrained by temperance and wisdom; when that education is public and universal, it is an aristocracy to which all can belong. (p. 44)

All that remains is to introduce each of the ten chapters of this book. They are collected in three sections: Contexts, Curricula, and Assessments.

In the first section, *Contexts*, are three chapters that locate education for democracy within particular national cultures.

Chapter 1, "Democratic Education and the American Dream: One, Some, and All." Few parents in the United States disagree with the goal of using state power to shape the education of children in such a way that they might have the "type of character" appropriate to democracy, as Aristotle put it, and "their minds . . . improved to a certain degree," as Jefferson hoped. Few parents, that is, take issue with curriculum and instruction that are aimed deliberately at the development of virtuous democratic citizens as long as other goals are not sacrificed to that endeavor. These multiple goals and their implications for highly contentious school practices—school funding, curriculum tracking, and differential group treatment—are the subject of this volume's first chapter by Jennifer Hochschild and Nathan Scovronick.

Chapter 2, "Citizenship Education: Anti-political Culture and Political Education in Britain." Elizabeth Frazer asks why there has been no tradition of "education for democracy" or "citizenship education" in the school curriculum of the United Kingdom, and she contrasts that absence to the presence of such a tradition in the schools of the United States. The most important set of reasons, she argues, lies in the lack of any wide consensus on or dominant account of the nature of politics, civic life, or constitutionalism in the U.K., combined with a marked preference for non-political "values education" over political education in the schools. This avoidance of politics, she notes, is undemocratic. In democratic societies, we all have to contend with strangers who may very well be antagonists, and the aim of citizenship education is to enable people to participate in these webs of democratic relations. Values, Frazer argues, such as justice and tolerance, are "necessary background" to these relations, and if they are corrupt or distorted, then certainly the political relations will be, too. "However, it is not the case that getting the politics right is simply a matter of getting the values right."

Chapter 3, "The Irony of Exclusion: Citizenship Education in Seattle During the Japanese American Incarceration." Yoon Pak examines a collection of classroom compositions written by seventh and eighth-grade Japanese American students at a public school in Seattle, Washington, during World War II. Writing to their homeroom teacher, the students reflected on the school assembly held the day before, Monday, which was the day following the bombing of Pearl Harbor on December 7, 1941. The content of the assembly expressed the Seattle Public Schools' progressive emphasis on democratic citizenship, tolerance, and intercultural friendship. A few months later, these children were sent with their families to prison camps in Idaho and California. Pak also examines a second collection of their compositions—letters written to the same teacher on the eve of their departure, in which they are struggling to make sense of their citizenship and their impending incarceration.

In the second section, *Curricula*, are five chapters that consider proposed and enacted plans for educating democratic citizens. Both descriptive and prescriptive works are included.

Chapter 4, "Education for Democratic Citizenship: One Nation's Story." When Elizabeth Frazer asserts in chapter 2 that there is broad consensus in the United States, unlike in the U.K., for the schools to teach about democracy and to prepare students to be effective democratic citizens, she is using as the basis for her comparison the study of the civics curriculum in the United States that is the subject of chapter 4 by Carole L. Hahn. This is one of 24 national case studies that were completed by researchers involved in the multinational Civic Education study of the International Association for the Evaluation of Educational Achievement (IEA). In this chapter, Hahn describes what U.S. students are expected to learn from civic education across four domains: democracy, political institutions, and rights and responsibilities of citizens; national identity; social cohesion and diversity, including attention to what students learn about discrimination against a range of groups; and the connection between the political and economic systems. Data for these descriptions were gathered from multiple sources: focus group interviews with students and with social studies teachers, a survey of the 50 state social studies curriculum coordinators, a content analysis of textbooks, and interviews with experts in the four domains. What emerges is the richest big-picture portrayal of education for democratic citizenship in the U.S. now available.

Chapter 5, "Issue-Centered Education for Democracy through *Project Citizen*." Citizenship educators perennially debate whether the most powerful civic education comes through the study of powerful content or through participation in powerful experiences, or some combination of the two. This is the knowledge/engagement debate, sometimes termed the transmission/participation debate. John Patrick and his colleagues note that a particular curricular approach called "issue-centered education" has always promised to balance the two emphases. Study and discussion of controversial public issues and democratic ideals are at the core of this approach. Still, they contend, the approach has its difficulties—mainly, getting off balance and falling into extremist swings. Here they evaluate a prominent middle-school citizenship education curriculum, *Project Citizen*, and argue that it represents the best of a balanced issue-centered approach.

Chapter 6, "Political Tolerance, Democracy, and Adolescents." Tolerance has to be learned and practiced, writes Patricia G. Avery. Intolerance is easier because we tend naturally to categorize people as belonging to "in groups" (us) and "out groups" (them). Education is necessary, therefore, for developing young people's understanding of what tolerance is and how it supports democratic living, especially liberty, justice, and minority rights. Avery reviews curriculum intervention studies that suggest tolerance can be taught. Successful curricula provide concrete cases in which civil liberties issues are at the forefront, students are encouraged to discuss multiple perspectives and positions on the issues, and the classroom climate supports the free expression and exchange of opinions.

Chapter 7, "Teaching for Diversity and Unity in a Democratic Multicultural Society." James A. Banks notes that citizenship education in the United States as well as in many other nations has long embraced an assimilationist ideology. In the United States, its goal was to fit students into "a mythical Anglo-Saxon Protestant conception of the good citizen," which required the subjugation, even eradication, of other races, religions, community cultures, and languages. Generally it was multicultural educators such as Banks himself, not mainstream educators, who brought attention to this most illiberal practice and described how the school curriculum privileged some students while alienating others and submerging their histories. Here Banks also considers insights from the Social Identity and Cooperative Learning literatures that suggest ways to improve intergroup relations in schools and classrooms. As he shows, such improvement does not "just happen" through contact and interaction alone but is the result of careful planning and deliberate action by teachers and principals. At the core of these efforts is the creation of equal-status cooperation among students of diverse groups along with the creation of superordinate group memberships. Both help mitigate pre-existing animosities while fostering new, shared identities.

Chapter 8, "Educating 'World Citizens': Toward Multinational Curriculum Development." I coauthored this chapter with global education scholars at Hiroshima University (Akira Ninomiya) and the University of Minnesota (John Cogan, the Principal Investigator on the project). We asked the question: Has the time not come to create multinationally, rather than nationally or locally, some portions of the school curriculum? In particular, would it not be wise to develop multinationally that part of the school curriculum that is concerned to teach young people to grapple democratically with multinational issues? Results from a nine-nation study are presented. They indicate that there are very difficult international crises coming in the next 25 years (e.g., a water shortage) and that students will need to be knowledgeable about them and skilled at deliberating solutions together across national, cultural, and linguistic boundaries. These are called "world citizens," and an issue- and inquiry-centered curriculum is recommended to help cultivate them.

In the third section of the book, *Assessments*, are two chapters that capture important dimensions of students' democratic learning through very different kinds of assessment tools. The first is a large-scale, multinational survey; the second is a small-scale classroom assessment guide for use in evaluating students' participation in discussions of controversial public issues.

Chapter 9, "An Assessment of what 14-year-olds Know and Believe about Democracy in 28 Countries." Judith Torney-Purta and Wendy Klandl Richardson report on the most comprehensive large-scale assessment to date of adolescents' civic knowledge, skills, attitudes, and engagement: the IEA Civic Education study. This study, foreshadowed in chapters 2 (Frazer) and 4 (Hahn), is a remarkably high-quality, multinationally-negotiated survey of democratic learning and participation in 28-nations. It involved 90,000 14-year-olds and 10,000 teachers. Readers are afforded a unique opportunity to learn how students are being prepared to take on the role of citizen in various democracies, new and old. Students' civic content knowledge and skill are assessed along with their attitudes about the rights of women and immigrants and the degree to which they feel free to express opinions in class. Readers can consider various models of civic education in light of these findings; for example, the relationship between civic knowledge and community participation (these findings suggest that explicit instruction in civics is likely to increase participation). And, of special relevance to the issue-centered model of civics instruction highlighted in chapters 5, 8, and 10, an open classroom climate for discussion was a positive predictor of students' civic knowledge.

Chapter 10, "Classroom Assessment of Civic Discourse." In the final chapter by David E. Harris, we move from large-scale assessment to a classroom assessment tool for evaluating students' performance in discussions of controversial public issues. Issue-centered education typically involves learning to engage in oral discourse on public issues involving value conflicts and other disagreements. Harris's assessment guide is powerful both for judging students' ability to engage in oral discourse on public controversies and for clarifying the criteria that define a successful discussion of this kind. That is, the guide simultaneously clarifies the curricular goal and helps students and their teacher determine whether or not their performance hits the mark. Both substantive and procedural criteria are included in the guide; students should be knowledgeable about the issue (e.g., they not only state opinions but offer explanations and analogies) and able to engage one another skillfully in a serious exchange of views (e.g., they invite others into the discussion and avoid personal attacks).

NOTES

1. The debate between capitalist and social democracy is important, especially now that the former is ascendant and nearly indistinguishable from globalization.

See the discussions in Bhagwati (1995), Hardt and Negri (2001), Mouffe (1992), and Rorty (1998).

2. Hereafter, for convenience, I use the term *democracy*. *Liberal democracy*, however, is more precise: *Liberalism* refers to civil liberties (individual rights), the rule of law, equality, and limited (constitutional) government, which includes limits on majority power. *Democracy* refers to the selection of legislators and executives by universal suffrage in fair, competitive elections. "Illiberal democracies" and "liberal autocracies" are among the alternatives to which liberal democracies are preferable. See the discussions in Zakaria (1997), Plattner (1999), and Young (1990).

REFERENCES

Aristotle (1958). *The politics*. (E. Barker, ed. & trans.). London: Oxford University Press.

Bhagwati, J. (1995). The new thinking on development. *Journal of Democracy, 6*(4), 50–64.

Barber, B.R. (1993, November). America skips school. *Harper's Magazine, 287*, 39–46.

Gutmann, A (1996). Democracy, philosophy, and justification. In S. Benhabib (Ed.), *Democracy and difference* (pp. 340–347). Princeton, NJ: Princeton University Press.

Hardt, M., & Negri, A. (2001). *Empire*. Cambridge, MA: Harvard University Press.

Jefferson, T. (1954). *Notes on the State of Virginia*. New York: Norton (originally published in 1787).

King, M.L., Jr. (1963a, August). *I have a dream* (address). The Martin Luther King, Jr. Papers Project at Stanford University. Retrieved October 27, 2000 from the World Wide Web: http://www.stanford.edu/group/King/speeches/.

King, M.L. Jr. (1963b). Letter from Birmingham Jail, *Why we can't wait* (pp. 76–95). New York: Mentor.

King, M.L., Jr. (1964, December). Nobel Peace Prize acceptance (address). In C. Carson & K. Shepard (Eds.), *A call to conscience:* The landmark speeches of Dr. Martin Luther King, Jr. New York: Warner Books (collection published in 2001).

Mouffe, C. (Ed.). (1992). *Dimensions of radical democracy: Pluralism, citizenship, community*. London: Verso.

Parker, W.C. (2002). *Democracy, diversity, and deliberation in the classroom: From idiocy to citizenship*. New York: Teachers College Press.

Plattner, M.F. (1999). From liberalism to liberal democracy. *Journal of Democracy, 10*(3), 121–134.

Rorty, R. (1998). *Achieving our country*. Cambridge, MA: Harvard University Press.

Shklar, J.N. (1991). *American citizenship: The quest for inclusion*. Cambridge, MA: Harvard University Press.

Wiebe, R.H. (1995). *Self rule: A cultural history of American democracy*. Chicago: The University of Chicago Press.

Young, I.M. (1990). *Justice and the politics of difference*. Princeton, NJ: Princeton University Press.

Zakaria, F. (1997). The rise of illiberal democracy. *Foreign Affairs, 76*(6), 22–43.

ACKNOWLEDGMENTS

My thanks to Series Editor, Merry Merryfield, for her invitation to conceptualize this volume and gather the chapter authors. I was fortunate to receive a positive response from each author I approached; consequently, this is a collection of exceptional quality. These authors are uniquely qualified to write on the subject of education for democracy by the depth of their scholarship as well as their diverse experiences and perspectives. I am grateful to them for their good work. Note that some of the chapters are adaptations of work previously published. Where this is the case, an acknowledgment is provided at the end of the chapter.

Part I

CONTEXTS

CHAPTER 1

DEMOCRATIC EDUCATION AND THE AMERICAN DREAM:

One, Some, and All

Jennifer L. Hochschild and Nathan Scovronick

> *Nothing can more effectually contribute to the Cultivation and Improvement of a Country, the Wisdom, Riches, and Strength, Virtue and Piety, the Welfare and Happiness of a People, than a proper Education of youth, by forming their Manners, imbuing their tender Minds with Principles of Rectitude and Morality, [and] instructing them ... all useful Branches of liberal Arts and Science.*
> —Benjamin Franklin (1749/1962, pp. 152–53)

INTRODUCTION

As Franklin believed it should be, the education of children is the United States' most important social policy.[1] Public schooling involves more people, both as providers and as recipients, than any other government program for social welfare. Its provision absorbs a larger share of the gross domestic product than almost any other social program.[2] It is the main governmental activity, both financially and operationally, at the local level and a central activity of all state governments.[3] It is America's answer to the European social welfare state,[4] to massive waves of immigration, and to demands for the abolition of structures of immobility based on race, class or gender.

THE GOALS OF PUBLIC EDUCATION

As the epigraph from Franklin also implies, this massive effort devoted to public education is intended to accomplish a variety of purposes. Virtually all Americans hold two broad goals for schooling that shape most choices for educational policy and practice.[5] First, education plays a key role in the ideology of the American dream—Franklin's "Wisdom, Riches, and Strength, Virtue and Piety, the Welfare and Happiness of a People." Most briefly, the American dream is the promise that all residents of the United States have a reasonable chance to achieve success as they define it (material or otherwise) through their own efforts and resources, and to attain virtue and fulfillment through that success (Hochschild, 1995). Equality of opportunity to become legitimately unequal is an essential part, though not the whole, of the American dream. From this perspective, publicly provided education is intended to enable individuals to succeed.

The second core value, Franklin's "Cultivation and Improvement of a Country," is a commitment to democracy or the collective good, broadly defined. By democracy we mean a governance system in which control over policy choices is chiefly vested in elected officials chosen through fair and frequent elections in which virtually all adult citizens may participate. Alternatively, citizens may choose policies directly through some fair and frequent electoral mechanism. In either case, the practice of democracy presumes a degree of civility, shared knowledge, the ability to communicate beyond face-to-face encounters, willingness to play in accord with the rules of the voting game, tolerance or even respect for disparate views, equal opportunity to attain full citizenship, a common culture, and commitment to the polity even if one's electoral choice loses. From this perspective, publicly provided education is intended to provide benefits for the society as a whole.

Surveys, campaign platforms, Fourth of July speeches, and other indicators of popular culture show that most Americans ascribe to the ideology of the American dream, and believe that democracy is the best form of government (Hochschild, 1995, chap. 1; McClosky & Zaller, 1984; Verba & Orren, 1985).[6] Similarly, the vast majority of Americans agree that schools should both enhance the chances for individual students to succeed in life and provide the skills and viewpoints necessary for engaging in democratic politics.

At various points in American history, and especially during the past decade, some Americans have also demanded that schools fulfill a third goal—responding to the claims of particular groups. This goal is based on the belief that members of marked racial, ethnic, religious, sexual or other disadvantaged groups cannot have the same chance to succeed or be full participants in the American democratic polity unless their group identity is recognized, publicly respected, and treated differently from that of unmarked citizens. Thus public education must provide distinctive benefits for children in particular groups, different from and perhaps at the expense of benefits to other groups, individual students, or the collectivity as a whole. This claim on behalf of "some" is distinct from the focus on the "one" of the American dream or the "all" of democracy, but it shares features of both of the core claims. It can appeal to those who seek success for their children, and it can resonate with those who seek democratic participation and the collective good. Nevertheless, it has very different implications and demands, and uses different means from the individual or collective goals of education. Americans show least support for this goal and it is the most controversial in practice.

In principle, Americans want schools to help individuals as well as to strengthen the collectivity, and some also support group differentiation. But in practice, anyone who reads the newspaper knows that endorsement of general goals does not translate into comity on when or how to pursue them. Let us examine the three values in a bit more detail before exploring the ways in which disputes among them play out in choices of education policies.[7]

Schools and the Dream of Individual Attainment

Good schools should and can help individuals attain success. Virtually all Americans share that belief. That shared belief does not, however, resolve all difficulties because "success" can have several meanings with different pedagogical implications (Hochschild, 1995, pp. 16–17). One form of success is *absolute*—reaching some threshold of well-being higher than where one started. Absolute success is, in principle, available to everyone. In schooling it would consist in teaching all students the skills they need to live satisfactory adult lives, such as literacy and numeracy, the ability to find and use desired information, the ability to plan and discipline oneself, and the pleasure of exercising one's mind. As that list suggests, enabling all individuals to achieve absolute success would be a triumph indeed; no society has attained it. The serious pursuit of this goal can be controversial because it can imply the provision of more educational resources to some students than to others so that all may have a chance of success regardless of their initial endowments or family context.

For most parents, absolute success is a threshold that they want their children to move beyond. This desire comports with a second, *relative* definition of success—attaining more than a comparison point such as one's parents or classmates. Relative success is egalitarian if it applies an equal standard of measurement to all, but it is inegalitarian in the sense that some individuals will do better than others. Most Americans assume that in a properly functioning system of relative success in schooling, some—but not all—children will achieve permanent upward mobility or in some other way be better off than their parents (they seldom consider the possibility of corresponding downward mobility or declines in satisfaction).

Some parents go even further, and expect schools to provide their children with an advantage over other children. That is the third form of success—*competitive*—in which my success implies your failure. A system of district boundaries and a method of school finance based on local wealth can, for example, create or maintain a privileged competitive position for some children. Competitive success might (but need not) imply initial equality of opportunity to seek victory, but beyond that starting point opportunities are to be taken and advantages used, not redistributed to those with fewer.

The pursuit of success for individual students is further complicated by different visions of the American dream, and thus disagreement over what schools should teach. Some share the Puritans' view: "The mind of man is a vast thing, it can take in, and swallow down Heaps of Knowledge, and yet is greedy after more; it can grasp the World in its conception" (Miller, 1954, p. 66). Children thirst for knowledge, and schools should nurture that thirst while teaching students how to slake it. Some are more instrumental, along with Benjamin Franklin: "In Europe, the Encouragements to Learning are ... great.... A poor Man's Son has a chance, if he studies hard, to rise ... to gainful Offices or Benefices; to an extraordinary Pitch of Grandeur; ... and even to mix his Blood with Princes" (Franklin, 1749/1987, p. 326). In this view, children thirst for wealth or power rather than for knowledge and schools should give them the tools they need to improve their status. The ideology of the American dream is itself agnostic on what counts as success, but its liberal neutrality can lead to disputes over whether teachers should be drilling students in the basics or encouraging them to follow their imaginations and let the correct spelling come later.

Schools and the Promotion of Democracy

Just as most Americans endorse some variant of the American dream, most agree that schools are a crucial locus for training children to become democratic citizens. "Democracy" is usually conceived very broadly, to encompass everything from republican virtue to participation in elections to neighborliness. Thus, schools are supposed to provide at least five collective outcomes.

The first is a *common core of knowledge*. Americans abhor the perhaps apocryphal boast of the French administrator that at 10:00 a.m. he could know just which page of Virgil all students of a certain age were construing throughout the nation. But they do generally agree that all students in the United States should end their schooling with some shared learning. They should know the rudiments of American history; they should be able to communicate in English; they should have basic literacy and numeracy; and they should understand basic rules of politics and society such as the purpose of elections and the meaning of the rule of law.

Closely allied with the goal of a common core of knowledge is the desire for students to graduate with a *common set of values*. Those values include loyalty to the nation, acceptance of the Declaration of Independence and Constitution as venerable founding documents, appreciation that in American constitutionalism rights sometimes trump majority rule and majority rule is supposed to trump intense desire, belief in the rule of law as the proper grounding for a legal system, belief in equal opportunity as the proper grounding for a social system, willingness to adhere to the discipline implied by rotation in office through an electoral system, and so on. They also include economic and social values such as the work ethic, self-reliance, and trustworthiness.

The *ability to deal with, if not warm to, diverse others* is a third collective value that Americans want schools to inculcate. At the time of the founding, the most volatile dimensions of diversity were varying Christian faiths and different views of monarchical governance. In subsequent generations, the list of things we expect students to learn to tolerate and cope with has lengthened to include differences by political and social ideology, class, region, race, ethnicity, gender, sexual orientation, and disability. Most people agree that the best way to teach mutual tolerance is to have students learn in casual contact with others unlike themselves; that is why public schools have always been under great pressure to admit all students within their duly designated district. Private schools were permitted to be parochial, but public schools were not. (The greatest exception to this point, of course, was racial segregation, which we address below.) Schools are increasingly expected to teach through a multicultural curriculum so that children will understand and appreciate each other's racial or cultural background as well as their own.

A fourth collective goal of schooling is *teaching democratic practices*. These include: following properly designated procedures, negotiating rather than using violence to secure what you want, respecting those who disagree, taking turns, expressing your own views persuasively, organizing with others for change, competing fairly, and winning (or losing) gracefully. There is, of course, always tension between maintaining educators' authority and teaching democratic practices through actually permitting students to make decisions. Schools and teachers negotiate this tension differently, depending mostly on the age and social class of their students, although they can never resolve it.

Fifth, Americans expect schools to participate in the broad social goal of *providing equal opportunity* for all children. Equality of opportunity is a protean goal; it is as important in the American dream of individual success as in democratic governance. We discuss it here because its collective implications require more change in schooling policy than do its individual implications (see our discussion below of school desegregation for justification). Most Americans now agree, at least in principle, that schools should offset some unfair disadvantages (such as disability), and should provide at least equal treatment to those with other social disadvantages (such as those occasioned by racial minority status, poverty, or lack of facility in English). After all, if unfair disadvantages into which one is born persist into adulthood, one is unlikely to be able to participate fully in public affairs. For some people that is a matter of simple injustice that should be rectified if it can be. Others calculate, more instrumentally, that even if they themselves do not suffer these disadvantages, they do not want their children to have to confront the specter of second-class citizens and to compensate for their social, economic, and political drawbacks. Thus it is in the interests of everyone for schools to do what they can to transform inequalities of birth into equality of adult citizenship.[8]

As with the American dream, the more specific goals within Americans' broad democratic commitment have never been fully achieved for all, or even most, students. And strong efforts to promote one or several of these specific goals are likely to conflict with strong efforts to promote others of them. But the deepest dilemmas for public schools lie not within each of these two values but between them, and among them and the third, most contentious, one.

Schools and Respect for Groups

Claims to distinctive treatment for particular groups have two roots. One origin is the demand for respect of the educational rights of individual children who were treated unjustly because of some ascriptive trait. In the nineteenth century, for example, reformers insisted that girls deserved access to public schooling just as much as boys did. In the twentieth century, *Brown v. Board of Education* held that once a state committed itself to a system of public education black children were unconstitutionally deprived if they could not participate in that system on the same terms as white children. In some cases and especially in the 1990s, such claims to individual rights have been broadened into an insistence that the child cannot attain an equal education unless the child's group is treated distinctively—for example, the claim that blacks would be better off if members of their own race controlled their educational system. Only that arrangement, in this view, can provide the same autonomy, respect, and cultural self-definition that whites have always enjoyed (Bell, 1976).

The second root of group-based claims is itself based on group identity rather than individual treatment. In the mid-nineteenth century, Catholic leaders vigorously opposed the Protestant pedagogy of the new public schools. They proposed either that schools be religiously neutral, that they teach Catholic doctrine to Catholic children (Macedo, 1999), or that the state provide public funds for a system of Catholic schools parallel to that of the Protestant "public" schools (Kaestle, 1983, pp. 136–181; Viteritti, 1998, pp. 664–675). A century later, some proponents of bilingual education argue that helping to maintain a foreign student's culture is just as important as teaching that student to study and speak in English.[9] These are examples of a more general claim: schools must not only include students with particular characteristics, provide for their needs, and teach other students to accept their presence, but also either change their practices in deference to the distinctive group or enable its members to be taught separately in accord with their own distinctive values (*The Good Society*, 1996).

Demands for respect for group identities are highly volatile. They emerge from an unstable mix of the desire for inclusion but on terms distinctive of and specified by that group, the desire to use public resources to be educated outside the mainstream, the desire to change the educational mainstream to accommodate the group, and the desire to be left alone or to remove one's children from the mainstream.

Some of these desires affect schooling practices but do not speak to the purposes of education. Teachers may be asked to change their pedagogical techniques to accommodate what is presumed to be the more cooperative style of girls or the more physically-oriented learning preferences of young African American boys. Other proposals for accommodating group distinctiveness do, however, affect the purposes of schooling. Educators may be asked to change the curriculum, to teach in more than one language, or to describe American history as a story of oppression rather than unbridled progress. In its most drastic (and rare) form, policymakers may be asked to provide a separate education for particular groups, as in all-male Afrocentric schools, "leadership training" schools for young black girls, schools with no technology for fundamentalist Christians, or schools for gay teens.

Group advocates' points of intersection or conflict with proponents of individual success or democratic training are not always predictable. What is predictable is that all of these efforts can expect sooner or later (probably sooner) to be discordant with the highest priorities of those focused on other groups, and with the priorities of educators and parents focused on the two most basic values.

PUTTING THE CORE VALUES INTO PRACTICE

Many of those who have thought most carefully about the purposes of public education have insisted with Benjamin Franklin that the core goals of individual success and democratic governance must be united and that neither may supercede the other. Thomas Jefferson (1819/1856), for example, offered six "objects of primary education," in order "to instruct the mass of our citizens in these, their rights, interests, and duties, as men and citizens":

- To give to every citizen the information he needs for the transaction of his own business;
- To enable him to calculate for himself, and to express and preserve his ideas, his contracts and accounts, in writing;
- To improve, by reading, his morals and faculties;
- To understand his duties to his neighbors and country, and to discharge with competence the functions confided to him by either;
- To know his rights; to exercise with order and justice those he retains; to choose with discretion the fiduciary of those he delegates; and to notice their conduct with diligence, with candor, and judgment;
- And, in general, to observe with intelligence and faithfulness all the social relations under which he shall be placed.

The first three focus on varied forms of individual success. The fourth and sixth focus on participation in the public arena. The fifth combines both goals. Based on these principles, Jefferson designed an elaborate system of public elementary and secondary education for all (white) children of Virginia, to be publicly subsidized for those who could not afford it.

Almost 200 years later, the Supreme Court echoed the framers' assumption that both individual and collective goals jointly and equally constitute the purpose of public schooling: "The 'American people …' have recognized 'the public schools as a most vital civic institution for the preservation of a democratic form of government,' and as the primary vehicle for transmitting 'the values on which our society rests'…. In addition, education provides the basic tools by which individuals might lead economically productive lives" (*Plyler v. Doe*, 1982).

Public opinion surveys similarly demonstrate Americans' commitment to using the schools simultaneously to promote individual success and democratic engagement. Almost everyone supports the mastery of basic skills, endorses teachers and principals who will "push students to ... excel," and wants every student to be given a chance to successfully complete a high school curriculum. More than eight in ten also agree that schools must "teach values such as honesty, respect, and civility," and believe that "the percentage of students practicing good citizenship" is a very important measure of schools' success (Public Agenda, 1998, pp. 23, 25; Phi Delta Kappa, 1998, pp. 17, 18; Public Agenda, 1994, pp. 43–49). Most want textbooks and lesson plans to teach racial and ethnic respect as well as gender equality; 70% want schools to teach that "democracy is the best form of government" (Public Agenda, 1994, pp. 43–49). Between one-half and three-quarters of Americans endorse teaching "the diverse cultural traditions of the different population groups in America" even when that implies "decreas[ing] the amount of information on traditional subjects in U.S. ... history" (Phi Delta Kappa, 1994, pp. 55, 56; *Time*/CNN, 1994, p. 54).

Finally, Americans occasionally endorse schooling claims of particular groups in ways that are inconsistent with their general verbal support for the goal of democratic inclusiveness. Thus on several surveys a majority think that "special public schools for young black males should be allowed." Similarly, on one survey almost nine out of ten women favor single-sex education for part of a student's career in school, so that girls attain the kind of information that will enable deeper knowledge and informed choices later in life (*Los Angeles Times*, 1991, p. 34; CNN/*USA Today*, 1994, p. 70; National Black Politics Study, 1993–94, p. D6d; *Redbook*, 1994, pp. 7, 8).

Some school practices can in fact foster the two basic values, or even all three values, simultaneously. Enabling the brightest students to learn as much as they can not only bolsters them as individuals but also increases the possibility that they benefit the nation through discoveries, insights, or leadership. Ensuring that all students are verbally and mathematically competent helps them to live satisfying lives at the same time that it makes them better democratic citizens. Teaching immigrant students to speak English makes their transition into the American workplace easier as well as reinforcing the cultural core so essential to a huge and diverse democracy. Showing respect for the identity of students outside the racial or cultural mainstream encourages them to achieve while teaching all students to be mutually tolerant. Allowing some children to be educated separately might enhance their individual success as well as respecting their distinctiveness.

However, amity and balance do not usually reign. In the actual practice of schooling, fostering what is good for all may divert resources from one or some; what shows respect for the identity of some may violate the convictions of others or distort democratic practices; what encourages success for the brightest or luckiest may deny opportunity for the weakest or most disadvantaged. When choices must be made and priorities determined—under pressure from demographic change, political demands, fiscal limits, global competition, competing values, or fear—one goal or another is likely to take precedence.

The history of previous tradeoffs among goals itself shapes the context within which new choices must be made. In the first decades of this century, for example, many citizens saw immigration as a frightening challenge to democracy and demanded that schools be transformed in order to "Americanize" these future citizens. In the 1980s, with many people fearing economic challenges from abroad and reduced chances for success at home, the emphasis shifted even more to individual achievement, and parents engaged in an intense competition for advantage in educational or fiscal resources. Most recently, demands for group respect that started as a drive for integration in the 1960s have sometimes been transformed into advocacy for separate schools or distinct treatment within common schools.

Over time, the combination of multiple goals, competing interests, and a fragmented governance structure has created considerable incoherence in policy and instability in decision making. As one goal takes precedence and then is replaced by another, some policies, institutions, and practices continue to function well in the new environment. Others become relics that create an inappropriate policy emphasis, use a disproportionate amount of resources, or otherwise distort the system. Too much bureaucracy may remain from Progressive era attempts to deal with demographic change; too much willingness to accept an unequal educational system or to jettison public schooling entirely may be the legacy of fear from the 1980s; too much separatism may be the consequence of the newest demand for group rights and respect.

INTERACTION AMONG GOALS IN EDUCATIONAL POLICY AND PRACTICE

We cannot in this chapter analyze the layers remaining from previous emphases on one goal or another, or sort out the many ways in which the values combine, coincide, or conflict. We will, instead, look briefly at several major policy disputes in which the interaction among values has crucially shaped schooling policy, practice, and outcomes.

School Desegregation

The elimination of de jure segregation was essential to permit equal educational opportunity for all children. In principle, it provided a greater chance for children of all races to attain success, enhanced the ability of the United States to become a fully democratic community, and insured that African Americans would be recognized as full citizens. Thus, the elimination of de jure segregation reinforced both of the values central to American public education.

Most Americans concur on the need for and even desirability of desegregated schooling. In the two decades after 1964, the proportion agreeing that black and white children should attend the same schools rose from fewer than two-thirds to over 90%. More than 40% of whites were unwilling to send their child to a school in which half or more of the students were black in 1964; that figure has since declined to fewer than 20% (Hochschild & Scott, 1998, p. 84).

In one important sense the practice of school desegregation did in fact promote the two basic values. The most careful studies of desegregated schools indicate that when properly implemented, the African American children involved showed improved achievement scores, more attainment of schooling, greater college attendance, and more adult participation in integrated jobs and neighborhoods. There is no systematic evidence that desegregation hurt the achievement of white children and arguably it made them more inclined to respect and live among African Americans as adults (Lissitz, 1994; National Center for Education Statistics 1998b, pp. 13–14, 62–63,112–113,160–161; Schofield, 1995; Sigelman, Bledsoe, Welch, & Combs, 1996; Wells & Crain, 1994). Most Americans now recognize the gains for blacks, and a plurality perceive gains for whites as well. In 1971, four in ten Americans thought desegregated schools had improved the quality of education for blacks; by 1996, six in ten did. The proportion agreeing that desegregated schools had improved the quality of education for whites increased over the same period from one quarter to almost one half. Similarly, in 1971, four in ten thought that desegregated schools had improved the quality of race relations (though almost as many thought it had "worked against better relations"). By 1994, two-thirds saw improvement, and fewer than three in ten saw worsening (Hochschild & Scott, 1998, p. 102).

School desegregation has, of course, been tried only in a limited way and was often implemented in a fashion that seemed designed to ensure its academic and political failure (Berg & Colton, 1982, p. 45). It has rarely been used to remedy de facto segregation or racial separation across district lines, even though cross-district remedies have in many ways been the most successful of all. Too often it has been imposed without sensitivity to the real allegiance of both blacks and whites to local governance, neighborhood schools, or well-known teachers and administrators. Frequently it did not sufficiently recognize that parents were worried that their children would be uncomfortable, unable to learn, or even physically endangered if they were in the minority in a tense situation. Legitimate opposition occurred for all of these reasons, among others.

Thus, in a different and larger sense the policy of mandated school desegregation has not succeeded in fostering the basic goals of education. White opponents argued that individual white children would suffer, and that the pursuit of collective goals could not be allowed to outweigh the pursuit of individual success. More recently, black opponents have argued that individual black children also are harmed, or at least that they are not benefitted enough to offset the costs imposed on individuals or the damage that desegregation does to the racial identity of children and the black community.[10] Despite support for desegregation in principle, the opposition to its vigorous pursuit, especially through busing, is almost as strong as ever. In 1988, three quarters of Americans rejected busing even if "white children were bused to top quality schools in the inner city and black children were bused to equally good schools outside of where they live" (NAACP Legal Defense and Education Fund, 1988, p. 21). A decade later, four in ten black parents and twice as many white parents were opposed to "busing children to achieve a better racial balance in schools" (Public Agenda, 1998, p. 57).

By the mid-1990s, about one third of black children were educated in majority white schools, but another third continued to attend schools that approach 100% minority (black and Hispanic) population. About a third of Latinos also attended schools that contain almost all non-Anglos. For the typical Anglo student in the mid-1990s, the population of his or her school was about 9% black and about 7% Latino (Orfield & Yun, 1999). African Americans' and whites' achievement test scores converged somewhat in the 1970s and 1980s (largely because blacks' scores rose more than whites' scores did), but the convergence has been arrested in the 1990s. There are no consistent trends with regard to the Hispanic-white achievement gap (National Center for Education Statistics, 1998b, pp. 38–40).

Thus school desegregation brought Americans part but not all of the way toward putting into practice their ideals of using schools to enable individual success and prepare for democratic governance. Mandated desegregated schooling may be the right policy for a democratic society; it may be the best way to guarantee the same educational opportunities for children of all races; and it may have been a successful method to enhance the chances of individual success. It is not, however, a viable policy option because individual fears as well as concerns about group identities have overwhelmed broader, collective values.

Equitable School Funding

Once it became clear that opposition to mandated racial desegregation would prevent most further efforts, reformers shifted their focus from the redistribution of students to the redistribution of resources. They argued that equal school funding, or at least funding at a level to permit absolute and relative success for most students, was essential for the American dream to be something other than a hypocritical cover for maintaining class privilege. If education had to be separate for most poor, often black, children, they wanted it at least to be equal. They believed that these children warranted the same training to enable them to pursue success as better-off children, and that poor communities have the same claim to public respect as wealthy ones.

As with school desegregation, most Americans agree, in theory. Since 1990, between 70 and 90% of Americans have endorsed an equal allocation of public education funds to all students regardless of their wealth (Hochschild & Scott, 1998, pp. 112–113). Results are similar in state-level polls that ask about support for particular measures to equalize funding. But as with school desegregation, many politicians who have tried to redistribute funds have been punished in the next election. Legislatures have found it very difficult politically to redistribute school funds except under threat of court order. Again, as in the case of school desegregation, the courts moved into the void. Of the 43 state supreme courts that have considered this issue, almost half have found grounds in their state constitutions to require greater equality in funding school districts. Some (for example, in New Jersey and Texas) have made such a finding at least several times or have sent legislatures back to the drawing board in order to see the court's mandates carried out. Even when the public has approved new funding formulas, the new ratios of funding have often proved insufficient or difficult to sustain.

In short, although a great deal more money is now available for education, and some places have achieved much greater equity, there has been an acrimonious debate for twenty-five years about the level of funding to which all children should be entitled and particularly about the obligation of all citizens to pay for the schooling of poor children. Like the controversy over school desegregation, the debate over funding equality has involved other issues, such as corruption, management efficiency, program impact, and especially the relationship between financial reform and achievement outcomes (Burtless, 1996; Corcoran & Scovronick, 1998; Ladd, Chalk, & Hansen 1999; Ladd & Hansen, 1999). But underlying particular disputes over school funding has been the conflict between enabling one's own child to achieve the American dream, defined competitively, and enhancing democratic outcomes for all Americans. Many parents, particularly those who worked hard to move to a district with better schools, see little reason to subsidize the districts they left. Many parents, anxious for the success of their children, have little desire to use their resources to level the playing field; privileged parents naturally want to pass on their privileges to their children. Thus while all adults accept responsibility to finance a basic education for everyone, there is little consensus beyond that on the proper relationship between the pursuit or maintenance of competitive advantage and the goal of equal opportunity (Reed, 1997).

Distinctive Group Treatment

As most commonly understood, multicultural education seeks to be inclusive and mutually respectful by exposing all students to the array of cultural heritages represented in the school, district, state, or nation. It is an attempt to redefine American culture away from that of the culturally dominant Anglo-Saxon Protestant majority, and thereby to enrich it. During the 1990s, most Americans came to endorse this understanding of multiculturalism. Typically, more than seven in ten respondents agree with survey questions asking if schools should "increase the amount of coursework, counseling, and school activities ... to promote understanding and tolerance among students of different races and ethnic backgrounds," to quote one unusually specific question (Phi Delta Kappa, 1992, p. 41).[11] This is a fairly new conviction for most Americans; the rapidity of its acceptance is a testament to Americans' belief in the need for mutual tolerance and respect in order to promote democracy.

Even thus understood, multicultural education is difficult to implement well. At a minimum, schools do not have time to do everything; if they teach the history of African Americans and Hispanics as well as that of European immigrants, they are leaving out Asian Americans and Native Americans (not to speak of variations within each category). The more inclusive school curricula and activities become, the sharper the exclusion of those remaining outside the fold. And absent a lot of thorny intellectual work, the more inclusive the curriculum becomes, the more superficially it treats all subjects. Finally, the more inclusive it becomes, in the usual sense of adding another cultural dimension to those already taught, the more difficult it is for teachers and students to retain any focus on the culture that was traditionally considered American—or any other common core.

But there is a deeper complexity, which moves the concept of multiculturalism away from promoting the good of all into promoting the good of some. Some advocates have altered their position from a call for inclusion and respect to a demand for separate and distinctive schooling appropriate to the particularity of their group. They often begin from a perception of power imbalance: "the nation's predominantly white educators have been slow to recognize that their own backgrounds—and the culture of the school—have a bearing on learning. And, rather than think of minority students as having a culture that is valid and distinct from theirs, they sometimes think of the youngsters as deficient" (Viadero, 1996, p. 1). To that perspective they add a distinct pedagogical philosophy, claiming that pedagogy must change to fit the cultural context of particular types of children, preferably by having a teacher from the same culture (Delpit, 1995).

The most assertive advocates of, for example, cultural maintenance programs for bilingual education, Afrocentrism, or fundamentalist Christianity may insist on the unique merit of their group's heritage and identity, and implicitly or explicitly reject the value of other cultures or the idea of a common culture. "Public school integration and the associated demolition of the black school has had a devastating impact on African American children—their self-esteem, motivation to succeed, conceptions of heroes or role models, respect for adults, and academic performance. Unless rational alternatives are devised that take into account the uniqueness of the African American heritage, ... compulsory school integration will become even more destructive, ... ultimately to the nation as a whole" (Wilkinson, 1996, pp. 1, 3). Most African Americans do not share that view (nor do most whites, not surprisingly). But almost half agree that African American students are not doing as well as white students because "schools are often too quick to label black kids as having behavior or learning problems," and in most surveys blacks no longer place a high priority on racial integration in schooling. Their priorities instead lie in higher achievement, safety and discipline, and sometimes political control of black schools by members of their own race (Henig, Hula, Orr, & Pedescleaux, 1998, pp. 69–77; Smith, 2001). About one fifth of whites also blame schools' behavior for black students' problems (Public Agenda, 1998, pp. 13, 20–28, 34). Thus a significant segment of the population is available to be mobilized by advocates who value group differentiation more strongly than they do, but who are concerned about cultural loss and frustrated by the failures or the discriminatory practices of some public schooling.

Other programs for separating students focus less on group identity and more on satisfying particular needs. Advocates of these programs typically begin with an emphasis on the core values of promoting individual success or enabling full participation in the democratic community. But they sometimes end up seeking distinctive treatment for a particular group of students if they come to believe that conventional educational practices cannot satisfy those students' needs. Thus, for example, some advocates for children with disabilities fight to get many more disabled children into a regular classroom on the grounds that "individuals of varying achievement levels and competency and behavioral patterns can learn together. Although they may learn different things at different times, their learning is enhanced by contact and interaction" (Brantlinger, 1997). But others argue that the goal of promoting the good of some requires their separation from all. Thus, for example, the Learning Disabilities Association of America (1993):

> does not support "full inclusion" or any policies that mandate same placement, instruction, or treatment for all students.... The regular education classroom is not the appropriate placement for a number of students with learning disabilities who may need alternative instructional environments, teaching strategies, and/or materials that cannot or will not be provided within the context of a regular classroom environment.... The placement of all children with disabilities in the regular classroom is as great a violation of IDEA [Individuals with Disabilities Education Act] as the placement of all children in separate classrooms on the basis of their type of disability.

Contests over whether and how to provide distinctive group recognition are played out at all levels of government. The federal Department of Education issues regulations on special education and bilingual education, and the Supreme Court rules on religion in the schools; state legislatures and local school boards debate the use of particular books in classrooms; principals and teachers contend over appropriate pedagogy and student placement; some parents demand to have their child included in all-black classes, and others demand to have their children removed from them. All of these disputes take place without regard to the bits of compelling evidence about the actual educational benefits of various programs and sometimes in the absence of any achievement data at all.

There is, in fact, almost no evidence on the outcomes of some forms of group-distinctive schooling such as Afrocentric schools or schools for gay and lesbian students. The lack of evidence is unfortunate but not surprising; few advocates, or opponents, seek systematic evaluations that might turn up distressing results. Even when researchers do seek dispassionate measures of outcomes of distinctive group treatment, many programs are too variable in quality or design to be compared, or the desired outcomes are too subtle to be clearly measured. Thus, for example, the evidence for sustaining many bilingual programs beyond the point of basic English proficiency is not clear, since "the major national-level evaluations suffer from design limitations; lack of documentation of study objectives; conceptual details and procedures followed; poorly articulated goals; lack of fit between goals and research design; and excessive use of elaborate statistical designs to overcome shortcomings in research designs" (August & Hakuta, 1998; Walters, 1998). For similar reasons, scholars produce contradictory conclusions on the benefits of separate classes for children with learning disabilities or emotional disturbances.¹²

Although there are relatively few advocates of group-distinctive education in the American population as a whole and relatively little evidence about their claims, they have a disproportionate impact on debates over educational policy for several reasons. First, their claims are sufficiently close to the core values that they cannot be dismissed as illegitimate, but they are sufficiently antagonistic that they do not fit well into most reform efforts. Second, their claims do not sort neatly into a consistent liberal or conservative framework¹³ or into a consistent demand for inclusion or separation, so educators must usually deal with the advocates of "some" one group or even one school at a time. Finally, a substantial part of the American public can sometimes be mobilized into support for distinctive treatment for some students, usually because they are frustrated with schools' efforts to promote individual success or the collective good.

Tracking

Tracking is the issue that brings all these themes together. Sorting students by ability group is almost universal, and children who are white or Asian, or come from upper class or professional families, almost always dominate the high tracks (Lucas, 1999, pp. 49–60). In many places, therefore, it is a race issue, like desegregation, or a class issue, like funding; it is by definition about the separation of students. Tracking may be the price paid for desegregation; in many districts, white students attend school with black students but rarely go to class with them. Tracking may also be the price paid to keep the children of the elite in the public schools; many wealthy parents will forego private schools as long as their children are educated separately in the high track and have access to the best teachers and the most resources. Finally, while bilingual education is about students whose language fluency may affect their ability to learn with others, and special education is about students whose disability may affect their capacity to learn with others, tracking is actually about the ability of all students to learn with others. In this way, it is a more fundamental issue than all of those we have discussed so far.

Tracking is different from most of the other controversies because it is also a matter of pedagogical practice and, for that reason, rarely the subject of action by the legislatures or the courts, except as part of a desegregation case. People genuinely disagree about the educational benefits or costs of tracking. According to much of the academic literature, however, the chief impact of ability grouping seems to be the educational disadvantage at which it puts those in the low tracks. Being in the high track is certainly preferable when the best teachers, smallest classes, and most resources are available there, and there is evidence that everyone would be better off in such a track (Gamoran & Mare, 1989). In the same way, being in the lower track when resources and expectations are low is not a prescription for success, and we have evidence that this, too, is the case (Oakes, 1985). In general, when the studies on tracking are fairly evaluated and the number of cases is large enough to deal with the impact of resource and other factors, much evidence indicates that tracking per se helps very few (Mosteller, Light, & Sachs, 1996; Slavin, 1990). With some exceptions, even the best students would be as well off in properly taught, heterogeneous classrooms.

We have witnessed not only generalized policy debates about tracking but also school by school warfare every time someone tries to eliminate it. It is difficult to eliminate for several reasons. First, tracking is compatible with the way many teachers have been trained, and it is very hard to teach well in heterogeneous classrooms without the proper preparation. Second, many parents were themselves taught in tracked classrooms and sincerely believe, despite the evidence, that it is the only proper way for children to learn (Public Agenda, 1994, p. 19). As we know, it is very hard to change schools in any manner that is a dramatic departure from the adult image of how they should look (Tyack & Cuban, 1995). Third and perhaps most important, tracking is often supported by elite or politically powerful parents whose children occupy the high tracks and who seek to maintain an advantage for them (Fine, 1997).

Like the other issues discussed here, this one involves matters of policy as well as of implementation. Tracking is more questionable when it is mandatory and begins in the primary grades than when it is voluntary and occurs late in high school. Tracking is less necessary, but also less pernicious, when students at all levels are given access to a challenging curriculum and good teaching. The harms of tracking can be ameliorated, but at root the tracking debate represents a conflict between a policy that is believed to be good for individual achievement, at least for those at the top, and one that is probably better for equal opportunity.

Although it is so embedded in practice, some districts have been at least partly successful in detracking (Shore, 1996; Wells & Serna, 1996). And on all the other policy issues discussed here, real changes have been made in the last fifty years. There is a much higher level of integration than before *Brown* as well as a striking transformation in the way schooling is organized in the South (Orfield & Yun, 1999, pp. 13–15). In part because of desegregation, there has been a substantial growth in the black middle class. School funding, similarly, is at a much higher level than before 1974, and in many states it is much more equitable (Murray, Evans, & Schwab, 1998). Children with disabilities have been brought much more into the mainstream, and parents continue to challenge the separation of disabled and other students when they believe justification for it is weak. National Assessment of Education Progress (NAEP) scores, although uneven, have shown improvement for most age groups in most subjects over two of the past three decades despite many more children with language and other problems. Black and Hispanic students have made the greatest gains (Krueger, 1998, pp. 30–31). Through it all, Americans have sustained a remarkable commitment to the public schools. The conflicts over education policy are serious, but movement on these issues is not impossible.

These changes have, to be sure, taken place in the context of a sustained prosperity that has made it much easier to dedicate more resources to education and to broaden opportunity. They have also been shaped by wider political and demographic developments. Yet in part they can be explained by the fact that Americans truly believe in the vision inherent in the American dream. Cumulatively, the changes have been remarkable.

ACKNOWLEDGMENT

This chapter is adapted with permission from the publisher from our "Democratic Education and the American Dream" in Lorraine M. McDonnell, P. Michael Timpane, and Roger Benjamin (Eds.), *Rediscovering the Democratic Purposes of Education* (Lawrence: University Press of Kansas, 2000, pp. 209–265). Copyright 2000 by the University Press of Kansas.

NOTES

1. Our deep thanks for her invaluable assistance to Smriti Belbase. Thanks for excellent suggestions also go to Rainer Baubock, Elaine Bonner-Tompkins, Thomas Corcoran, Jeffrey Henig, Christopher Jencks, Lorraine McDonnell, Richard Murnane, David Paris, Harry Stein, Clarence Stone, Michael Timpane, and the participants in a seminar at Harvard University. This chapter is an early version of our argument; the complete version is in *The American Dream and the Public Schools*, forthcoming 2003 from Oxford University Press.

2. About five million people, more than half of all local governmental employees, hold jobs in schools. By comparison, only about 1.3 million Americans are in the armed forces. The U.S. spends roughly $315 billion a year on elementary and secondary public education, compared with $190 billion for Medicare and $365 billion for Social Security (National Center for Education Statistics, 2000, p. 18; National Center for Education Statistics 1998a, Table 4; U.S. Department of Commerce, 1998, Tables 251, 543, and 582).

3. In 1996, local governments spent $292 billion on education (including higher education), compared with $42 billion on hospitals, $38 billion on police, and $33 billion on public welfare (http://www.census.gov/govs/estimate/96stlus.txt).

Almost a quarter of all state expenditures go to K-12 schools (National Association of State Budget Officers, 1999, p. 12).

4. In 1994, for example, the United States spent $5,944 per student in elementary and secondary education. Among the G-7 countries, the next highest was Germany at $5,262 per student. The lowest in this group was the United Kingdom, at $3,914 per student (National Center for Education Statistics, 1998c, Table 56-4).

5. "Education" here is elementary and secondary schooling that is universal, mandatory, and directly provided or otherwise ensured by public authorities. We do not address private or religious schools, college or postgraduate schooling, vocational training, preschool or after-school child care, or other such programs.

6. Many Americans who do not believe that the values of the American dream or of democratic governance are actually practiced are among those most committed to the values (Hochschild, 1995; Huntington, 1981).

7. Analysts who share our core framing that disputes over educational pedagogy and policy are really disputes over the nature and priority of a few core values, include Cuban (1998); Labaree (1997); Gutmann (1987); and Paris (1995).

8. Economic purposes of education, official and unofficial, are outside our discussion.

9. "The loss of language ... causes [children] to be cut off from their past and their heritage.... A sense of group belonging ... is badly needed in today's American schools which are mainly Eurocentric, competitive, individualistic, and materialistic" (Pewewardy, 1997, p. 2).

10. In an 1998 survey, only half of blacks and 28% of whites said that it was "very important" that their child's school be racially integrated. Similarly, 82% chose "raising academic standards and achievement" over "more diversity and integration" as their preferred priority for their children's school (Public Agenda, 1998, pp. 2, 13).

11. Typically, the less specific the query and the more generic its focus on "teaching respect for people of different racial and ethnic groups," the higher the rate of support, which sometimes reaches 90% or more.

12. Heller, Holtzman, and Messick (1982) found special education classes to be "ineffective and discriminatory," and Baker, Wang, and Walberg (1994) find that inclusion in regular classrooms leads to academic and social benefits for disabled and special needs children. However, Kavale (1990), Carlberg and Kavale (1980), and Sindelar and Deno (1979) find that separation improves the academic achievement of learning disabled and emotionally disturbed children.

13. Fundamentalist Christian requests for curriculum changes are on the conventionally-defined right; schools for gay and lesbian students or Afrocentric schools for black boys are on the conventionally-defined left. No proposal for distinctive group treatment is "liberal," as conventionally understood. In contrast, one can plausibly begin with the assumption that people concerned about individual success will be more conservative in conventional terms than will people concerned about the community as a whole.

REFERENCES

August, D., & Hakuta, K. (Eds.). (1998). *Educating language-minority children.* Washington DC: National Academy Press.

Baker, E., Wang, M., & Walberg H. (1994). The effects of inclusion on learning. *Educational Leadership, 52*, 4.

Bell, D. (1976). Serving two masters: Integration ideals and client interests in school desegregation litigation. *Yale Law Journal, 85*, 470–516.

Berg, W., & Colton, D. (1982). Budgeting for desegregation in urban school systems. *Integrated Education, 20*, 40–48.

Brantlinger, E. (1997). Using ideology: Cases on nonrecognition of the politics of research and practice in special education. *Review of Educational Research, 67*, 425–459.

Burtless, G. (Ed.). (1996). *Does money matter?: The effect of school resources on student achievement and adult success.* Washington DC: Brookings Institution.

CNN/U.S.A. Today. (1994, April 22–24). Poll conducted by the Gallup Organization.

Carlberg, C., & Kavale, K. (1980). The efficacy of special versus regular class placement for exceptional children: A meta-analysis. *Journal of Special Education, 14*, 295–309.

Corcoran, T., & Scovronick, N. (1998). More than equal: New Jersey's Quality Education Act. In M. Gittell (Ed.), *Strategies for school equity: Creating productive schools in a just society* (pp. 53–69). New Haven, CT: Yale University Press.

Cuban, L. (1998, January 28). A tale of two schools. *Education Week*, p. 48.

Delpit, L. (1995). *Other people's children: Cultural conflict in the classroom.* New York: New Press.

Fine, M. (1997). Communities of difference: A critical look at desegregated spaces created for and by youth. *Harvard Educational Review, 67*, 247–284.

Franklin, B. (1962). Constitutions of the publick academy in the city of Philadelphia. In J. Best (Ed.), *Benjamin Franklin on education* (pp.152–158). New York: Teachers College Press (originally published 1749).

Franklin, B. (1987). Proposals relating to the education of youth in Pennsylvania. In J.A. Leo Lemay (Ed.), *Writings* (pp. 323–344). New York: Library of America (originally published 1749).

Gamoran, A., & Mare. R. (1989). Secondary school tracking and educational inequality: Compensation, reinforcement, or neutrality? *American Journal of Sociology, 94*, 1146–1183.

The Good Society. (1996, Spring). *Symposium on group rights* (pp. 1–37). College Park: Committee on the Political Economy of the Good Society.

Gutmann, A. (1987). *Democratic education.* Princeton NJ: Princeton University Press.

Heller, K., Holtzman, W., & Messick, S. (1982). *Placing children in special education: A strategy for equity.* Washington, DC: National Academy of Sciences Press.

Henig, J., Hula, R., Orr, M., & Pedescleaux, D. (1999). *The color of school reform: Race, politics, and the challenge of urban education.* Princeton, NJ: Princeton University Press.

Hochschild, J. (1995). *Facing up to the American dream: Race, class, and the soul of the nation.* Princeton, NJ: Princeton University Press.

Hochschild, J., & Scott, B. (1998). The polls—trends: Governance and reform of public education in the United States. *Public Opinion Quarterly, 62*, 79–120.

Huntington, S. (1981). *American politics: The promise of disharmony.* Cambridge, MA: Harvard University Press.

Jefferson, T. (1856). Report of the Commissioners appointed to fix the site of the University of Virginia &c. In *Early History of the University of Virginia, as Contained in the Letters of Thomas Jefferson and Joseph Cabell* (pp. 432–447). Richmond: J.W. Randolph (originally published in 1818).

Kaestle, C. (1983). *Pillars of the Republic.* New York: Hill and Wang.

Kavale, K. (1990). Effectiveness of special education. In C. Reynolds & T. Gutkin (Eds.), *The handbook of school psychology* (2nd ed., pp. 868–98). New York: Wiley.

Krueger, A. (1998, March). Reassessing the view that American schools are broken. *FRBNY Economic Policy Review,* pp. 29–43.

Labaree, D. (1997). *How to succeed in school without really learning.* New Haven, CT: Yale University Press.

Ladd, H, Chalk, R., & Hansen, J. (1999). *Equity and adequacy in education finance.* Washington DC: National Academy Press.

Ladd, H., & Hansen, J. (1999). *Making money matter: Financing America's schools.* Washington, DC: National Academy Press.

Learning Disabilities Association of America. (1993). Inclusion, position paper. (http://www.ldanatl.org/positions/inclusion.html).

Lissitz, R. (1994). Assessment of student performance and attitude, year iv—1994, Report submitted to Voluntary Interdistrict Coordinating Council, St. Louis, Missouri.

Los Angeles Times. Poll conducted Sept. 21–25, 1991.

Lucas, S. (1999). *Tracking inequality: Stratification and mobility in American high schools.* New York: Teachers College Press.

Macedo, S. (1999). *Diversity and distrust: Civic education in a multicultural democracy.* Cambridge, MA: Harvard University Press.

McClosky, H., & Zaller, J. (1984). *The American ethos: Public attitudes toward capitalism and democracy.* Cambridge, MA: Harvard University Press.

Miller, P. (1954). *The New England mind: The seventeenth century.* Cambridge, MA: Harvard University Press.

Mosteller, F., Light, R., & Sachs, J. (1996). Sustained inquiry in education: Lessons from skill grouping and class size. *Harvard Educational Review, 66,* 797–842.

Murray, S., Evans, W., & Schwab, R. (1998). Education-finance reform and the distribution of education resources. *American Economic Review, 88,* 789–812.

NAACP Legal Defense and Education Fund. (1988). *Unfinished agenda on race.* Poll conducted by Louis Harris and Associates, June 3-Sept. 12, 1988.

National Association of State Budget Officers. (1999). *State expenditures report 1998.* Washington, DC: National Association of State Budget Officers.

National Black Politics Study. (1993–94). Michael Dawson and Ronald Brown, principal investigators. Ann Arbor: University of Michigan, ICPSR.

National Center for Education Statistics. (1998a). *The digest of education statistics 1998.* Washington, DC: U.S. Department of Education.

National Center for Education Statistics. (1998b). *NAEP 1999 trends in academic progress.* Washington, DC: U.S. Department of Education.

National Center for Education Statistics. (1998c). *The condition of education: 1998.* Washington, DC: U.S. Government Printing Office.

National Center for Education Statistics. (2000). *State profiles of public elementary and secondary education, 1996–97.* Washington, DC: U.S. Department of Education.

Oakes, J. (1985). *Keeping track: How schools structure inequality.* New Haven, CT: Yale University Press.
Orfield, G., & Yun, J. (1999). *Resegregation in American schools.* Cambridge, MA: Harvard University, The Civil Rights Project.
Paris, D. (1995). *Ideology and educational reform: Themes and theories in public education.* Boulder, CO: Westview Press.
Pewewardy, C. (1997, January 20). Melting pot, salad bowl, multicultural mosaic, crazy quilt, or Indian stew. *Indian Country Today,* p. A7.
Phi Delta Kappa. (1992). Attitudes toward the public schools 1992. Survey conducted by the Gallup Organization, April 23-May 14, 1992.
Phi Delta Kappa. (1994). Attitudes toward the public schools 1994. Survey conducted by the Gallup Organization, May 10-June 8, 1994.
Phi Delta Kappa. (1998). Attitudes toward the public schools 1998. Survey conducted by the Gallup Organization, June 5–23, 1998.
Plyler v. Doe, 80–1538 U.S. 102S. Ct. 2382 (1982).
Public Agenda. (1994). *First things first: What Americans expect from the public schools.* New York: Public Agenda Foundation.
Public Agenda. (1998). *Time to move on: An agenda for public schools survey.* New York: Public Agenda Foundation.
Redbook. (1994). *Redbook Poll.* Conducted by E.D.K. Associates, Feb.7–10, 1994.
Reed, D. (1997). *Court-ordered school finance equalization: Judicial activism and democratic opposition.* Georgetown University, Department of Political Science, www.ed.gov/NCES/pubs97/9753g.html.
Schofield, J. (1995). Review of research on school desegregation's impact on elementary and secondary school students. In J. Banks & C. McGee Banks (Eds.), *Handbook on multicultural education* (pp. 597–616). New York: Macmillan Publishing.
Shore, A. (1996). *Detracking: The politics of creating heterogeneous ability classrooms.* Princeton, NJ: Princeton University, Woodrow Wilson School of Public and International Affairs, Senior Thesis.
Sigelman, L, Bledsoe, T., Welch, S., & Combs, M. (1996). Making contact? Black-white social interaction in an urban setting. *American Journal of Sociology, 101,* 1306–1332.
Sindelar, P., & Deno, S. (1979). The effectiveness of resource programming. *Journal of Special Education, 12,* 149–177.
Slavin, R. (1990). *Achievement effects of ability grouping in secondary schools: a best-evidence synthesis.* Madison: National Center on Effective Secondary Schools.
Smith, S. (2001). *Boom for whom? Education, desegregation, and development in Charlotte.* Charlotte, NC: Winthrop University, Department of Political Science, book manuscript.
Time/CNN. (1994). Poll conducted by Yankelovitch Partners, Inc., Dec. 7–8, 1994.
Tyack, D., & Cuban, L. (1995). *Tinkering toward utopia: A century of public school reform.* Cambridge, MA: Harvard University Press.
U.S. Department of Commerce. (1998). *Statistical abstract of the United States, 1998.* Washington, DC: U.S. Department of Commerce.
Verba, S., & Orren, G. (1985). *Equality in America: the view from the top.* Cambridge, MA: Harvard University Press.

Viadero, D. (1996, April 10). Culture clash. *Education Week*, p. 1.
Viteritti, J. (1998). Blaine's wake: School choice, the first amendment, and state constitutional law. *Harvard Journal of Law and Public Policy, 21*, 657–718.
Walters, L. (1998). The bilingual education debate. *Harvard Education Letter, 14*(3), 1–4.
Wells, A., & Crain, R. (1994). Perpetuation theory and the long-term effects of school desegregation. *Review of Educational Research, 64*, 531–555.
Wells, A., & Serna, I. (1996). The politics of culture: Understanding local political resistance to detracking in racially mixed schools. *Harvard Educational Review, 66*, 93–118.
Wilkinson, D. (1996). Integration dilemmas in a racist culture. *Society, 33*, 27–31.

CHAPTER 2

CITIZENSHIP EDUCATION:

Anti-political Culture and Political Education in Britain

Elizabeth Frazer

INTRODUCTION

In this chapter I discuss reasons why there has been no well established tradition of "education for citizenship," "education for democracy," or "political education" in United Kingdom (U.K.) schools' curriculum. The most important set of reasons, I argue, lies in the lack of any wide assent to, consensus on, or even well articulated dominant account of the nature of politics, civic life, or the constitution.

Several constituents of this dissensus are salient. One is the weakness of the discourse or ideal of citizenship in U.K. political culture and institutions. A second is the fact that with the discrediting of a (crudely speaking) "Whig" view of British history no very robust conception of political processes has been substituted for it in history teaching in schools. Third, even though politics is construed only vaguely, nevertheless its negative connotations are extremely powerful. This factor is connected, I believe, with the fact that in the course of recent discussions about "citizenship education" and "education for democracy" commentators from markedly different political and pedagogical positions have argued that the important thing is not education in politics but education in values.

Nick Tate (then Chief Executive of the England and Wales Schools Curriculum and Assessment Authority, now Chief Executive of the Qualifications and Curriculum Authority which has replaced it) has been personally identified with the promotion of "values education" and "moral and spiritual education" in schools. In a speech on the subject of "education for citizenship" he linked the "promotion of moral reasoning" and consideration of "core values and virtues" to basic knowledge of history, geography and economy, but steadfastly avoided mentioning either "politics" or "citizenship" (Citizenship Foundation, 1997, pp.17–20). Richard Pring, Professor of Education at the University of Oxford has taken a different argumentative route to the same conclusion. Pring (1999) argues against any "instrumentalist" approach to education at all: "education for citizenship" like "education for parenthood" or "for work" or "against drugs" misses the educational point which is to foster students' capacities for knowledge, for reason and for independence. "Education for citizenship" is particularly suspicious when it is legislated for by a government with unprecedented levels of centralized control over curriculum, teaching methods, assessment and the governance of schools. Instead, according to this view, education should itself be democratic in its structures and pedagogy. "Democratic education" in the humanities would enable people to acquire the ability to reason about "issues of supreme political importance: sexual relations, social justice, the use of violence, the respect (or disrespect) for authority, racism and so on. . . . There is no need for a subject set apart" (p. 81).

It is my contention in this chapter that the emphasis on "values," in the U.K. context, is an explicitly depoliticising move in the debate about political education.

"CITIZENSHIP EDUCATION" IN RECENT BRITISH GOVERNMENT POLICY

In the last two decades there has been a steady stream of projects with the aim of having education for citizenship and democracy taken seriously in schools and other educational institutions, such as youth clubs (e.g., British Youth Council, 1986; Citizenship Foundation, 1997; Commission on Citizenship, 1990; Fogelman, 1991; John, 1991; Lansdown, 1995; Lynch, 1992; Review Group on the Youth Service in England, 1982; Smith, 1989; Smith, Southworth, & Wilson, 1985; Williamson, 1997). Promoters of this educational effort must have been pleased when "citizenship" was named as a "cross-curricular theme" in the National Curriculum and curriculum guidance was drawn up (National Curriculum Council, 1990). However, citizenship went the way of all attempts to institutionalize political education in previous decades, and, indeed, the way of all cross-curricular themes (although one recent commentator remarks that it does seem to have been the one that was ignored most often! [Davies, 1999]). A survey of how, if at all, "citizenship education" was being delivered in schools, conducted in 1989 as the curriculum guidance was being drawn up, elicited reports of volunteer projects and general studies sessions—courses that are notably light on political content (Fogelman, 1991, 1997). In the last decade there have been debates about "values education," concern about the aims and objectives of "personal and social education," the promotion (and denigration) of sex education, legal education, and environmental awareness, and official enthusiasm for "moral and spiritual education" in schools (Schools Curriculum and Assessment Authority, 1995; Schools Curriculum and Assessment Authority, 1996).

After all this determined evasion of "politics" the Labour government's white paper published two months after they came into office seemed to strike a distinctive note (Secretary of State for Education and Employment, 1997). It expressed a determination that schools should "help to ensure that young people feel that they have a stake in our society and the community in which they live by teaching them the nature of democracy and the duties, responsibilities and rights of citizens" (Secretary of State for Education and Employment, 1997, p. 63). It identifies citizenship education as "part of schools' wider provision for personal and social education, which helps more broadly give pupils a strong sense of personal responsibility and of their duties toward others" (p. 63). But it explicitly emphasizes that "citizenship" is not exhausted by "values" or "moral and spiritual" or "personal and social" education. "Citizenship" is a specific issue which, it is implied, has been left "undeveloped" (p. 62). The white paper committed the Department of Education and Employment to setting up "an advisory group to discuss citizenship and the teaching of democracy in our schools." Its purpose was

> to provide advice on effective education for citizenship in schools—to include the nature and practices of participation in democracy; the duties, responsibilities and rights of individuals as citizens; and the value to individuals and society of community activity. (Advisory Group on Citizenship, 1998, p. 4)

Its terms of reference mentioned:

> the teaching of civics, participative democracy and citizenship, and may be taken to include some understanding of democratic practices and institutions, including parties, pressure groups and voluntary bodies, and the rela-

tionship of formal political activity with civic society in the context of the U.K., Europe and the wider world. (p. 4).

These terms of reference with their mention of "civics" and "civic society," of "practices" and "institutions" and "formal political activity," already bear something of the stamp of the Chairman of the Advisory Group on Citizenship, Bernard Crick. In the 1970s Crick was a leading figure in that decade's most prominent campaign for serious political education in schools—the Programme for Political Education, supported by the Hansard Society, and with considerable overlap of personnel with the Politics Association—organized around the motif of "political literacy" (see Crick & Porter, 1978). The idea of the specificity of political relations and political processes, their non-assimilability into the generality of morals and values, or social relations, is the key point of much of Crick's work (e.g., Crick, 1993) It seems significant that the then Labour Secretary of State for Education and Employment, David Blunkett, had been Crick's student.

It is not possible to generalize from studies of schools in England and Wales to those in Northern Ireland or Scotland. The questions and problems regarding "political education" or "education for citizenship" in the sectarian and divided society of Northern Ireland are distinct, focused as they are on the political and social outcomes of the churches' and the state's delivery of education to Catholic and Protestant children, and on the prospects for the "common school" (Dunn, 1993). The Scottish curriculum differs somewhat from that of England and Wales, with Scottish Highers based on examination in a wider range of subjects than the counterpart English and Welsh Advanced Level qualifications. However, neither "civics" nor anything like it has been a standard fixture on the Scottish curriculum (although some relevant material may be covered in "Modern Studies"). Anyway, judging by recent relevant publications, "citizenship" and so on have not been a preoccupation, or even a concern, of educators in Scotland. A report on *Promoting Social Competence* in schools focuses on "emotions, behaviors and social skills," "contact with the local community," and the importance of access to "role models for the full range of roles to be found in the world of work . . . professional people, graduates, skilled workers, carers, entrepreneurs, disabled people . . ." (Scottish Office, 1998, Tables 3.1 and 5.1). The importance of social competence for citizenship is not mentioned and this list of salient roles and role models is striking for the absence of roles from public life, such as representatives, campaigners or volunteers. A report on Scotland from Her Majesty's Inspectors of Schools makes a number of comments about "religious and moral education "health education and "enterprise education" (H.M. Inspectors of Schools, 1999, para. 2.1). In the section on "school ethos" students' opportunities to "take responsibility" for example by participation in pupils' councils is mentioned, but none of the terms "politics," "democracy," or "citizenship" are used, although "charity" and "partnership with parents and the local community" are (para. 2.5). By contrast, the white paper on Scottish education bears the stamp of the Labour government with the striking addition of "citizenship" to educational objectives:

> [We are committed to] ensuring that we have a world class schools system in Scotland where young people will:
> - Be confident, motivated and well rounded.
> - Be literate and numerate—to a level at or above their peers in the rest of the world.
> - Fully understand and be able to play their part as citizens of a democratic society.
> - Seize opportunities open to them regardless of their background, culture or race.
> - Be able to work flexibly and to embrace change on a continuing basis.
> (Secretary of State for Scotland, 1999, p. 14).

I discuss an even more recent Scottish document—a discussion and consultation paper by the Review Group on Education for Citizenship (2001)—later in this chapter.

CITIZENSHIP EDUCATION IN THE U.K. AND THE UNITED STATES

Differences between the constituent countries of the U.K. mean that it is difficult to generalize about educational policy. Indeed, the political salience of those very differences, and the antagonisms and tensions they generate, is one major factor explaining the difficulties in establishing political education in schools in Britain generally and England in particular. The explanation certainly cannot be that there has been no interest in, or no perceived need for, political education, education for citizenship, education for democracy, civics or constitutional studies in the U.K. I remarked earlier that in the last two decades there has been a constant stream of projects to promote such education. But the same applies to every decade this century, and, indeed, every decade since a widened franchise prompted anxieties about the capacity of uneducated or poorly educated people to vote responsibly (Goldman, 1999; Harris, 1993). The anxiety tends to come in waves—prompted by constitutional changes such as the extensions of suffrage (for instance, the Hansard Society project of 1970 was prompted by worry about the lowering of the age of majority to 18 years in the *Representation of the People Act of 1969* [Stradling, 1977]; by threats such as totalitarianism in the 1930s; and by social changes conditioned by the end of wars [see Brindle & Arnot, 1999]).

It is interesting and notable that "citizenship" is the term that has invariably been used by promoters of political education, to underline and to propel into the debate ideals and values such as responsibility, political equality, participation, duty and public service. It is a curious choice of term because equally notable is that it either lacks salience for significant sections of the intended audience, or invokes an antipathetic response. In comparative research in England and the United States Conover, Crewe, and Searing (1991) found that English respondents did not use the concept "citizenship" themselves in connection with their own political identities; for some there was clear discomfort with its connotations of "foreignness" (Citizenship Foundation, 1997, p. 4). That in Britain "we are not citizens but subjects" became a commonplace critical point in debate about British political culture and constitution in the 1980s and 1990s. The implications of this and other relevant factors in the British political system, political history, and current political culture, can be traced by looking at research which allows comparison between Britain and the United States in particular and some European countries as well (Torney-Purta, Schwille, & Amadeo, 1999; and chapter 9, this volume).

In the United States "civics" is a ubiquitous item in school curricula. Although not all states mandate "civics," "government," or "citizenship," those who do not tend to mandate "social studies," and in states where there is no state mandate some school districts do have such a mandate. Thus Hahn (1999; and chapter 4, this volume) and her colleagues calculate that by age 15–16 most students will have had "deliberate instruction" in government. Furthermore, most 14–15 year olds will have been taught about democracy, political institutions, and rights and responsibilities in a course in U.S. history. The significance of "civics" in U.S. schooling is clear from the fact that it is evaluated in the National Assessment of Educational Progress (NAEP 1990, 1999).

Hahn (1999) reports that "There is a broad consensus in the country that it is the responsibility of schools to teach about democracy and to prepare students to be effective democratic citizens" (p. 588). Students in the United States focus groups were able to talk about "democracy," reported that they had learned about branches and levels of government (a few using the terms "executive," "legislature," "local, state, and national levels" and the like), while others mentioned "people who make laws" and "courts." Most reported learning about the U.S. Constitution and the Bill of Rights, some about "checks and balances," and the history behind the Constitution such as the Magna Carta, the Declaration of Independence, and the Articles of Confederation. They also mentioned rights, jury duty, voting, and military service. They also mentioned a predictable enough list of notable individuals including presidents (for instance Washington, Jefferson, Roosevelt, Kennedy) and also Martin Luther King Jr., Rosa Parks, Harriet Tubman and others. Data from these focus groups, and those with teachers, suggest that although there is variation in the statutory situation from one state and district to another, there is little variation between classrooms. History and civics teachers reported teaching about democracy when they teach about the Mayflower Compact, Magna Carta, the colonial period, the Articles of Confederation, the Civil War, the Constitution, the Bill of Rights, landmark Supreme Court cases, and the denial of rights to women, black people, and native Americans.

But Hahn (1999) comments that most content (in "teaching democracy") is presented as uncontested, and that the teaching of democracy is done in a very conventional pedagogical fashion with little emphasis on critical thinking or controversy. In Hahn's sample the teachers themselves seemed to be conscious of "superficiality" and worse. They commented on the need for these subjects to be treated critically, and some commented on issues such as the difficulty of "teaching democracy" in schools where the values of docility and quietness were uppermost.

One factor explaining hostility to launching a similar civics curriculum in the U.K. is skepticism about the effectiveness of the kind of "deliberate instruction" in government and related topics that is imparted in U.S. schools, and a sense that the resulting "knowledge" is superficial. It is clearly true that although education as such has a powerful effect on a range of political outcomes including "political knowledge" or "expertise," as well as political attitudes and levels of political engagement, the difference that explicit political education makes has been rather unclear. A number of studies failed to find any clear difference in knowledge, attitudes, or engagement between students who have studied politics at A Level or sat through civics classes and those who have not (Furnham & Gunter, 1983; Langton & Jennings, 1968; Lister, 1973; Mercer, 1972; Stradling, 1977). However more recent analysis of the 1988 NAEP data by Niemi and Junn (1998) suggest these findings may have been influenced by research design and questionnaire design. Niemi and Junn show that discussing current events in class and studying "government" or "civics" (and studying a decent range of topics under these headings) do have independent effects on school students' ability to correctly answer questions about the U.S. polity (pp. 120–3, 142–5).

In any case, I would argue that it does not follow from the lack of a direct and strikingly measurable effect on knowledge that formal political education is insignificant. For one thing, teaching mathematics in schools often has rather disappointing results, but nobody infers from those results that we should not bother to teach mathematics. For another, I take it that to have heard and ignored, or to have listened and forgotten, or to have tried but not understood, is not epistemically the equivalent of never having been told at all. With this in mind, the important thing is that whereas U.S. school children are told important things about the system of government under which they live, U.K. children for the most part have been told nothing at all.

However, critics might argue, despite the established place of civics in the school curriculum, U.S. political culture and democracy are not in noticeably better shape than our own. Superficiality of knowledge outcomes is likely to be connected to superficiality in the material taught. The depiction of U.S. history as progressively enlightened, just, and democratic is culpably romantic. The discourses of rights, equality, and freedom are naive and uncritical. Basic work needs critical content and must be supplemented by participation in decision making, the experience of political debate and conflict, and the critical study of political power.

The striking point is that whereas in the United States there can be, and is, an argument about how to take a more critical and practical approach to the basic study of constitution, political institutions, political processes, and political history, in the British case there is no such "basic study" to take a critical and practical approach to. The consensus on the key events and texts that form the narrative of U.S. history as taught to school children in all the states has no counterpart in Britain or England. Although it is conceivable that a group of politics and history teachers would come up with a fairly definite list of key events—including perhaps the Magna Carta, the Commonwealth, the Restoration, 1689, the Reform Bills—two things are notable. One is that such a list is in no way a constituent of a widely promulgated or articulated political culture. Another is that any such list will be highly controversial or, rather, that the meaning of the various events will be highly and systematically contested. The role of capital and the nature of class rule, imperialism and the colonial oppression of Welsh, Scots, and Irish people, the dominance of Protestantism over Catholicism—these are all features of British history that tend to underline division and oppression rather than convergence and agreement.

Now this fact of the controversial nature of the events that can be seen as ingredients of the long and messy process of British "state formation" should not in itself be a bar to their place in the school curriculum. After all, U.S. teachers must deal with slavery, segregation, the fate of native American people, contests between rich and poor, employers and labor. A number of teachers mentioned to Hahn the process of discussing with pupils "when democracy doesn't work," the negative experience of being Black in a racist society, and the different meanings of "citizenship" to migrant and non-migrant children. These episodes are subject to competing theories and value interpretations, just as much as are the execution of

Charles I or the long delays before granting women the vote in Britain or recent patterns of migration to Britain.

But another striking aspect of the U.S. situation when viewed from a British perspective is that the Constitution, both the fact of its codification and its preeminent symbolic status in U.S. political and indeed social life, makes U.S. teachers' task of teaching the structures and functions of government, the nature of rights and duties, and the battles for representation and participation more straightforward than it would be in the U.K. The uncodified nature of the British Constitution does not entail that it is obscure. However, it is notable that study of the British Constitution is advanced, and optional, work only for university students in law, history and politics. Similarly, when it comes to teaching political values U.S. teachers have a number of obvious documents to use: the Mayflower Compact, the Declaration of Independence, Martin Luther King Jr.'s "I Have A Dream" speech. U.K. teachers would find it more or less impossible to put such a package together (they would have to have recourse to international documents such as the UN Declaration of Human Rights).

This obscurity of constitutional principles and the unarticulated nature of political ideals is reflected in the difficulties that research respondents have with the language and idea of citizenship. A recent survey of British trainee teachers before, during, and after their postgraduate Certificate of Education courses at two large teacher-education institutions in England suggests that, like Conover, Crewe, and Searing's (1991) respondents mentioned earlier, this group has difficulties with the language of citizenship (Wilkins, 1999). The idea of a "good citizen" prompted negative images such as "disgusted of Tunbridge Wells," "stiff upper lip and bowler hat," "neighborhood watch and writing letters to the parish council"—that is, stereotypes of a particular kind of English middle-class identity. Questions about "traditional values" prompted expression of fear that such values are imposed rather than being consensual or truly universal, as well as derisive references to "British bulldogs" and "roast beef" and skeptical references to "class deference" and "acceptance of hierarchy." When, at the end of their courses, these respondents were asked about "teaching citizenship" they were even more uncertain and skeptical than they had been at the beginning of the study, both because of continuing vagueness about what citizenship is, and because of recognition of the pressures on timetables and the preeminence of effort directed to basic skills in literacy and numeracy, and to "packaging and assessment." Perhaps most notable is that the younger students surveyed expressed cynical and negative attitudes to "politics" itself—as "not affecting me," as "a joke." Older students (26 years and over) often were involved in campaigns and action, but expressed a sense of disempowerment by conventional politics—that is, party and Parliament.

It is obviously difficult to come to grips with what these respondents (university degree holders) are really saying. Are they saying that it does not matter which party is in government in a political system—that policies affecting the fates of ordinary people are always the same? Are they assuming that however goes the competition for the power to govern the degree of physical and social security they enjoy will not diminish—that things could not be worse? Are they saying that it is satisfactory to leave politics to a special class of people? If so, how do they think politicians should be recruited and checked? Speculatively, it could be any of the above, or indeed none, that is being said.

ANTI-POLITICAL CULTURE

The research and analysis considered so far suggests a number of factors about British culture and politics that are obstacles to any easy reform of the curriculum. First, from one political and social perspective "citizenship" is a foreign concept which already goes some way to undermining the traditional constitutional relationships between ruler and ruled. Second, from a different political perspective citizenship is identified with a particular class identity and a deferential attitude to values such as hierarchy and respectability, which should be contested. Third, there is no widely assented to historical narrative or corpus of texts which would mean that the teaching of history and the teaching of "politics" or "civics" or "citizenship," were such a curriculum slot to be institutionalized, would reinforce one another. A fourth, and key, issue is that the meaning of "politics" itself is construed both vaguely and negatively, even by people with a high level of education.

In fact, we can see deep-seated antipathies to politics within both structured political discourse and within political theory. Take, for example, the common identification of "political" with "partisan." The *Education Act 1996* enjoined education authorities, governing bodies, and head teachers to forbid "(a) the pursuit of partisan political activities by registered pupils at maintained schools who are junior pupils and (b) the promotion of partisan political views in the teaching of any subject in the school" (para. 406). The point is that if educators find it difficult to specify a meaning of political that is distinct from partisan this proscription is likely to sweep political content out together with partisan content. Hahn (1998) reported to one teacher in an English school that her sixth formers had said they wished to know more about politics. The teacher was "surprised" and "admitted that the school does not do much with that in the sixth form course 'because it is difficult. If you have someone from one party then you have to have someone from the other parties too'" (p. 68).

This proscription was first enshrined in the *1986 No.2 Education Act* and was clearly prompted by suspicion that bias and even propaganda was present in subject teaching in some schools. Suspicion at that time came from the right wing of the political spectrum. It was fixed, of course, on socialism, marxism, and pacifism as doctrines that can be insidiously and subversively promulgated among vulnerable populations (the young being thought of as particularly vulnerable). But it is important that a comparable level of suspicion about political education also comes from the left wing. The subjects of "citizenship," "democracy," "constitution," "civics" and the like are interpreted as biased vehicles for a quietist ideology, as is "politics." For many left-wing thinkers and activists, not just marxists, economic relations are "real" and really significant in determining people's life chances. Democratic representation and parliamentary politics have not made, and perhaps cannot make, significant differences to people's economic fates. At worst, democratic government has been seen as a charade that distracts individuals and groups from a genuine understanding of the nature of economic power and their place in the structure (Freeden, 1996; Phillips, 1993). At best, "politics" for socialists has been working class, party politics, which as we have seen can have no place in schools. To the extent that the left-right axis has dominated debates in policy making and in society (and it certainly has for the larger part of the industrial period) then the kind of "political education" in schools discussed here has had determined and powerful opponents from both left and right.

Of course, this left-right axis, with conservatives and the interests of capital on one side, and liberals, socialists and the interests of labor on the other, has not been universally admired or participated in. Particularly since the 1960s a number of interests and articulated positions have emerged which say, more or less, "a plague on both your houses." Feminists in particular, environmentalists, some pacifist groups, those committed to solidarity with the developing world, anti-racists, all have found in both the ideas and theories of the traditional left and right, and in the policies of Labour and Conservative governments in power, gaps, silences and perversities. These positions identify structures which generate negative social outcomes—sexism and the disadvantage of women, militarism, racism, exploitation. These outcomes occur regardless whether ostensibly "right" or "left" pro-capitalist or pro-labor interests have governmental power.

In the 1980s in Britain as elsewhere two notable aspects of these interests and values, salient to this discussion, crystallized. First, a "critique of politics" was articulated. Tendencies to perverse and unjust outcomes such as sexism and racism were identified in the very structures of partisan politics, parliamentary procedures and values, and the conventions and values of public life. This analysis generated a positive emphasis on efforts to make changes in social and cultural relationships beyond the ambit of conventional politics with its structures of partisanship and emphasis on legislation. On the one hand, from these political efforts an *extension of the scope of politics* was derived. The concept and domain of politics was stretched beyond the bounds of state and governmental institutions to encompass social institutions and interpersonal and intimate relationships. On the other hand, these analyses generated a *skeptical and critical approach to politics altogether.* Politics in the sense of the conciliation of opposing interests through participation in public and representative institutions is thought to be unable to do justice to the needs and aspirations of those individuals and those values that are at stake in unequal societies. This ambivalence about politics, interestingly, has its counterpart in more dominant discourses which, on the one hand, are forced to acknowledge the scope of politics beyond the state and conventional governing institutions but, on the other, reserve the term "political" for rule and disputes about rule that are conducted through public and state institutions.

Second, oppositional values and analyses—pacifism, anti-nuclear power, feminism, anti-racism, social justice—were worked up into a range of teaching packs and educational programs which were successfully albeit patchily introduced into curriculum slots such as "personal and social education," "health education," "general studies" and the like by enthusiastic teachers and some local education authorities (Davies, 1999). Hostility to these programs and their perceived political bias undoubtedly galvanized the Conservative government's proscription of partisan politics in schools. But more interesting for my argument here is that this "critique of politics" means that educators who are or were committed to the kind of critical social education enshrined in these programs will no more be enthusiastic supporters of civic education or the study of political institutions and constitution than will the socialist and conservative parties and interests they criticize.

A further source of antipathy to politics stems from antipathy to government, and especially to government interference in education. Arguably any socially or politically instrumentalist approach to education—the requirement, for instance, that education prepares children for "economic realities," or for parenthood, or for a coming technological revolution—fundamentally undermines educational values, which should focus on the individual and her or his capacities and needs (Pring, 1999). Again, the burden of this argument is that governmental power is intrinsically oppressive, and it is important that social institutions, and individuals, are able to enjoy freedom from it. One important set of such social institutions are the educational institutions—these are the places where (ideally at least) individuals might be educated to become autonomous, to set their own goals for life, and to resist social and state power.

A final source of antipathy to politics looks back to the concern with "values education" with which this chapter opened. A number of strains of ethical theory emphasize the primary importance of moral values and human rights, uncontroversially enough, and link this commitment to a denial of the specificity or particular importance of political values, political relationships, and political processes. If values such as equality, tolerance of difference, political liberty, or free speech are truly valuable they are so because they are morally right, because they are values for human beings as such. Political processes and relationships cannot create values that do not already exist as moral values. This means that one important goal for education is the imparting of and the critical consciousness of these values. But, it is inferred, this means that the study of "politics" and discussion of explicitly political values is a diversion, at best, or positively undermines values education, at worst, because of the particular place of power and pragmatism in politics. The point, according to critics, is that if the perspective of politics is primary, then values such as autonomy, individual freedom, equality and justice might be compromised by the workings of power and the imperative of political stability. That is to say, the point of view of politics—teaching about particular state and institutional arrangements, and the values implicit and explicit therein—entails taking up the point of the view of the state or collective, with obvious dangers to the liberty of individuals, not only dissenters (Pring, 1999). Another way of putting the point is to say that the important thing is to get the values and morals right, then the politics will look after itself.

Recent debates about citizenship education in Britain are replete with protests that "just" teaching young people about institutions, constitutions, and democratic processes is "not enough." For example, the recent Scottish discussion paper (Review Group on Education for Citizenship, 2001) quotes the Scottish Consultative Council on the Curriculum:

> (A)n understanding of the political structures and processes, of rights, obligations, law, justice and democracy will not be sufficient. The curriculum should go further . . . by fostering a sense of active and responsible citizenship. . . . (n.p.)

Now every first year university student knows that necessity does not entail sufficiency. The problem, in my reading of this and other documents referenced in this chapter, is that their authors often seem to imply that insufficiency entails non-necessity. At least, one searches in vain in many of these discussion papers, and certainly in this one, for any clear recommendation that understanding of "structures, processes, rights, obligations, law, justice, democracy" is necessary or that, being necessary, clear plans have to be made for education in these fields.

The Scottish discussion paper, for instance, states "Finally, capability for citizenship, as envisaged here, includes ideas about 'political literacy'" But "ideas about political literacy" seems very different from "political literacy" itself. The recommendation of the Review Group (2001) is that it is inappropriate to think of a separate curriculum slot because "Education for citizenship is more than a simple expectation of political literacy. Civics lessons are not enough." But the analysis and recommendations of the Review Group don't seem to include any formal political education at all—not only is it insufficient, it seemingly has been rendered unnecessary. The emphasis on "environment," "thoughtful interaction," and involvement with "the wider community" are not, in this paper, supplements to an education which is clear about the specific nature of political relations; instead it is a substitute for it. The proposal to exploit the existing curriculum slots of "personal and social education" or "moral and spiritual" is bound to dilute, rather than encompass, any possible emphasis on political values, political relationships, and political skills.

CONCLUSION

Promoters of citizenship education, legal education, a greater emphasis on human rights, personal development and interpersonal skills, moral and spiritual education, health and parenting and preparation for economic realities, environmentalism, and education for racial, sexual and international justice can, coherently enough, share any or all of these antipathies to politics.

Real political societies are full of friction. Political actors play annoying games. Participants experience emotional difficulties and discomforts. The contest for political power is endless. Settlements of economic, social, ethnic, and religious conflicts are impossible or elusive. No wonder, perhaps, that many ideal models of politics are focused on the goal of reasoned settlement, harmonious social relations, rational cooperation, and the constraint of power by right. Yet this emphasis on nonviolent conciliation can foster the illusion that politics is less agonistic than it really is. Further it can foster the illusion of the non-necessity of politics—the idea that it is an unpleasantness that may sometime end.

But politics is non-optional. In political societies we all have to encounter fellow citizens who are strangers (not liked, not loved, not known; also "different" with different voices, different values, different ways of life and modes of conduct). These strangers may be antagonists. The aim of political education must be to enable people to participate in these webs of political relations, to understand the formal institutions that structure them, and, thereby, to be equal to the structures of power and authority that govern them. Of course values such as justice, nonviolence, autonomy, and democracy itself are a necessary background to such engagement. If the values are wrong, then the politics will, undoubtedly be wrong. However, it is not the case that getting the politics right is simply a matter of getting the values right.

REFERENCES

Advisory Group on Citizenship. (1998). *Education for citizenship and the teaching of democracy in schools.* London: Qualifications and Curriculum Authority.
Brindle, P., & Arnot, M. (1999). "England expects every man to do his duty": The gendering of the citizenship textbook. *Oxford Review of Education, 25*, 103–23.
British Youth Council. (1986). *The voice of young people.* London: Author.
Citizenship Foundation. (1997). *Colloquium on education and citizenship: Citizenship and civic education.* London: Author.
Commission on Citizenship. (1990). *Encouraging citizenship.* London: Her Majesty's Stationery Office.
Conover, P.J., Crewe, I., & Searing, D. (1991). The nature of citizenship in the United States and Great Britain: Empirical comments on theoretical themes. *Journal of Politics, 53*, 800–832.
Crick, B., & Porter. A. (Eds.). (1978). *Political education and political literacy.* London: Longman.
Crick B. (1993). *In defence of politics* (4th ed.). Harmondsworth: Penguin.
Davies, I. (1999). What has happened in the teaching of politics in schools in England in the last three decades and why? *Oxford Review of Education, 25,* 125–140.
Dunn, S. (1993). *The common school.* Coleraine: University of Ulster.
Fogelman, K. (Ed.). (1991). *Citizenship in schools.* London: David Fulton.
Fogelman, K. (1997). Citizenship education. In J. Bynner, L. Chisholm, & A. Furlong (Eds.), *Youth, citizenship and social change.* Aldershot: Ashgate.
Freeden, M.. (1996). *Ideologies and political theory.* Oxford: Clarendon.
Furnham, A., & Gunter, B. (1983). Political knowledge and awareness in adolescents. *Journal of Adolescence, 6,* 373–385.
Goldman, L. (1999). Education as politics: University adult education since 1914. *Oxford Review of Education, 25,* 89–101.
Hahn, C.L. (1998). *Becoming political: Comparative perspectives on citizenship education.* Albany: State University of New York Press.
Hahn, C.L. (1999). Civic education in the United States. J. Torney-Purta, J. Schwille, & P. Amadeo (Eds.), *Civic education across countries* (pp. 583–607). Delft: Eburon.
Harris, J. (1993). *Private lives, public spirit: Britain 1870–1914.* Harmondsworth: Penguin.
H. M. Inspectors of Schools. (1999). *Standards and quality in Scottish schools 1995–1998.* London: The Scottish Office.
John, G. (1991). *Education for citizenship.* London: Charter 88 (http://www.charter88.org.uk/pubs).

Langton, K.P., & Jennings, M.K. (1968). Political socialisation and the high school civics curriculum in the United States. *American Political Science Review,* 62, 852–867.

Lansdown, G. (1995). *Taking part: Children's participation in decision making.* London: IPPR.

Lister, I. (1973). Political socialisation and the schools: With special reference to the knowledge of political concepts of English sixth formers. *Teaching Politics,* 2, 2–9.

Lynch, J. (1992). *Education for citizenship in a multicultural society.* London: Cassell.

Mercer, G. (1972) Political interest among adolescents: The influence of formal political education. *Teaching Politics,* 1, 8–13.

National Assessment of Educational Progress 1988. (1990). *The civics report card.* Washington, DC: U.S. Department of Education.

National Assessment of Educational Progress 1998. (1999). *Civics report card for the nation.* Washington, DC: U.S. Department of Education.

National Curriculum Council. (1990). *Education for citizenship* (Curriculum guidance no. 8). London: Author.

Niemi, R., & Junn, J. (1998). *Civic education: What makes students learn.* New Haven, CT: Yale University Press.

Phillips, A. (1993). *Democracy and Difference.* Oxford: Polity.

Pring, R. (1999). Political education: The relevance of the humanities. *Oxford Review of Education,* 25, 71–87.

Review Group on Education for Citizenship. (2001). *Education for citizenship in Scotland: A paper for discussion and consultation.* Edinburgh: Learning and Teaching Scotland.

Review Group on the Youth Service in England. (1982). *Experience and participation* ("The Thompson Report"). London: Her Majesty's Stationery Office.

Schools Curriculum and Assessment Authority. (1995). *Spiritual and moral development* (Discussion paper no. 3). London: Author.

Schools Curriculum and Assessment Authority. (1996). *Education for adult life: The spiritual and moral development of young people* (Discussion paper no. 6). London: Author.

Scottish Office. (1998). *Taking a closer look at promoting social competence.* London: Author.

Secretary of State for Education and Employment. (1997). *Excellence in schools* (Cm3681). London: Her Majesty's Stationery Office.

Smith, D.I. (1989). *Taking shape: Development in youth service provision.* London: National Youth Bureau.

Smith, J. Southworth, M., & Wilson, A. (1985). *A course in political education for 14–18 year olds.* London: Longman.

Stradling, R. (1977). *A programme for political education: The political awareness of the school leaver.* London: Hansard Society.

Torney-Purta, J., Schwille, J., & Amadeo, P. (Eds.). (1999). *Civic education across countries: Twenty four national case studies from the IEA civic education project.* Delft: Eburon.

Wilkins, C. (1999) Making good citizens: The social and political attitudes of PGCE students. *Oxford Review of Education,* 25, 217–230.

Williamson, H. (1997) Youth work and citizenship. In J. Bynner, L. Chisholm, & A. Furlong (Eds.), *Youth, citizenship and social change.* Aldershot: Ashgate.

CHAPTER 3

THE IRONY OF EXCLUSION:

Citizenship Education in Seattle During the Japanese American Incarceration[1]

Yoon K. Pak

March 24, [19]42

Dear Miss Evanson,

Because of this situation, we are asked to leave this dear city of Seattle and its surroundings. I am sure I will miss my teachers and Mr. Sears. There was never a school like Washington School and I sure will miss it. As for me, the one I will miss the most will be you. You have been very patient and kind throughout my work. If the school I will attend next would have a teacher like you I will be only too glad. When I am on my way my memories will flow back to the time I was attending this school and the assemblies that were held in the hall.

Wherever I go I will be a loyal American.

Love,

Emiko

Loyalty to the ideals of democracy has always been a means of survival and resistance for Asian Americans. While systematic and structural discrimination have impeded civic participation for Asian Americans, their steadfast belief in the ultimate goals of democracy provided hope in the face of hopeless situations. As historian Gary Okihiro (1994) writes, "[R]acial minorities, specifically Asian Americans, have in the past repeatedly sought inclusion within the American community, within the promise of American democracy, within the ideals of equality and human dignity, and have, just as regularly, been rebuffed and excluded from that company and ideal" (p. 151).

For Japanese American, or Nisei, students of Seattle Public Schools, democracy, citizenship, and loyalty were weighted with meaning during World War II. As offspring of immigrants who had been denied citizenship and who had experienced a range of racial discrimination, many Nisei were cognizant of their parents' struggle for dignity. Understanding this struggle fostered Nisei children's appreciation for their U.S. citizenship.

With the signing of Executive Order 9066 by President Franklin D. Roosevelt on February 19, 1942, the imprisonment[2] of Japanese American and permanent residents on the west coast of the United States called into question the very meaning of citizenship for many Nisei. As expressed in the letter by Emiko, a seventh-grade student in Ella Evanson's homeroom class at Washington School, she would remain loyal to a government that questioned her very loyalty. Writing to her teacher in response to Executive Order 9066, the student was attempting to make sense of the dissonance between the idea of citizenship on the one hand, and the experience of being treated as an "enemy alien," on the other.

Here I share my investigation of the Seattle (Washington) Public Schools' approach to citizenship education at a time when the status of Japanese Americans as citizens was held suspect. As sites of cultural and social reproduction, schools could not shield themselves or their students from wartime hysteria. European Americans, as well as a number of minorities in the neighboring communities of Seattle, accused Japanese residents, or Nikkei, of having developed alliances with Japan and believed their presence to be a threat to safety.[3] Such fallacious allegations and the subsequent increase in racial incidents against Seattle's Nikkei grew in intensity after the bombing of Pearl Harbor. While the Seattle Public School system prided itself on promoting racial tolerance in its citizenship education curricula (Pak, 1997), democratic principles were put to the test. The tradition of progressive education in Seattle (Nelson, 1998) established by Superintendent Frank Cooper (1901–1922) underwent severe challenges.

This chapter draws from two primary historical works to investigate the Seattle schools' tradition of progressive democratic citizenship. The first is a popular curriculum guide for citizenship and character education utilized in the Seattle Schools from the late 1930s through the 1940s. *Successful Living* described the paths toward democratic citizenship and moral character by developing principles such as tolerance. The study of literature and composition exemplified successful classroom practices that promoted and cultivated tolerance among students of different ethnic and immigrant groups. The authors of *Successful Living* encouraged all teachers to extend to their students, topics of composition stemming from their own personal lives. Only by examining the circumstances of one's own life could a bridge toward greater understanding toward others be built. Such lessons on tolerance, however conceived and practiced in the classrooms, lends for deeper understanding of the writings by Nisei students.

The second, and the more significant, historical source is a collection of classroom composition by seventh and eighth-grade Nisei of Washington School in Seattle, Washington. In writing to their homeroom teacher, Ella Evanson, the students reflected on the content of the school's assembly held on the day after the bombing of Pearl Harbor. Included in their recollections was the moral leadership and message of their principal, Arthur Sears, on practicing citizenship and tolerance. Farewell messages to Ella Evanson, in response to the Executive Order 9066, provide critical insights into how Nisei students grappled with the irony of exclusion. Leaning on their lessons in citizenship education and the values taught at home and in the Japanese Language Schools, Nisei students expressed in compositions how they would remain loyal to the United States in spite of the public's view that they were not to be trusted.

SUCCESSFUL LIVING

The publication of *Successful Living* (*SL*) in 1935 aimed at implementing a cohesive set of ideals on citizenship. The authors of the guide, a committee of Seattle school teachers and principals, emphasized progressive social goals in two main ways: through character education and by seeing schools as actual societies and laboratories of democracy. They examined how public schools could serve to facilitate the process of living a democratic way of life. According to the authors, character education was to be thought of, "like health, as the productive way of living through which strength is acquired. Character education in America is the mastery of a truly democratic way of living . . . a way of living which conserves and produces as many values as possible for as many persons as possible over as long a time as possible. Character education is the facilitation of this way of life" (*SL*, p. 1). In their view, citizenship and character education were synonymous terms. One could not exist without the other. At the time, the effects of the Great Depression and political unrest overseas necessitated a broader understanding of how character was inextricably linked to citizenship (Goodenow, 1975; Moreo, 1996; Tyack et al., 1984).

Successful Living attributed some of its goals to John Dewey (1916) in that the school offered a place to equalize opportunities for all children. In the committee's view, schools, "serving all the children of all people, [have] a unique opportunity for overcoming snobbery, reducing racial and class prejudices, and teaching the brotherhood of man" (*SL*, p. 4). Furthermore, "The individual must gain a consciousness of his civic responsibilities. Dewey reminds us of the fact that school is not only a preparation for life; it is life itself. It may be so organized as to afford opportunity for the exercise of all the duties and obligations of citizenship" (*SL*, p. 4).

Successful Living approached the teaching of tolerance by highlighting stories of students who came from various racial, ethnic, class, and religious backgrounds. The "success" stories showcased how immigrant and second generation students should: (1) recognize their cultural or religious background as one that has value and not as subordinate or inferior; (2) not denigrate their parents for speaking a different language and practicing foreign customs; (3) exhibit character at home by practicing the habits of citizenship, thereby serving as Americanizing agents to one's parents; and (4) understand that there are two sides to every story.

Successful Living further articulated why a study of literature and composition augmented the development of character. Such an approach served two purposes: to increase students' understandings of others' experiences through literature, and to use writing as a means to express complex world situations.

LITERATURE AND COMPOSITION

Literature stirred the imagination of students by providing possibilities to envisage a moral life. In the Seattle schools, the writings of Louisa May Alcott, Maude Warren, Ralph Waldo Emerson, and Abraham Lincoln exemplified such moral goals. Certain kinds of literature not only provided a bridge for deeper understanding, but also provided moral guidance—another critical component in the development of character.

Composition extended naturally from the study of literature. According to *Successful Living*, writing was a gateway to one's conscience, to see how students made sense of their world in relation to larger contexts as gleaned from literature. It was also an individual piece of creativity, generated from their unique understanding of their immediate experiences. The process of composing built character and the principles for ethical and moral understanding:

> Someone has said that literature is the telescope through which we view human nature. We might add that compositions created by the pupils are the

instruments through which we see their innermost souls. Their composition is a piece of creative work built by the student from his own thoughts. If we can help him to strengthen right ideals and can direct him to new avenues of high thinking, we create a condition that makes for fine character building. (*SL*, p. 46)

Students' writing applied the lessons learned from literature to aspects of their own lives. A classroom writing assignment entitled, "Where Was Your Dad Born?" (*SL*, p. 46) aimed to integrate students' home culture to that of the school's. Examining the contributions of the country from which the students' parent immigrated deepened their understanding of how world cultures were interconnected. The aim was to make the strange familiar. "The whole unit was worked out on the assumption that we seldom hate those we really know. Interest, understanding, and sympathy should first be developed, and from that, friendship will follow" (*SL*, p. 59).

The writing by Nisei students added a critical dimension to the study of character education. Although students' modes of self-representation through composition are mediated and complicated by sociopolitical and racialized contexts, we are, in essence, peering into their conscience. What they write may not be articulate or detailed, but their expressions carry heavy meaning. Especially for Nisei students, the sense of self, or lack thereof, becomes salient. The affirmation in their writing of their American identity indicates that this identity was held suspect by others around them. The need to accentuate their loyalty to the United States came at a time when the government questioned Nikkei's loyalty as viable citizens. The prejudices against Nikkei in Seattle and nationwide escalated within a few months time. How students and schools reacted to outside pressures is revealed to varying degrees in the students' compositions and by the school district's response to wartime pressures. Ideals of understanding, sympathy, friendship and tolerance surfaced as wartime hostilities and anxieties created tensions between Nisei and non-Nisei students. The crisis became a test of the schools' tolerance, character, and democratic citizenship education programs.

SEATTLE PUBLIC SCHOOLS RESPONSE TO THE BOMBING OF PEARL HARBOR

December 7, 1941, has taken its place beside the dates in the life of America which will endure forever in the minds of the people. Never before in our history had there been so sudden and complete a transition from the ways of peace to the ways of war.

> On the morning of the 8th of December Seattle teachers and principals began quietly and thoughtfully to meet the challenge. The need for calmness and orderliness was discussed with children who the day before had listened to the broadcasts from Honolulu and who had participated in the first hurried blackout precautions. Tolerance toward Japanese classmates was stressed. One principal reminded her cosmopolitan student body: "You were American citizens last Friday; you are American citizens today. You were friends last Friday; you are friends today." (*Seattle Schools*, January 1942, p. 1)

The bombing of Pearl Harbor on Sunday, December 7, 1941 ruptured any semblance of normalcy. Never before did the possibility of war occur so close to the continental United States. School officials knew that they had to address what occurred on Sunday when students entered school the following morning. As the Seattle School newsletter indicates, teachers and principals prepared to meet the challenge by leaning on their tradition of democratic citizenship education. The school officials concentrated their efforts on promoting tolerance and citizenship, especially toward their Nisei student body. While they could not affect change in international politics, they at least controlled how schools should respond to the United States entrance into World War II.

In Washington School, Principal Arthur G. Sears instilled democratic principles in his young students early on. In describing this and Sears's response to the bombing of Pearl Harbor, Martha Mortensen, a teacher at Washington School, wrote, "The Principal, A.G. Sears, long ago laid the ground work for rooting out any existing prejudices. At all times he has tried to break down cultural barriers, establish mutual appreciation, and develop a program which would lead to a deep devotion to the American way of life. He has stressed a better understanding of all races and religions" (Mortensen, 1942, p. 7).

Arthur Sears emphasized the teaching of democratic citizenship and tolerance at Washington School during his tenure as the principal. And his approach to the understanding of ethnic traditions was highlighted in a *Seattle Educational Bulletin* article ("In the Language of their Fathers") in November 1937. The story described how Washington School students wrote individual letters to their parents inviting them to the school's open house. Many students were encouraged to write in English and in the language of their immigrant parents—Spanish, Hebrew, Japanese, or Chinese. Principal Sears upheld this practice:

> I use this device not only to get the message over to the parents, but also to dignify the parental background. Too often I have seen tragedies among the second generations. They feel frequently that they have reason to be ashamed of their parents when they can neither read nor write the English language. I believe we produce better Americans from the foreign-born if we

dignify their background, and while they should love America more, they should not lose their love of the land of their ancestry. (p. 1)

Principal Sears understood the importance of preserving one's ethnic heritage. He revealed that total assimilation, at the cost of forsaking one's ethnicity, created a rift not only between the parents and their children, but also within the children themselves. Thus, a careful balance between one's past and present identities marked a successful entre into the American way of life. Sears taught and maintained his views on the American way of life until his retirement in 1942.

WASHINGTON SCHOOL, 1941–1942

Washington school, where the writings by Nisei took place, bordered the multiracial "Central District" of Seattle, near a Jewish Settlement House, and served students from different ethnic backgrounds. The student body was composed primarily of Jewish immigrants from Eastern and Southern Europe, Asian Americans and immigrants, and African Americans. Washington School, from 1920 until 1942, was among those in which the highest numbers of Japanese American students attended.

Washington School originally was a grade school from 1912 to 1938. In 1938 Washington became a seventh and eighth grade center and remained so through World War II. In 1945, it became a junior high school. Washington, according to published reports, embodied cosmopolitanism. A 1961 Seattle School publication describes the history and tradition of the school as follows:

> Washington School, as a separate unit, in and of itself, presents a close approximation to the great American ideal which the fathers of the American Constitution hoped to achieve. A visitor to Washington School would find around one thousand children between the ages of 12 to 15, or every race, every religion, and every economic status, working together and playing together, with no tensions between them due to their differences of race, religion, or economic background. Democracy, in the true sense of the word, is practiced from the principal right down through the office staff and faculty, the custodians, and cafeteria workers, and then is reflected back again through the students themselves. The school is truly a small United Nations, actually accomplishing democratic objectives in an extremely significant way. Teachers and students are fortunate and privileged to be able to participate in the democratic situation as it exists at Washington at the present time. (Seattle Public Schools, 1961)

Washington School's philosophy of promoting democratic ideals is admirable, yet to maintain that no tensions existed between students is questionable. The passage is romantic and borders on an imagined, color-blind democracy. Nevertheless, a survey of other schools' histories in the Seattle area revealed only Washington School explicitly emphasizing the promise and possibilities of the democratic ideal (Seattle Public Schools, 1961). Certainly the character of the school, its teachers and principal, and the student body contributed to its unique reputation. Nisei students, through their compositions, expressed the extent to which that was real.

Keisoo—Dec. 8, 1941[4]

Our Assembly

Today Mr. Sears talked to us about tolerance. As we know tolerance means to be friendly to other in any way.

When war broke out in the Far East situation yesterday some citizen of this country were intolerance. The people who are intolerant do not think before they speak.

Every person should be tolerant to different nationality if they have enemies.

Fumiko—December 8, 1941

Morning Assembly

The morning assembly was good for it tells to be good friends or neighbors wither our skin are different. That skin does not count by shelf but our spirit for helping people and cleaned heart count more for America and honesty too counts more for defending and best of all is love one another. We are all brothers and sisters even our parents and teachers but they are sent to take care of us and to give us more education and to become a better boy and girl.

The poem was good also and that all make to become American.

I wish sometimes if there were no war or evil thing, that do now happen were stop we should be friendly with country more and more until the end of the world than people would be like neighbor, no war, no unclean heart, but all clean and cheerful voice in this world.

Katsu—December 8, 1941

This Morning Assembly

In this morning assembly Mr. Sears experimented about having the morning assembly in the second period and next week it would be the third period because we always miss the first period class.

He spoked to us about not hating each other first because we have mixed nationalities in this school. But instead cooperate with each other and think of other people as our neighbors.

He also told us a story about a German boy and a Italian boy being a good American Citizens and even if their country is in war they are very good friends.

Mr. Sears read us a poem copied from a bulletin that a boy from Miss Fritzgerald's room. Then he mentioned about the paper drive. After he was through with his speech we sang America from the bottom of our hearts and we also saluted the flag.

Betty—Dec. 8, 1941

Assembly

This morning we had a assembly in the hall. Mr. Sears told us that if even we have a different color face, it's alright because we're American Citizen. We all should be American Citizen.

He read us a poem of prayer because in school or outside the school the people might not be friendly with the other people which as (Japanese people) cause the war is going to be. When I heard Mr. Sears read that poem I was proud to be a American Citizen. And I'll (I am) always be American Citizen.

This year is the second world war in many years if it goes on.

When we were saluting the flag I was proud to salute the flag. Some people were crying because they were proud of there country.

The language of tolerance and citizenship expressed by these students is clear. They understood Principal Sears's message of maintaining a steady course through friendship and understanding in light of international turmoil. Their school needed to operate as a bastion of democracy. While teachers and administrators could not affect change in the community's response to the war—through threats of increased racial violence—they could at least influence how students should act toward each other. Lessons in character and citizenship education became pronounced even more.

The meaning of citizenship weighed heavily in the minds of Nisei. Betty's statement, "When I heard Mr. Sears read that poem I was proud to be a American Citizen. And I'll (I am) always be American Citizen," reemphasizes the importance of citizenship and an American identity. At a tenuous moment in her life she needed to remind her teacher, Ella Evanson, and herself that she, too, was an American citizen worthy of the rights of citizenship. While Betty's teacher and principal taught those values, the government's exclusionary, race-based policy could not be changed.

The concepts of difference and race, and how they fit within the concept of citizenship, was central in the minds of Nisei. The students' interpretations of race, conceived either by them or by Sears, were noted by their use of "different color face or skin" or "mixed nationalities" in their writings. In that regard, citizenship meant an acceptance of individuals from various ethnic backgrounds and racial characteristics, most notably differentiated by skin color. Race as a social and cultural construct permeated scientific communities and popular culture to create an artificial social hierarchy (see for example Gossett, 1997; Gould, 1981; Omi & Winant, 1994; Takaki, 1990). For Sears to express the idea of equality of races, despite skin color, could have come as a surprise, as well as a welcome message, for some students.

The idea of race in the 1940s, especially in the Seattle area, can be understood in context by examining the minutes of a 1939 meeting of the Council of Jewish Women (CJW) and its work in the Settlement House near Washington School. One of the meetings of the CJW brought an anthropologist from the University of Washington to speak on Franz Boas' concept of the word "race" and why the term should no longer be used:

> Dr. Rose Ostrow introduced the speaker of the evening, Dr. Melville Jacobs of the U of W who spoke on "An Anthropologist's Point of View on Race." He explained that Dr. Franz Boas, noted authority on anthropology, urges the elimination of the use of the word race from the English language. He argues that there is really only one race on the face of the earth—the human race—that the gradual shadings from region to region are scientifically unjustifiable as 'races'—he suggests the use of the term 'varieties' or 'regional types.' (Council of Jewish Women, 17 April 1939)

It is not known if Sears was influenced by the theoretical concepts of race at the time. However, Sears' approach to racial tolerance was congruent with the ideas of leading progressive and intercultural educators, such as William H. Kilpatrick, George S. Counts, Harold Rugg and Rachel Davis Dubois, within the Progressive Education Association and the Bureau for Intercultural Education (Montalto, 1982). Time and again, his principles of racial equality, of one race—the human race, and the need for tolerance and brotherly love were reflected in the writings of Nisei. The students' compositions address how the concept of race should be focused more on the commonalities in the human race rather than one's facial features. The following essays by *non*-Japanese American students are illuminating.

Maurice—Dec. 8, 1941

American's

In our first assembly, Mr. Sears our principal spoke on the friendly attitude toward the pacific crisis. He said, "We are all American's and we here at Washington want no part of race hated. We are all under the same roof."

In the short time he spoke he *accomplish* very much.

He spoke of 23 years ago, of how he work in the naturalazion dept., and of two gents (men), one a Italian and a German who at the same time as Germans were fighting Italians were still good neighbors and good Americans. We should now be that way here at Washington school.

Shirley—Dec. 8, 1941

Assembly

In assembly this morning Mr. Sears told us about being intolerant he said that now because of the war different races might fight with each other and say that they started the war. He said that no matter what race or color you are that you are all American citizens and that even if your parent came from country that are fighting aganest us that we had nothing to do with it.

Mr. Sears also read a peom that a boy in our school made up it was very patreotic and expressed the feeling that and imagrant might have coming to America.

Mr. Sears said that people said to him that they thought he would have trouble with the children of Washington School because of the many different races and Mr. Sears said that he trust us and knew that we would not be intolerant.

These classmates of Nisei students articulated in their compositions the message of tolerance in the assembly conducted by Sears. Leaning on his past experience working for the Naturalization department during World War I, Sears emphasized and reiterated the need to continue the friendships developed between students of different cultures. Intercultural understanding was the ideal for those attending Washington School. Nevertheless, the reality of the war and the impending incarceration of Japanese residents and citizens would soon take its toll. Nisei students of Washington School prepared for their departure and for a future entirely outside their control.

LOYALTY AND DEMOCRACY IN THE FACE OF EXCLUSION

Let us turn to Nisei students' writing on the eve of the incarceration and in this way try to understand the actions of the government in the lives of the affected students. The following farewell essays portray young Americans grappling with the conflicting messages of citizenship and exclusion, tolerance and prejudice, loyalty and distrust, and democracy and totalitarianism. Nisei were suddenly thrust into a situation where their racial identity became a major determining factor for exclusion. Children found themselves dealing with issues generally confronted by adults. The message of tolerance did not extend much beyond the boundaries of the school. What they faced outside of school was to be overwhelming. Within a few months time, their schools, homes and all their belongings had to be abandoned for a tenuous life behind barbed wire. These entries are a lasting reminder of how everyday young people were attempting to reconcile and negotiate the ideal of democracy with racism.

March 29, 1942

Dear Miss Evanson,

We are leaving our city, to where I am going I am wholly ignorant. However I am not unhappy, nor do I have objections for as long as this evacuation is for the benefit of the United State. But I do am regreting about leaving this school and the thought that I shall not see for a long while pains me extremely. Your pleasant ways of teaching had made my heart yearn for the days when I was in your classroom. Your kind smile and your wonderful work you did for me shall be one of my pleasant memories.

Tooru

Mar. 20, 1942

Dear Miss Evanson,

I well start out my letter by writing about the worst thing. I do not want to go away but the goverment says we all have to go so we have to mind him. It said in the Japanese paper that we have to go east of the cascade mt. but we were planning to go to Idaho or Montana.

Now that the war is going on many Japanese men, women, and girls are out of jobs. And a lot of my friends fater are in consentration camp. If I go there I hope I well have a teacher just like you. And rather more I hope the war well be strighten out very soon so that I would be able to attend Washington school.

Sincerely Yours,

Sadako

Mar. 25 1942

Dear Miss Evanson,

I am very sorry I will have to leave Washington School so soon. As long as I am here I will try in some way to appreciate what you've taught me.

We all hope we will win this war (not the Japs) and come back to Seattle for more education.

Sincerely Yours,

James

Mar. 19, 1942

Dear Miss Evanson,

I am writing to you today because I am expecting to move away with in very short time. As you always know the Japanese people has been asked by our goverment to evacuate. I do not know yet where we will go. I hope there will be some good school in which I can continual, my school work. I am very sorry to leave Seattle and Washington School. And most especially to lose you for my teacher. I am hoping the war trouble will be soon over and I could come back to Seattle and be in your school and have you for my teacher again.

Sincerely yours,

Chiyoko

March 20, 1942

Dear Miss Evanson,

I am very sorry that I will soon be leaving Washington School and the teachers I have. As you know we have been asked to evacuate. My parents still haven't decided where to go. Where I am going I hope there will be a school like Washington School. I also hope to have a good teacher like you. I don't want to leave Seattle because I have been in Seattle from the time I was a little baby. I hate to lose you for my teacher and Mr. Sears as my principal. I know I am going to miss everybody. I am hoping the trouble will be over soon so we will not have to evacuate.

Sincerely,

Yurido

The Nisei students made it clear that they were American born, and distinguished themselves from the Japanese or the pejorative "Japs" as James makes explicit. At the same time, however, the students also underscore the reality that they indeed, look like the "enemy" and their evacuation was taking place because of their ethnic heritage. The dissonance of being a citizen, yet not a "true" United States citizen, rings in the tone of their writings.

Ideas of loyalty, democracy, citizenship, the threat of possible violence, and how school officials were helping to cope are unveiled. The most expressive ideas disclose feelings of uncertainty at what the future will hold and of the sadness of having to leave their home. Being uprooted from their birthplace to a place unknown created extreme anxieties. Proof of loyalty and American identity became a focal point for many Nisei as they were preparing to leave Seattle. Perhaps the opportunity to express the chaotic experiences of being uprooted provided a vehicle for students to attempt to make sense of dissonance. In the end, there was not much that could be done.

Shikata-ga-nai

"It cannot [could not] be helped." This was the phrase often used by Japanese immigrants to express the situation surrounding the imprisonment (see Houston &Houston, 1973; Sone, 1995; Uchida, 1991). Acts of loyalty toward the United States government would come in acquiescing to the "evacuation" orders. What else could be done? Since one's loyalty was already in question, the only loyal thing to do was to obey the government's orders. One of the cultural values Japanese immigrant, or Issei, parents, instilled in their children was a sense of loyalty to their home country (the United States). They also encouraged their children to accept, to a degree, voices of authority (Kitano, 1993; Miyamoto, 1972). For those who challenged the very ideals of democracy at the time, their civil liberties were quickly stripped away (Daniels et al., 1991). For the Nisei students of Washington School, writing about their immediate anxieties afforded a limited opportunity to wrestle with the democratic ideal of equality. They believed that the government would take care of them because, after all, they were citizens.

CONCLUSION

Seldom can schools change world events. At best, schools can offer opportunities for students to make sense of the dissonant world around them. Washington School, with teachers such as Ella Evanson and Principal Arthur Sears, provided a context in which students could express how they were making sense of Pearl Harbor and the news of the incarceration. While school officials themselves were powerless to overturn Executive Order 9066, they reminded their students that everyone was an American.

Many powerful ideas emerge in the students' compositions. Nisei students emphasized their loyalty to the United States in spite of what was happening to their lives with moving phrases such as "I am an American" and "wherever I go I will be a loyal American." As citizens, they trusted the government as they felt that the forced incarceration would be for the "benefit of the United States." The government in turn informed them that their individual sacrifices were necessary for the collective good of all Americans.

Schools continued to remind their students that everyone was an American, regardless of which countries were at war with the United States. However, many Nisei still faced chaotic home lives. Some of their fathers were arrested by the FBI and interned in Fort Missoula, Montana. Many of their mothers were left to resolve the final details of their removal from Seattle. Most of their belongings had to be sold. Family memorabilia were either burned—for it might have been deemed "suspect" by the FBI—or sold to the lowest bidder.

The strength and persistence of Nikkeis to survive the years behind bars is also a testament to their faith in the power and promise afforded in a democracy (Takezawa, 1995). The Civil Liberties Act, signed by President Ronald Reagan in 1988 acknowledged the findings, of the Commission on Wartime Relocation and Internment of Civilians, stating that the imprisonment of Japanese Americans was motivated largely by racial prejudice, wartime hysteria, and failure of political leadership (United States, 1997, p. 459). This government report signified, for the first time, the undemocratic act of forced incarceration during wartime against its own citizens and residents. Moreover, it became an admission of an anti-democratic policy. The lessons of the Japanese American incarceration during World War II are lost if confined only to the history of Japanese America. The exclusion of Japanese American students from the democratic education curriculum of Washington School, by their incarceration, is a particularly ironic example of a long record in the United States of denying basic, democratic rights to over two-thirds of its citizens based on race, nationality and gender (Smith, 1999). It is a vivid reminder that our fragile democracy is always a work in progress.

ACKNOWLEDGMENT

This chapter draws on an article published earlier in *Theory and Research in Social Education*, vol. 28. No. 3, pp.339–358, with permission of the National Council for the Social Studies. I would like to thank the editorial assistance of Janie Wu.

NOTES

1. An elaborated version of this chapter appears in Yoon K. Pak, *Wherever I Go, I Will Always Be A Loyal American* (Routledge Falmer, 2002).
2. As a point of clarification and accuracy, I shall be using the terms "incarceration" and "imprisonment" over "evacuation" and "internment." According to David Takami (1998), "Evacuation" was a government euphemism for the forced removal of Japanese Americans on the West Coast. It conveyed the idea that the removal of citizens was for their own safety. "Internment" is a technical term applied to prison camps run by the United States Justice Department for suspect Issei, immigrant Japanese, just after Pearl Harbor and to more permanent army-run camps for some of these detainees. The internment of enemy aliens during a war has a basis in law—specifically the Alien and Sedition Act of 1798—and it is governed by international accord in the form of the Geneva Conventions. The roundup and incarceration of American citizens had no legal precedent and singled out a race of people.
3. A content analysis of newspaper articles in *The Seattle Times*, from December 8, 1941 through May 1942, revealed escalating discrimination against Seattle's Nikkei. Some reports in the beginning indicated that tolerance, especially toward Nisei should be practiced, but as the war drew on, public opinion in favor of the imprisonment and the ouster of all Nikkei along the west coast grew. A comparative analysis of *The Los Angeles Times* revealed similar stories.
4. All the entries are transcribed in the exact manner in which they were written by the students, including spelling and grammar errors. Only the students' first names are used. This approach was used to maintain anonymity while focusing on each individual student as real and historical participants. The students' compositions are all from the Ella Evanson Papers at the University of Washington's Manuscripts and Archives Division. The students' compositions were originally the personal collection of their homeroom teacher, Ella Evanson, of Washington School.

REFERENCES

Campbell, E.W. (1942, January). Schools prepare for war emergencies. *Seattle Schools, 18*(5), 1. Seattle, WA: Seattle Public Schools.

Council of Jewish Women. (1939, April 17). *Minutes of the business and professional women's evening committee of the Seattle Council of Jewish Women*. Council of Jewish Women. University of Washington Manuscripts and Archives, Accession No. 2089-29, Box 6, Folder 25.

Daniels, R., Taylor, S.C., & Kitano, H.H.L. (Eds.). (1994). *Japanese Americans: From relocation to redress* (rev. ed.). Seattle: University of Washington Press.

Dewey, J. (1916/1985). *Democracy and education* (Vol. 9). In J.A. Boydston (Ed.), *John Dewey, the middle works, 1899–1924*. Carbondale: Southern Illinois University Press.

Ella Evanson Papers. University of Washington Manuscripts and Archives Division, Accession No. 2402.

Goodenow, R.K. (1975). The progressive educator, race and ethnicity in the Depression years: An overview. *History of Education Quarterly, 15*(4), 365–394.

Gossett, T.F. (1997). *Race: The history of an idea*. New York: Oxford University Press.

Gould, S.J. (1981). *The mismeasure of man*. New York: W. W. Norton & Company.

Houston, J.W., & Houston, D. (1973). *Farewell to Manzanar.* New York: Bantam Press.
In the language of their fathers. (1937, November). *Seattle Educational Bulletin,* 4(2), 1. Seattle, WA: Seattle Public Schools.
Kitano, H.H.L. (1993). *Generation and identity: The Japanese Americans.* Needham Heights, MA: Ginn Press.
Miyamoto, S.F. (1972). An immigrant community in America. In H. Conroy & T.S. Miyakawa (Eds.), *East across the pacific: Historical and sociological studies of Japanese immigration and assimilation* (pp. 217–43). Santa Barbara, CA: Clio Press.
Montalto, N.V. (1982). *A history of the intercultural educational movement, 1924–1941.* New York: Garland Publishing, Inc.
Moreo, D.W. (1996). *Schools in the Great Depression.* New York: Garland Publishing, Inc.
Mortensen, M. (1942, May). War and the children. *Seattle Principal's Exchange,* 6(7), 7–8. Seattle, WA: Seattle Public Schools.
Nelson, B. (1988). *Good schools: The Seattle public school system, 1901–1930.* Seattle: University of Washington Press.
Omi, M., & Winant, H. (1994). *Racial formation in the United States: From the 1960s to the 1990s* (2nd ed.). New York: Routledge.
Okihiro, G. (1994). *Margins and mainstreams: Asians in American history and culture.* Seattle: University of Washington Press.
Pak, Y.K. (1997, March). *Japanese Americans and the public school Americanization program of the progressive era.* Paper presented at the annual meeting of the American Educational Research Association, Chicago.
Parker, W.C. (Ed.). (1996). *Educating the democratic mind.* Albany: State University of New York Press.
Seattle Public Schools. (1961). *Histories of the Seattle public schools.* Seattle, WA: Author.
Seattle Public Schools. (1942). *1941–1942 Seattle Public Schools' Directory.* Seattle, WA: Author.
Seattle Public Schools. (1935). *Successful living.* Seattle, WA: Author.
Smith, R.M. (1999). *Civic ideals: Conflicting visions of citizenship in U. S. history.* New Haven, CT: Yale University Press.
Sone, M. (1995). *Nisei daughter* (rev. ed.). Seattle: University of Washington Press.
Takaki, R. (1990). *Iron cages: Race and culture in 19th-century America.* New York: Oxford University Press.
Takami, D.A. (1998). *Divided destiny: A history of Japanese Americans in Seattle.* Seattle: University of Washington Press.
Takezawa, Y. (1995). *Breaking the silence: Redress and Japanese American ethnicity.* Ithaca, NY: Cornell University Press.
Tyack, D., Lowe, R., & Hansot, E. (1984). *Public schools in hard times: The Great Depression and recent years.* Cambridge, MA: Harvard University Press.
Uchida, Y. (1991). *The invisible thread.* New York: Simon and Schuster.
United States Commission on Wartime Relocation and Internment of Civilians. (1997). *Personal justice denied: Report of the Commission on wartime relocation and internment of civilians: With a new foreword by Tetsuden Kashima.* Seattle: University of Washington Press.

Part II

CURRICULA

CHAPTER 4

EDUCATION FOR DEMOCRATIC CITIZENSHIP:

One Nation's Story

Carole L. Hahn

INTRODUCTION

In the United States educators have traditionally told the young that theirs is a nation committed to liberty, justice, and equality and that they live in a pluralistic democracy where citizens of diverse backgrounds share a common set of civic values, enshrined in the Constitution. Additionally, educators have often taught that the country's strength is nurtured by the complementary nature of democracy and capitalism. At the beginning of a new millennium, the Civic Education (CivEd) study of the International Association for the Evaluation of Educational Achievement (IEA) provided an opportunity to assess the current nature of civic education in the United States. Begun in 1993, the IEA CivEd project was conducted in two phases. In the first phase, which is the focus of this chapter, researchers in 24 countries gathered data on civic education in their countries for the development of case studies describing the context in which young people acquire their civic knowledge and attitudes (Torney-Purta, Schwille, & Amadeo, 1999). In the second phase of the study, nationally representative samples of 14-year-olds in 28 countries were assessed for their civic knowledge, skills, concepts, attitudes, and experiences (Torney-Purta, Lehmann, Oswald, & Schulz, 2001, and chapter 9, this volume). In this chapter I also will include the findings from Phase 2 that extend our understanding of the context of civic learning in the United States beyond that found in the initial case study.

CIVIC EDUCATION AND THE SCHOOLS

In all countries, civic education occurs in many out-of-school as well as in-school settings. However, in the United States, the school's role is particularly important—a fact that is often taken for granted by civic educators. This tradition becomes more apparent when compared to countries such as England, Portugal, and the Netherlands where there is no tradition of deliberate education for citizenship (Hahn, 1998; Torney-Purta et al., 1999). In the early days of the republic, Thomas Jefferson wrote of the need to educate citizens for democracy, and as the system of public education in the country grew, citizenship education was central to the mission of public schools.

Since the 1890s, the school subject called "social studies" has been designated to play a key role in citizenship preparation. Social studies has been viewed variously as the social sciences simplified for pedagogical reasons, an integrated subject that draws on history and the social sciences to help students deal with social problems, or the transmission of the nation's heritage (Barr, Barth, & Shermis, 1978). However, regardless, of the particular approach used, the subject has been seen to bear a particular responsibility for preparing young people for their role as citizens of a democracy (Hertzberg, 1981). For that reason, the IEA case study of civic education in the United States gives particular attention to social studies. Other aspects of the curriculum and the general school ethos, as well as out-of-school experiences, complement that focus.

Within that context, answers to a set of questions posed by the international steering committee of the IEA project frame the case study. What are 14- to 15- year-old students expected to learn in four domains? The domains are: (1) democracy, political institutions, and rights and responsibilities of citizens, considering messages in the hidden as well as overt curriculum; (2) national identity, including treatment of heroes and core documents; (3) social cohesion and diversity, including attention to what students learn about discrimination against a range of groups; and (4) the connection between the political and economic systems.

RESEARCH METHODS

To develop the case study, the research team collected data from multiple sources.[1] Those included a survey of the 50 states, a content analysis of textbooks, focus group interviews with 14- to 15-year-old students, focus group interviews with middle and high school social studies teachers, and interviews with experts in the particular domains being investigated (Hahn, Dilworth, Hughes, & Sen, 1998). Additionally, we drew on a survey of relevant literature (Hahn, Dilworth, & Hughes, 1998) and the insights of members of the National Expert Panel that advised the project (Hahn, Hughes, & Sen, 1998).[2] Later, information was added from a survey of a nationally representative sample of ninth graders in the United States (Baldi, Perie, Skidmore, Greenberg, & Hahn, 2001).

State Survey

In the United States, states and local school districts are responsible for schools. Consequently, unlike the situation in countries with a centralized curriculum (as for example, in Greece), there is considerable variety in curricular policy among the 50 states and over 15,000 school districts. For that reason we sent surveys to the 50 state social studies specialists or their equivalents. Ultimately we received responses from individuals in 48 states who were knowledgeable about statewide influences on social studies and civic education. The questionnaire asked about statewide policies that might impact upon civic education, such as requirements for particular courses for high school graduation, textbook adoption, and competency testing. We also asked the state social studies specialists to estimate whether a majority of school districts in their state taught particular courses from Grades 6 to 12 and, if so, at what grades.

Textbook Analysis

In the United States, it is a challenge to identify the most widely used textbooks. There is no official textbook (as there is, for example in Cyprus), no list of centrally approved textbooks (as exist, for example, in the Czech Republic), and no agency that keeps track of numbers of textbooks sold. About half of the states have textbook adoption policies. Notably, all of the southern states have such policies and none of the northeastern states do, according to respondents to our state survey. Even in states with an adoption policy, once a committee has adopted several textbooks for possible purchase with state funds, it is left to personnel in each school district, or even each school, to make the final selection.

To identify widely used textbooks for the subjects and grade levels of interest we triangulated information from several different sources.[3] Two specialists in social studies at the University of Minnesota conducted the content analysis of the textbooks using a rubric that focused on the four domains of interest in this study.

Student and Teacher Focus Groups

We conducted two focus groups with eighth- and ninth-grade students (approximately 14 years old) who attended four different schools in the metropolitan Atlanta area and two with students of the same age in two different communities in Texas. We conducted three focus groups with middle and high school teachers in the metropolitan Atlanta area, one in the Seattle area, and one in the Minneapolis area. We deliberately included in our groups students and teachers from both urban and suburban schools and from schools with differing racial and ethnic compositions. Focus groups contained from five to eight individuals and met for about two hours. Researchers in social studies education conducted the interviews using semi-structured interview protocols that focused on the four domains of the study. The purpose of these focus groups was to identify a range of meanings, experiences, and perceptions related to civic education to develop plausible hypotheses for testing with representative samples of students in Phase 2 of the IEA study and by other researchers in the future.

Individual Interviews

Additionally, we conducted several interviews with individuals. Three scholars were interviewed who are nationally known for their writing on citizenship education, history education, and economics education. In addition to being knowledgeable about research related to the domains of the study, these scholars had much experience conducting in-service education programs for teachers. We also interviewed a state social studies specialist and coordinators of state networks in law-related and economics education.

Student and School Surveys

In Phase 2 of the IEA CivEd study, questionnaires were administered to a representative sample of 2,811 ninth-grade students in 124 U. S. schools in October, 1999.[4] The student questionnaire was designed to measure civic knowledge, skills, concepts, attitudes, and experiences. Additionally, a school administrator completed a school questionnaire. In this chapter, I refer to data obtained from the two questionnaires that help us to see the extent to which themes identified in the initial case study are generalizable to representative samples of schools and students in the United States.

PERSPECTIVES ON THE CORE INTERNATIONAL FRAMING QUESTIONS

As we drew on the varied data sources described above, the review of literature (Hahn, Dilworth, & Hughes, 1998), and the knowledge of members of our National Expert Panel (Hahn, Hughes, & Sen, 1998), a general picture of civic education in the United States emerged. Each of the next sections begins with a discussion of the general context then summarizes findings from data collected by project staff for Phase 1 (Hahn, Dilworth, Hughes, & Sen, 1998). Additionally, I discuss relevant data from the Phase 2 survey of ninth graders (Baldi et al., 2001) and findings from other recent studies.

Domain 1: Democracy, Political Institutions, and Rights and Responsibilities of Citizens

There is a broad consensus in the United States that it is a responsibility of the schools to teach about democracy and to prepare students to be effective democratic citizens (Rose & Gallup, 2000). Nevertheless, there is considerable variety in how that is done. Because the curriculum of the schools is set at the local level within parameters set at the state level, there is variation from one state to the next and among school districts within a state about what is taught, when, and how. Even when teachers in the same school follow a common written curriculum, the way in which it is delivered often varies greatly (Hahn, 1991).

In many elementary classes students are taught about democracy when the class establishes class rules or votes to do something from among several alternatives. In the elementary grades students often learn about famous presidents and sometimes they learn about local government services when they study communities. Although most direct instruction about democracy, political institutions, and rights and responsibilities of citizens usually does not occur before middle or high school, some elementary classes or schools have had special citizenship programs. Moreover, in most school districts, children study some United States history—often in the fifth grade—during which they are taught about the founding of political institutions in the country.

Courses

In our state survey we asked the 50 state social studies specialists (or their equivalents) if there was a statewide requirement that United States government or civics/citizenship be taught in Grades 6 through 12. Respondents from 36 states said there was such a requirement in their state. Several noted that although civics, government, or citizenship was not specifically mandated, there was a state mandate for two or three years of high school social studies and within that, or in addition to that, some school districts mandated a course in civics or government. In other districts it was simply a tradition that most students took one such course. Additionally, in four states (Illinois, North Dakota, Washington, and Wyoming) there was a mandate that the United States Constitution be taught, but it was left up to districts to decide where and when they would do that.

In the state survey, we asked the state social studies specialists at which grades, between 6 and 12, they estimated that the majority of districts in their state taught particular courses, whether or not they were required. In order to address the international framing question related to student learning about democracy, institutions, and citizenship, we were interested in courses on state government, United States government, United States history, and civics or citizenship. Respondents from 45 states estimated that the majority of school districts in their state offered United States government or civics sometime between Grades 6 and 12. Additionally, respondents from 34 states said the majority of districts in their state taught state and local government—often in courses combined with either state history or United States government. Furthermore, respondents from 16 states estimated that courses in law, covering such topics as civil, criminal, consumer, and juvenile law, were taught in a majority of districts.

As for the grades at which students are most likely to be enrolled in civics, government, or law courses, respondents from 32 states estimated that the majority of districts teach United States government at the 12th grade and 20 estimated the 9th grade. In some cases, several grade levels were identified by the same person, for example, if he or she thought the majority of districts in the state taught civics as a required course in Grade 9 and government as a 12th-grade elective.

Seventeen respondents to our survey reported that state and local government tended to be taught in the eighth grade. Thirteen said they were taught in the 9th grade, and 13 said they were taught in 12th grade. The most frequently cited grade for teaching law courses was 12th grade.

The picture that emerges is similar to ones reported by other researchers. For example, Tolo (1999) identified statutes in 11 states that require the teaching of civics (no course specified) and another 10 that require specific courses before high school graduation. He also found that in recent years, states have adopted new curriculum standards and corresponding assessments, some of which may lead to increased teaching of civics and government. In analyzing transcripts from high school seniors in 1994, the National Center for Education Statistics (1997) reported that approximately 75% of students took at least one semester course in government. However, that tended to be in Grades 11 or 12. By examining that and other studies of high school transcripts, Niemi and Smith (2001) concluded that 17% of U. S. students take a ninth-grade course in civics or government; another 65% take such a course in Grades 10 through 12.

Overall, it appears from our survey that students in the majority of districts in 20 states might have had the opportunity to take a course in civics or government in Grade 9. Those in only 10 states are likely to have had such a course in Grade 8. Furthermore, students in a majority of districts in 17 states may have had instruction in state and local government in Grade 8; in 13 states it would have been in Grade 9. This means that students in many districts across the country will not have had deliberate instruction about local, state, and/or national government by the time they are 14- to 15-years old—the target age for the IEA study. A sizable number, however, are likely to have had such instruction. Moreover, most students will have learned about democracy, political institutions, and rights and responsibilities of citizens in a course in United States history before they are 14- or 15-years old. Indeed, respondents from 32 states estimated that the majority of districts in their state taught United States history in Grade 8; 12 said they did in Grade 9, and 7 in Grade 7.

It should be emphasized that because there is not a uniform pattern within states, the social studies specialists were only able to estimate at which grade a majority of districts in their state tended to teach particular courses. The variations in courses at particular grades even within the same state were illustrated by the difficulty we had in finding teachers of 14- to 15-year-olds in one state to participate in our focus groups. In the Atlanta metropolitan area alone, one school district taught Georgia history in Grade 8 and civics in Grade 9. Another district taught Georgia history in Grade 8 and one quarter each of civics, economics, and geography in Grade 9; a third district taught civics in Grade 8 and western civilization in Grade 9, and a fourth taught no civics, with government at Grade 12. In conducting focus groups and making phone calls to state social studies specialists for our survey, we found similar variations among districts within other states.

In Phase 2 of the IEA study, 55% of the school administrators who completed a school questionnaire reported that ninth-grade students were required to take five to six periods a week in various civic-related subjects (Baldi et al., 2001). However, that could be any social studies subject. Twenty percent of the respondents said that only one period or less of a civic-related subject was required.

The point is that most—but not all—students in the United States will have had some deliberate instruction related to democracy, political institutions, and rights and responsibilities of citizens by the time they are 14- or 15-years old. That is an important consideration because past researchers have found that students who are the most knowledgeable about government and politics are those who have had courses in civics or government (Niemi & Junn, 1998; Patrick & Hoge, 1991). However, the mere fact that students took a course in civics and government, does not tell us what they learned. One indication of the content to which they may have been exposed can be obtained from an examination of the most widely used textbooks for Grades 7 through 9.

Textbooks

For students who take a course in civics or United States history in Grades 7 through 9, the content and sequencing of topics is similar across the country. That is, to the extent that textbooks can be taken as indicative of what is actually taught in the classes where they are used, different books convey almost identical messages (Avery & Simmons, 2000/2001).

The three widely-used civics textbooks examined for this project emphasize the structure and function of national, state, and local levels of government. All three books begin with a discussion of representative democracy and introduce the United States Constitution as the foundation for government. They then move through the three branches of government in the same sequence: Congress, the Presidency, and finally, the Courts. The three widely used United States history books describe the development of democracy chronologically. They proceed from English antecedents through colonization, to the Revolutionary and Civil Wars, to the present. The history texts, like the civics texts, all define federalism and describe the functions of the three branches of government (Avery & Simmons, 2000/2001; Hahn, Dilworth, Hughes, & Sen, 1998).

In the textbooks, individual rights play a prominent role; general references to citizens' responsibilities are much less frequent. Additionally, the textbooks teach about the two major political parties, as well as about their historical forerunners. None of the texts, however, discuss advantages and disadvantages of a multiparty system (Avery & Simmons, 2000/20001). To determine whether the messages in the textbooks are actually those that are conveyed to students, we asked teachers in our focus groups what they taught and students what they learned.

Perspectives

When asked what "democracy" meant to the 14- to 15-year-olds in our focus groups, they said "the form of government that we have," "freedom," and "electing people to represent us." Several explained, "We don't have an exact democracy. If we did, even children could participate and it would take a lot of time." Rather, students emphasized, "We choose the people who have the same ideas as us and we elect them and they make the choices. Hopefully they make the choice we would make." Although one student distinguished a democracy from a monarchy, no student in our focus groups mentioned parliamentary or social democracies.

The 14- to 15-year-old students in our focus groups reported that in their social studies classes they had learned about the branches and levels of government; a few used the terms "executive," "legislative," and "judicial" branches, and referred to local, state, and national levels. Other students said "the people who make the laws," "courts and trials," and "the President, governor, and mayors." Most of the students reported learning about the United States Constitution and its amendments, especially the Bill of Rights. Several stated they had learned about "checks and balances" and some history behind the Constitution, such as the Magna Carta, the Declaration of Independence, and the Articles of Confederation. In regard to citizens' rights and responsibilities, most students mentioned voting either as a right that people in some "other countries don't have" or as a responsibility. They mentioned jury duty and "in case of war, to serve in the military" as responsibilities. Students noted that rights included the right "to have whatever religion you want, to free speech, and to bear arms." They recognized, however, that citizens disagree about the meaning of the latter right.

Teachers in our focus groups mentioned several other ideas that their students bring to the class about democracy. One said, "Kids come in with the idea that democracy is freedom of opportunity, especially to use your talents." Another reported that some of his African American male students who had encounters with the police came to his class with negative ideas about democracy and political institutions. Others commented that their immigrant students had ideas about rights based on their experiences in their home countries, particularly if they were refugees from repressive regimes.

Most of the teachers said that they taught about the distinction between direct and representative democracies. One said that he emphasized "in a democracy, power derives from the people," and "if people do not participate, they risk losing their freedom." Some of the eighth- and ninth-grade teachers said they compared democracy to communism, socialism, dictatorships, and monarchies. Additionally, several sixth- and seventh-grade teachers said that when they were teaching world regions, they would make comparisons between another country's form of government and that of the United States. Several teachers noted that they tried to point out not only the strengths but also the difficulties associated with democracy, such as its being inefficient and time consuming. Teachers also noted departures from the ideal of democracy, as when women could not vote and when Native Americans were put on reservations. Several teachers said that when students learned about the rights denied to colonial women, they complained, "that's not fair; that's not democracy."

Middle school teachers who did not explicitly teach civics or citizenship courses said they sometimes taught about political institutions and processes in the context of discussing current events with sixth and seventh graders. For example, one teacher said that if her class was talking about legislation being considered in the state legislature she would explain "how a bill becomes a law." Many of the social studies teachers who did not specifically teach civics classes said they had taught lessons related to this domain when they discussed the presidential elections with their students. Furthermore, teachers of eighth-grade state history courses explained that because "you can't study the state without the nation," they gave attention to colonial history and Constitutional principles. Teachers of eighth-grade United States history said they taught about democracy when they taught about the Mayflower Compact and colonial America.

Teachers of ninth-grade civics or citizenship courses said their course began with the background to democracy in the United States, including ancient Greece, the ideas of John Locke, the Magna Carta, the colonial period, and the Articles of Confederation. All of the teachers reported spending much time on the United States Constitution and the Bill of Rights and to a lesser extent the other amendments. One teacher, who taught the Constitution in depth said, "By the time I'm through with [the students] they can cite chapter and verse of all articles and sections of the Constitution."

All the civics teachers in the focus groups taught the three branches of government and several taught landmark Supreme Court cases. After studying the right to free speech, one teacher divided the class in half to consider two fictional scenarios. In one, students were to decide whether Nazis should be allowed to march and in the other, they were to decide if a homosexual group should be permitted to march. Most of the civics teachers reported that they taught a great deal of vocabulary, from "legislature" and "impeachment" to "subpoena" and "habeas corpus."

Several of the teachers in our focus groups said that their students had much interest in citizens' rights. That led one teacher to spend more time on rights than on other topics; it led another to talk about responsibilities that are associated with the Bill of Rights. Several teachers deliberately emphasized "one person can make a difference" and "you don't have to wait until you are 18" to become an active citizen. One teacher wanted her students to become "citizens who are willing to make sacrifices for the whole." Another teacher expressed the feeling that citizens should develop tolerance; for that reason, she used a curriculum project that was designed to teach tolerance for groups with diverse beliefs. Several teachers from different schools said that they wanted students to understand the tension between individual and group rights and, therefore, they would draw their students' attention to that perennial tension as they discussed a variety of issues.

Taken together, data from the textbook analysis and student and teacher focus groups suggest that when students have courses in United States history and civics, the topics differ very little from one classroom to the next. Moreover, it appears that most content in this domain is often presented as uncontested, for example, when teachers draw students' attention more to vocabulary and facts than to controversial historical and contemporary issues.

Many social studies educators since the 1940s have called for issues-centered instruction (Evans & Saxe, 1996; Parker, 1996). Furthermore, there is considerable evidence that students are more likely to develop knowledge about and an interest in the political arena if they have the opportunity to discuss controversial issues in a supportive environment (Ehman, 1980; Hahn, 1998; Niemi & Junn, 1998). Nevertheless, I found little evidence in our focus groups of such an approach being widely used. Students are told democracy rests on freedom of thought and that society values the "free marketplace of ideas." Additionally, much professional literature says that to develop democratic citizens social studies instruction should emphasize inquiry, critical thinking, and discussion of controversial issues. Yet, such inquiry and discussion does not appear to be prevalent in the schools from which our focus group participants came. Other researchers have made similar observations about social studies in the United States (Goodlad, 1984; McNeil, 1986).

Moreover, many of the themes that emerged from the focus groups and the textbook analysis in Phase 1 of the IEA study were also apparent in the questionnaire data obtained from the nationally representative sample of ninth graders in Phase 2. For example, with respect to topics studied, 79% of ninth graders reported studying the United States Constitution over the previous year. Keeping in mind that CivEd questionnaires were administered in October, students were reporting on their experience in eighth grade and only the first six weeks or so of the ninth grade. Seventy-five percent said they studied Congress and how laws are made (the first topic in many civics classes, according to our textbook analysis and focus groups). Slightly fewer—66 to 71%—reported studying the President and cabinet, state and local government, the court system, and political parties. In contrast, fewer than half reported studying other countries' governments (49%) and international organizations (43%). Similar data were obtained from the National Assessment of Educational Progress (NAEP) Civics assessment, which was administered in April 1998. Over 70% of students at both Grades 4 and 8 said that they had studied the Constitution and Congress in the current school year. Less than half said they had studied other countries' governments or international organizations, such as the United Nations (Lutkus, Weiss, Campbell, Mazzeo, & Lazer, 1999).

With respect to classroom climates that support democratic discourse, interesting data were obtained from the CivEd survey. Eighty-five percent of ninth graders reported that in their social studies classes they were encouraged to make up their minds, and close to 80% said that teachers present several sides of an issue and encourage students to express their views. Furthermore, almost 80% said they felt comfortable expressing their views. However, fewer—69%—reported that teachers encouraged them to discuss political or social issues about which people have different opinions (Baldi et al., 2001). It appears that students may be encouraged to express their opinions on minor matters in their classes, but they are not encouraged to explore the controversial issues that divide society. Our textbook analysis and focus group data point to that possibility.

Experiences

Students learn about democracy and the citizen's role not only from what is taught in social studies classes but also from co-curricular and extracurricular activities. The most common experiences are mock elections. All of the students in our 1997 focus groups said that they participated in mock presidential elections in 1996. Students also said that by electing peers to leadership positions in the band, clubs, and student government, they learned about democracy and citizens' rights and responsibilities.

Middle schools sometimes have programs for the purpose of developing responsibility in young citizens. In one district, the middle school teachers selected a "Citizen of the Month" at each school. In another district, middle school students were given citizenship grades prompting a teacher to explain,

> If you were quiet and didn't bother anybody, you got an A. We've tried to change that now so that the criteria are that you do that, plus you participate.

You make a better environment for other people, or you reach out and do something in an active way to change and make this a better place.

Other middle school teachers described programs in conflict resolution and peer mediation, whereby students learned to resolve conflicts nonviolently. At one school with such programs, there was also a community service program; student volunteers worked in nursing homes, with the Food Bank, and in homeless shelters "to learn good citizenship."

Interestingly, three middle school teachers in different urban schools with largely African American populations commented that it was difficult to teach about democracy and speaking one's opinion when the atmosphere of the school worked against that. They said that although they encourage their students to speak out, many of their colleagues told students to be quiet, listen, and take notes or work on assignments at their seats. Furthermore, the students had to be quiet in the halls and the lunchroom, where a "quiet lunch" policy was enforced. A teacher in another part of the country also expressed concern that when she taught in one urban school,

> There was no sense of responsibility put on the kids other than to be in class and to be on time. What the administrators in our building were most concerned about was order, and the last thing they wanted was for kids to speak out on issues.

In contrast, other teachers described ways in which their students were learning to be participatory citizens. In one middle school, each year students undertook a different project to connect them with governmental institutions, such as when one class made the arrangements to paint warning signs on storm drains. At another school during an election students were given the option to interview voters at the polls, work for a political party, or invite candidates to speak at the school.

At some schools, students participate in state and nationally sponsored experiential programs, such as mock trials, Kids Voting, Lobby Day, Close Up, and other programs that introduce young people to legislative and judicial processes. The Center for Civic Education sponsors two programs that have involved millions of students nationwide. *We the People ... The Citizen and the Constitution* engages students in mock legislative hearings on constitutional issues. *Project Citizen* (chapter 5, this volume) teaches middle school students to identify a problem in their community, research the issue, and develop a solution. Students participating in the program present portfolios of their projects in local, state, and national competitions. Another program to teach civic action skills is the Constitutional Rights Foundation's program *Active Citizenship Today* (ACT). It has been widely used, particularly in urban communities. Additionally, many schools and individual teachers have encouraged students to get involved in community service or service learning programs (Hepburn, 2001; Hodgkinson & Weitzman, 1997; Nolin, Chaney, Chapman, & Chandler, 1997; Torney-Purta, Hahn, & Amadeo, 2001; Wade, 1997).

The IEA CivEd Phase 2 surveys provide information about the percentage of schools in the United States with a ninth grade that offer various civic education programs. School administrators in 48% of schools reported that their schools had service clubs and conflict resolution or peer mediation programs. From 38 to 39% of respondents said their schools offered Girls/Boys State or Junior Statesmen programs (involving students in the legislative process), and character or values education. Twenty-five percent offered mock trial programs and 24% offered some form of service learning or community service program. Twenty-one percent of the schools offered Close Up, Presidential Classroom, or another program that takes students to Washington, DC, and 20% offer programs in which students work in the state legislature. Close to 18% sponsored History Day competitions, a debate team, and Kids Voting or other mock election program (Baldi et al., 2001). It is important to remember that administrators were reporting on whether their school offered programs, not the percentage of students who participated. Further, it is likely that many of the ninth graders who completed the surveys would not participate in particular programs until later in high school.

The survey did provide some information about the kinds of extracurricular activities that students had already participated in by October of the ninth grade—the kinds of activities from which our focus group participants told us they learned about democracy. Eighty-one percent of ninth graders said they had participated in a sports team or organization, 62% had participated in an art, music, or drama organization (most likely a school band, according to our focus group members). Fifty percent (considerably higher than the international mean of 18%) had worked with a group conducting voluntary activities to help the community. Additionally, 44% of ninth graders said they had participated in an organization sponsored by a religious organization, 40% had collected money for a charity or social cause, and 39% had participated in Scouts. Thirty-three percent had been on the student council or student government. Fewer reported participating in an environmental organization (24%), a school newspaper (21%), a computer club (16%), or other organization (Baldi et al., 2001).

Consistent with our focus group students' reports that they learned about democracy from participation in extracurricular activities, ninth graders who participated in extracurricular activities scored higher on both the content and skills sub-scales of the IEA knowledge test than students without such participation. Moreover, neither the type of activity nor the frequency of participation seemed to matter (Baldi et al., 2001). Of course, it is possible, that some other variable, such as socioeconomic status, may influence both participation in extracurricular activities and achievement, rather than participation directly influencing achievement. Further studies are needed to establish any cause-effect relationship.

In summary, for the first domain of the study only a small percentage of 14- to 15-year-old students in the United States are likely to have taken a course deliberately designed to teach them about political institutions and processes. (That is not unusual internationally. As in many other countries, most students will have had courses in history and/or integrated social studies in which they will have acquired information related to democracy, political institutions, and citizens' roles.) Regardless of the state or school district in which they live, students who take courses under similar titles are likely to have been exposed to similar information. It should be kept in mind that curriculum and instruction is not all that matters. Much of the learning that is relevant to this domain occurs through the hidden curriculum and experiences outside of the classroom. In that, there is clearly much variation from one school to another and even from one class to another in the same school. Some students participate in student government, clubs, community service projects, and special programs sponsored by civic education organizations; however, many do not. For example, the 1988 NAEP revealed that 52% of 12th graders said they had never participated in mock elections, councils, or trials (National Assessment, 1990). In the IEA CivEd study 50% of ninth graders had not participated in community service activities and almost 70% had not participated in student government. Similarly, while some students are in classes in which they are encouraged to discuss public policy issues and in schools in which they have input to decision making, many other students are not.

Domain 2: National Identity

Students acquire a sense of national identity from many out-of-school experiences, but schools also make a contribution. From the time they enter school in the first grade, children in the United States learn about their national identity from celebrations of holidays, literature, and history lessons. Additionally, a large flag hangs on a pole in front of most schools and smaller flags often hang on the wall at the front of classrooms. A morning flag salute is a common, but not universal, practice at the elementary and middle school levels in the United States.

To ascertain 14- to 15-year-olds' sense of national identity, we asked students in the focus groups what it meant to them to be an American. In all four groups, students said "freedom" or "being free." One young woman explained, "We have a lot more freedom to express our beliefs than [people in] other countries." Several Latino students in Texas noted that being an American meant being a citizen or legal resident, as opposed to "not legal." In that group, as well as the others, students expressed pride in being Americans at the same time they described ways in which the totality of the nation's history has not lived up to the ideal of freedom and equality for all.

The history education expert we interviewed reported that in her studies of students in Grades 5 and 8, there was a clear belief in "American exceptionality." That is, students perceive the United States to be different from and better than other countries. She explained that students tend to organize their understanding of what it means to be an American around the Bill of Rights. They see the nation's history as a story of progress that includes the struggles for women's rights and civil rights as bringing the country closer to achieving its ideals.

We heard similar themes in our student focus groups. Students said they associated being an American with democracy, various political institutions, and rights and responsibilities of citizenship—topics developed in the last section. Additionally, because the development of national identity is related to one's identification with the nation's history, the following discussion focuses on history teaching and learning.

Courses

All of the social studies specialists who responded to our survey of the states reported that United States history is taught in the majority of school districts in their state. Indeed, United States history is the social studies course for which there is most likely to be a statewide mandate, with 85% of the respondents to our state survey reporting that students were required to take such a course. Most of the social studies specialists—89%—said it is taught in the 11th grade when students are typically 16 or 17 years old. Eighth grade (13- to 14-year-olds) was the second most common grade to teach United States history, with 68% of the respondents estimating the majority of districts in their state taught it then. Twenty-one percent reported it was taught in Grades 6 or 7.

Textbooks

Because national identity is formed, in part, through a connection to a nation's "story"—its birth, celebrations, struggles, heroes, and villains—the story passed on to students in their textbooks is of particular relevance (Avery & Simmons, 2000/2001). Across the civics and history books examined, there is a common story of significant events, people, and documents. Events related to the country's founding and to armed conflict dominate the history books, and to a lesser extent, the civics books. The United States Constitution is the document at the center of the country's narrative. All six of the widely used textbooks include copies of the Constitution, the Bill of Rights, and the Declaration of Independence.

The people most frequently mentioned in the textbooks, with only a few notable exceptions such as Martin Luther King, Jr., were European American males who held political offices. Over half the individuals mentioned were presidents of the United States. Not surprisingly perhaps, the people presented in the textbooks seem to be the ones who are most remembered by students and teachers.

Perspectives

Most United States history courses are organized and taught chronologically (Jenness, 1990). Topics covered in the classes of teachers and students in our focus groups included the colonial period, the French and Indian War, the Revolutionary War, the War between the United States and Mexico, and the Civil War. As one Texas student replied when asked about big historical events, "the Civil War, Civil War, Civil War." In many school districts, students study about United States history up to the Civil War in Grade 5 and/or Grades 8 or 9. Eleventh-grade courses emphasize the period from the Civil War to the present. Perhaps it is because we did not interview students over age 15 that we did not hear much about events in the 20th century.

Focus group students identified a number of national heroes they had studied in school. They included presidents (Washington, Jefferson, Adams, Lincoln, Franklin Roosevelt, Kennedy, Lyndon Johnson, Nixon, and Carter), military leaders (Generals Lee and Grant from the Civil War period and General Colin Powell from the Gulf War), and civil rights leaders (Harriet Tubman, Dr. Martin Luther King, Jr., and Rosa Parks). Benjamin Franklin and Eleanor Roosevelt were also mentioned. There seems to be a mixed amount of criticism or skepticism with respect to national leaders. On the one hand, students are told that leaders are not infallible or above criticism; on the other, there seems to be little critical assessment of contemporary leaders and issues. Students in one group said they had learned about Nixon and the Watergate scandal (the focus group interviews were conducted prior to the impeachment proceedings against President Clinton; otherwise, he also might have been mentioned). One of the teachers who said she tries to teach both the positive and negative sides of United States history explained, "I think it is very important to show that negative things happened but things are changing or have been changing."

Students in the United States associate a number of core documents with their nation's heritage. In addition to making frequent mention of the Constitution and Bill of Rights, the students we interviewed cited the Articles of Confederation, the Declaration of Independence, and Martin

Luther King, Jr.'s "I Have a Dream" speech. Teachers in our focus groups confirmed the importance placed on the Constitution, particularly in civics classes, as noted previously.

In referring to events in the nation's past, students frequently used terms such as "we," "us," or "our." Clearly, they identified with the narrative they were told in their history books—even when they knew that their own personal ancestors were not part of the dominant group at the time of the event to which they referred. This interesting trend has been found by other researchers also (Barton & Levstik, 1998).

This is not to say that students hold totally positive feelings toward the history of their country. Indeed, U.S. students' feelings toward their country and its symbols, like those of students in other countries appear to be positive, but not excessively so. On the CivEd survey, students from the United States scored at the international mean on the three-item scale measuring attitudes toward the nation. Although 92% of the U.S. ninth graders said that the United States should be proud of what it has achieved, fewer—84%—said they had a great love for the country or that the national flag is important to them. Interestingly, on this scale there were no statistically significant differences between white and black students, male and female students, nor students from various socioeconomic levels, as measured by number of books in the home. However, Hispanic ninth graders were less likely than their white peers to agree with the items on this scale, and foreign-born students were less likely than native-born students to agree with these statements (Baldi et al., 2001). I am reminded of the lack of attention to Hispanics in the textbooks that we analyzed and the discussion of what it means to be an American in the focus group containing Latinos in Texas. As the 2000 census indicates the growing size of the Hispanic population in the United States, it is especially important that future social studies researchers explore the context of civic education that might have an impact on the complex development of national identity for students in this and other ethnic groups.

Domain 3: Social Cohesion and Diversity

The third domain investigated in the IEA project focuses on what students are expected to learn about those belonging to groups that are seen as set apart or discriminated against (as for example, by ethnicity, race, immigrant status, mother tongue, social class, religion, or gender).

Courses

In our survey of state social studies specialists, respondents from only nine states reported that the majority of districts in their state teach distinct ethnic studies courses. However, 73% of the respondents said that ethnic studies are infused into other courses. Most of that is probably done through instruction in United States history. If the experiences of people in our focus groups are typical, then the greatest integration of ethnic studies content and multiple perspectives is in United States history courses.

Textbooks

In earlier periods, social studies textbooks were criticized for giving insufficient attention to minorities and women. Through the 1980s researchers reported that books were becoming more inclusive (Patrick & Hoge, 1991). Our analysis of textbooks suggests, however, that some problems persist (Avery & Simmons, 2000/2001).

The United States is depicted in all of the civics and United States history textbooks examined as a "nation of immigrants." The civics texts describe the country's immigration policies, including graphic representations of the naturalization process. The history texts present an historical overview of waves of immigration, with some discussion of why immigrants came to the United States. The history texts describe the earliest immigrants as those who arrived in the Americas across the Bering Straits and then present information on early civilizations on the continent. The history texts describe later immigrants' experiences during different periods of history. Each history book discusses slavery, attending to the living conditions, religion, education, artwork, and music of slave culture.

Ethnic minorities receive little attention across the texts. The few mentioned are generally cited for their roles as advocates for political rights. Very few Hispanics or individuals with Asian ancestry are cited. Women receive substantially less coverage than men, particularly in the civics textbooks. Further, although the disparity between men and women in the political realm is noted, there is little discussion of the implications. Women are more often discussed in the history texts than in the civics texts, although even there, few women are mentioned when compared to the number of men cited. Very few women of color are described in either the civics or history textbooks.

Perspectives

Since the 1960s, numerous writers have argued that social studies curriculum and instruction should be more inclusive of diverse perspectives. In the early 1990s some people argued that the pendulum had swung too far in emphasizing diversity at the expense of unity. In the midst of national debates over this issue, there was little empirical evidence of what students were actually learning about cultural diversity and social cohesion, so we turned to our focus groups for insights. Most teachers and students in our groups reported that United States history courses included information on the treatment of Native Americans and of blacks under slavery and segregation, as well as the Civil Rights movement. Fewer teachers and students described attention to Hispanics and Asian Americans in United States history courses. One teacher in the Northwest explained,

> We usually start with our state history and discuss the people who populate our region. We discuss who was in our state first ...we look at the Native Americans, and then we begin to look at the people who came later ...If we are talking about the building of railroads we discuss the arrival of the Chinese. When we talk about the expansion of our farmlands we discuss the Japanese arrival and involvement with the expansion. We talk about the arrival of African Americans into our region.

Several teachers said that, in their history classes, they talked about discrimination against women in colonial America and the suffragist movement. Also, teachers reported discussing discrimination against religious minorities and immigrants. The students in our focus groups mentioned those topics in general terms only. In one focus group in Texas, which contained several Mexican American students, students also cited discrimination against Mexicans. In addition to receiving instruction in the context of United States history, students in the various focus groups mentioned lessons about discrimination that they had in conjunction with Martin Luther King, Jr.'s birthday and with Black History Month. These findings are similar to those obtained by the history education expert we interviewed. She said that in her research on students' historical understanding, by the end of eighth grade "all of the kids knew there was prejudice" and that "race, class, and gender were problematic" in the history of the United States.

None of the students in our focus groups mentioned particular extracurricular activities that contributed to their knowledge of diverse groups. Rather, most students reported learning about different groups by socializing with students at their school who were members of a cultural or racial group different from their own. This was especially true for students who attended schools in which members of ethnic "minority" groups made up a substantial part of the student population. These personal experiences taught young people about diversity in the contemporary context while their history lessons taught them about social diversity in the past.

Overall, unlike adults who fiercely debated the national unity versus cultural diversity choice, young people appear to feel that both unity and diversity exist simultaneously in their country. They describe contributions by diverse groups to the history of the nation. They cite inequities of the past and the present at the same time they refer to "our" country.

The CivEd survey from Phase 2 of the IEA study further reveals the positive attitudes that students in the United States are developing toward diversity. U.S. ninth graders were among students from only four countries who were highly supportive of rights for both women and immigrants (the other countries were Norway, Sweden, and Cyprus). More than 90% of ninth graders in the United States agreed that: women should run for public office and take part in government just as men do; women should have the same rights as men in every way; and men and women should get equal pay when they are in the same jobs (Baldi et al., 2001). Females were more supportive of these statements than males. Additionally, ninth graders born in the United States were more supportive of women's rights than those born out of the country, white students were more supportive than black students, and students with more books in the home (a proxy for socioeconomic status) were more supportive than those with fewer.

More than 90% of ninth graders said that immigrants should have the same opportunities for education as other children. Fewer, but still over 80%, agreed that immigrants should have the same rights as everyone else in the country, including the opportunity to keep their own customs and lifestyles, and the right to vote in elections (Baldi et al., 2001). On this scale, ninth graders born outside the United States were more supportive than those born within the country; Hispanic, Asian, and multiracial students were more supportive than white students; and females reported more positive attitudes than did male students. There were no statistically significant differences among students from different socioeconomic backgrounds, as indicated by number of books in the home.

Domain 4: Connections between the Economic and Political Systems

To many people, democracy and a market economy are intertwined and economic literacy is an important component of citizenship education. For that reason we were interested in what students learn about the connection between the economic and political systems.

Courses

It appears that students before the age of 14 or 15 are most likely to learn about any connection between economic principles and the government in elementary school social studies or in United States history, state studies, or world studies at the middle school level. Relatively few 14- to 15-year-olds will have had a separate economics course. On the survey, state social studies specialists in only 10 states estimated that the majority of districts in their state taught economics courses at the ninth grade. Additionally, no more than two respondents said they taught such a course at Grades 6, 7, or 8. However, respondents from 25 states estimated that an economics course was taught at the 12th grade. In 16 of those states economics was a requirement for high school graduation.

Textbooks

All three of the civics textbooks analyzed describe the economics system in the United States in terms of a free market system (Avery & Miller, 1998). Students are given information on the relationship of government to business and labor. The texts, both implicitly and explicitly, tend to support government provision of basic services, such as police, fire services, and garbage removal. One textbook quoted Abraham Lincoln: "The legitimate object of government is to do for people what needs to be done but which they cannot by individual effort do at all or do so well for themselves" (Avery & Miller, 1998). The authors continued with the statement that Lincoln knew that government could grow too large and spend too much money. However, the three civics textbooks did describe the agencies of the executive branch of government that attempt to ameliorate the effects of unemployment, illness, homelessness, and natural disasters.

Capitalism and communism are contrasted in all three of the civics textbooks. Capitalism is explained as a system in which all members of society make economic decisions. Communism is portrayed as leaving the citizen with few choices. There was little examination of poverty or unequal distribution of resources in the United States [or elsewhere] (Avery & Miller, 1998).

Perspectives

When focus group students were asked what democracy meant to them, many contrasted it with communism or socialism. However, when asked if they thought there was a connection between the economic and political system and what they learned about that, students tended to say that they didn't know. Furthermore, when asked if they had discussed whether the government ought to provide social benefits to people, a few students replied that such an issue had not been raised in any of their classes. A few other students, however, remembered talking about "welfare" and that the government was "supposed" to take care of the sick, homeless, and unemployed.

Only one of the teachers said that she tried to bring "a lot" of economics into her civics class. Middle school teachers in another focus group complained that they hardly ever got to teach economics. For the most part, teachers said that they taught about democracy and the economy without making a conscious attempt to connect the two; to them they were two separate spheres. In the school districts that offer a ninth-grade economics course taught by a specialist teacher, more deliberate attention might be given to the connection than was revealed in our focus groups.

Experiences

A few of the teachers in our focus groups mentioned that their schools had student stores and Junior Achievement programs in which students learned about business and economics. Students were more likely to mention out-of-school than in-school activities from which they learned about the connection between economic principles and government. Most students said they learned about different taxes from buying things and from their parents, as well as from teachers.

Overall, except in a few school districts, 14- to 15-year-olds are not likely to have received concentrated instruction in economic concepts and principles. Rather, they may have acquired some general knowledge about the relationship between the economic system and government indirectly from their school, family, and everyday experiences in the wider society.

Once again, the Phase 2 survey of a national sample of schools and students adds some information to this picture. On the school questionnaire, 37% of school administrators reported that their school offered the Stock Market Game, sponsored by the National Council on Economic Education; 12% said that they had a Junior Achievement program. However, we do not know what percentage of students at any particular grade level, such as ninth graders, participate.

Consistent with the view suggested by our textbook analysis and focus groups, it appears that most students learn that government should have a limited role in the economy. On the one hand 84% of ninth graders agreed that it should be the government's responsibility to keep prices under control. Close to 65% said it should be the government's responsibility to provide industries with the support they need to grow, guarantee a job for everyone who wants one, and reduce differences in income and wealth among people. Almost as many—59%—said the government should provide an adequate standard of living for the unemployed (Baldi et al., 2001). These percentages are lower than those reported by samples in the other 27 countries that participated in the IEA study (Torney-Purta, Lehmann, Oswald, & Schulz, 2001).

Instructional Activities and Assessment across Four Domains

The International Steering Committee for the IEA project posed questions about instructional activities and assessments. In the United States those factors influence civic education similarly, regardless of whether one is looking at the teaching of political concepts, national identity, social cohesion and diversity, or the connection between economics and politics.

Instructional Activities

In Phase 2 of the IEA study, 88% of ninth-grade students reported that when they studied social studies, they read from the textbook or filled out worksheets (Baldi et al., 2001). Seventy-seven percent reported writing reports and watching videos. Discussing current events (75%) and videos were other activities reported by most students. Fewer said they took part in debates or panel discussions (45%) or in role plays, mock trials, or dramas (40%).

Although some students in our focus groups reported that in their classes they "mostly read out of the book" and did not do other activities, the majority of students we interviewed said that they did some activities, such as projects and simulations, in their social studies classes. Students in one group mentioned many engaging experiential activities that one teacher used to stimulate reflection and discussion. Additionally, several of the teachers in our focus groups described activities they used that took students outside of the classroom. In reading the focus group transcripts the variation in the amount of instructional activities to which a student might be exposed from one teacher to the next and from one school to the next is striking.

Students and teachers alike mentioned the use of current events, notebooks, discussions, debates, position papers, and research projects. Simulations and role playing exercises were commonly mentioned activities. For example, several teachers and students described simulations of the Constitutional convention, elections, and "how a bill becomes a law." Some students experienced a simulation in which the teacher "discriminated" against some of the students based on an arbitrary criteria, such as eye color, and from that experience the class went on to study prejudice or segregation in the United States. In learning about the economy, some classes simulated a mini-society complete with stores and other businesses. At the middle school and high school level in one state, many students participate in the Stock Market Game.

However, not all classes use a wide range of activities. One teacher explained why he and his colleagues in an urban high school serving African American students did not engage students in a variety of activities and his concern for the consequences,

> Although they want us to be more creative, we do the traditional things—lectures and have students answer questions in the text.... We've got to do whatever we can to get the students to read the textbook, and answering questions is one way to guarantee that we can have a conversation about what they've read. The students are not reading it at home, so we end up having to do it in the classroom, which none of us likes. Number one, we'd rather be doing other things and number two, our students are falling behind. If somebody else's students are reading at home and then doing stuff in the classroom,

they're getting more than ours are. But we've got to play with the cards that we're dealt.

It appears from our interviews and from other recent studies of social studies classes in the United States (Hahn, 1991, 1998) that classes and schools differ widely as to how much variety there is in instructional activities. Some teachers provide much variety; others very little. Most students seem to be in classes that fall between the two extremes, with frequent teacher talk and student recitation related to the textbook and, periodically, a simulation, written project, or discussion of a current issue. Listening to the teachers and students in the focus groups, we wondered if students in classes in which there is special concern with basic skill development are likely to experience fewer engaging instructional activities than those in classes where there is less emphasis on basic skills, such as reading comprehension. It remains for future researchers to explore that hypothesis further.

Assessment

In the United States, unlike many other countries, there is no national examination that all students take. However, the National Assessment of Educational Progress (NAEP) periodically assesses the knowledge of students in a representative sample of schools in the country. Researchers analyzing NAEP assessments conducted in the 1970s and 1980s concluded that youth in the United States had a general, but not detailed understanding of government and political processes (Hahn, Dilworth, & Hughes, 1998). A similar conclusion can be drawn from recent assessments.

In Phase 2 of the IEA CivEd project, U.S. ninth graders overall performed well when compared to their counterparts in other countries, with respect to knowledge of democracy and democratic processes. They scored significantly above the international mean on the total civic knowledge scale; their average score on the content subscale was at the international mean, and on the skills subscale, U.S. ninth graders scored significantly above students in every other country (Baldi et al., 2001). However, NAEP researchers, using an instrument that measured specific knowledge of United States government and political processes, concluded that close to 30% of students at Grades 4, 8, and 12 did not have a basic understanding of civic content (Lutkus et al., 1999).

Statewide assessments in social studies are quite common in the United States. Indeed, they are required in 25 states, according to respondents to our 1997 state survey. Moreover, most said that the major change they saw on the horizon in their state was the development of new content standards with corresponding assessments.

According to participants in our focus groups, most assessment is done at the classroom level through chapter and unit tests and examinations at the end of a course. Most of these tests tend to be multiple choice and short answer with a few essays. They tend to be either teacher-developed or teacher-adapted from published tests that accompany the textbook. Teachers also reported evaluating projects, homework, and student participation in class discussions to complement test results. A few teachers encourage students to present their newly acquired knowledge in diverse forms, such as a play, song, or video presentation. Others said they try to use "authentic assessment," by asking their students to present their knowledge in ways that they might use in the future, such as in the form of a letter to the editor of a local newspaper or a petition to a local council.

CHALLENGES

Numerous challenges face civic educators in the United States. For example, state social studies specialists said that budget constraints and a crowded curriculum were obstacles to effective social studies. They also reported that a shortage of materials and inadequate teacher content knowledge were problems. Although a few teachers in our focus groups also mentioned lack of resources, and one said that setting priorities in a crowded curriculum was a challenge, others raised different issues. Several mentioned that teaching students who spoke little English or who had poor reading skills was a daily challenge. A few said lack of teacher knowledge and fear of controversy posed a problem in teaching about diversity. Others said that it was a challenge trying to teach about democracy and encouraging students to express their opinions when school policies aimed at "keeping kids silent and powerless." One teacher added,

> I think it's a hard job to teach kids about democracy and citizenship because you don't get results until much later, and the civics teacher alone isn't going to do it. It's got to be the whole building. It's got to be every teacher. Right now, I don't think that happens.

The results from Phase 2 of the IEA study and from the 1998 NAEP Civics point to the need to learn more about the quality of civic education for particular subgroups of students. In both those assessments, achievement was related to socioeconomic factors, as measured by eligibility for the free and reduced lunch program, parental education level, and number of books in the home. Students from low SES families and/or schools did not perform as well as students from high SES families/schools (Baldi et al., 2001; Lutkus et al., 1999). Additionally, at Grades 8 and 12, students in suburban schools had higher scores on NAEP Civics than their peers in central city schools (Lutkus et al., 1999).

Although there were no gender differences in knowledge on either assessment, in both there were significant differences by race and ethnicity; white students scored higher than African American and Hispanic students (Baldi et al., 2001; Lutkus et al., 1999). In a country that prides itself on valuing equality and justice for all, it is especially important that researchers, policy makers, and educators direct their attention to these glaring inequalities in the outcomes of civic education.

Importantly, as most states have revised content standards and developed new tests, some of which assess what students know in the area of civic education, it strikes me that the great need is less to equalize what students are taught than how they are taught. Listening to the students and teachers from different schools in our focus groups, it sounded as if students in urban schools serving families from lower socioeconomic levels may be less likely to experience varied instructional strategies and democratic school environments than students in schools serving higher socioeconomic groups. The messages they thus learn about democracy, national identity, and diversity are quite different.

ACKNOWLEDGMENT

This chapter is a revision of Hahn, C. L. (1999). Funding for the research reported here was provided by the National Center for Education Statistics of the United States Office of Education.

NOTES

1. Carole Hahn was the National Research Coordinator for the United States portion of the study. Paulette Dilworth, Michael Hughes, Trisha Sen, and Lois Wolfe assisted her in Phase 1 at Emory University. Patricia Avery and Annette Miller at the University of Minnesota conducted the textbook analysis. Gloria Contreras conducted student focus groups in Texas. Walter Parker and Theresa Johnson conducted teacher focus groups in Seattle and Minneapolis, respectively.

2. Members of the National Expert Panel for both phases of the project in the United States were: Patricia Avery, Margaret Branson, Gloria Contreras, Shielah Mann, Richard Niemi, Pat Nickell, Valerie Pang, Walter Parker, and John Patrick. Richard Sirvint was a member of the panel for Phase 1.

3. First, we asked state social studies specialists if their state had an adoption policy to provide us with a list of the adopted texts for social studies. We identified the civics and United States history textbooks for Grades 7 through 9 that appeared on the most lists, paying particular attention to the ones that were used in the states with the largest populations (California, Texas). We also asked three experts in civics and United States history teaching to name the books that they thought were

the most widely used in the country. Additionally, a staff member of the American Textbook Council, who could not give us specific figures, did give us what he believed to be a "short list" of widely used books. Finally, we selected the three books for United States history and the three books for civics/government for Grades 7 through 9 that appeared on the most lists.

4. Staff at Westat, Inc. selected a sample of 150 nationally representative public and private schools that contained a ninth grade. Within the selected schools, if a school required a social studies course of ninth graders, then one intact class of the required course was randomly selected. If there was no required ninth grade social studies course, then a ninth grade homeroom class was randomly selected. Useable data were obtained from 124 schools. Staff at the American Institutes of Research analyzed data from the student and school surveys.

REFERENCES

Avery, P.G., & Miller, A. (1998, April). *A content analysis of U.S. history and civics textbooks: U.S. national case study for the IEA civic education project.* Paper presented at the annual meeting of the American Educational Research Association, San Diego.

Avery, P.G., & Simmons, A.M. (2000/2001). Civic life as conveyed in U. S. civics and history textbooks. *International Journal of Social Education, 15,* 105–130.

Baldi, S., Perie, M., Skidmore, D., Greenberg, E., & Hahn, C. (2001). *What democracy means to ninth-graders: U.S. results from the international IEA civic education study.* Washington, DC: National Center for Education Statistics, U.S. Department of Education.

Barr, R., Barth, J., & Shermis, S. (1978). *The nature of the social studies.* Palm Springs, CA: ETC Publications.

Barton, K., & Levstik, L. (1998). It wasn't a good part of history. *Teachers College Record, 99,* 478–513.

Ehman, L.H. (1980). The American school in the political socialization process. *Review of Educational Research, 50,* 99–119.

Evans, R.W., & Saxe, D.W. (1996). *Handbook on teaching social issues.* Washington, DC: National Council for the Social Studies.

Goodlad, J. (1984). *A place called school.* New York: McGraw-Hill.

Hahn, C.L. (1991, November). *Social studies classroom climate, the media, and adolescent political attitudes: A case of the complementary roles of qualitative and quantitative methodologies in political socialization research.* Paper presented at the annual meeting of the National Council for the Social Studies, Washington, DC.

Hahn, C.L. (1998). *Becoming political: Comparative perspectives on citizenship education.* Albany: State University of New York Press.

Hahn, C.L. (1999). Challenges to civic education in the United States. In J. Torney-Purta, J. Schwille, & J.A. Amadeo (Eds.), *Civic education across countries: Twenty four national case studies from the IEA civic education project* (pp. 583–607). Amsterdam: The International Association for the Evaluation of Educational Achievement.

Hahn, C.L., Dilworth, P.P., & Hughes, M. (1998). *IEA civic education project phase 1: The United States—A review of literature* (Vol. I). Unpublished manuscript. ERIC Document Reproduction Service ED 444 885.

Hahn, C.L., Dilworth, P.P., Hughes, M., & Sen, T. (1998). *IEA civic education project phase 1: The United States—Responses to the four core international framing questions* (Vol. III). Unpublished manuscript. ERIC Document Reproduction Service ED 444 887.

Hahn, C.L., Hughes, M., & Sen, T. (Eds.). (1998). *IEA civic education project phase 1: The United States—Responses to 18 framing questions and annotated bibliography* (Vol. II). Unpublished manuscript. ERIC Document Reproduction Service ED 444 886.

Hepburn, M. (2001, July). *Service learning in civic education: Potential and pitfalls.* Paper presented at the annual meeting of the Social Science Education Consortium, Oxford, England.

Hertzberg, H. (1981). *Social studies reform-1880–1890. A report of project SPAN.* Boulder, CO: Social Science Education Consortium.

Hodgkinson, V., & Weitzman, M. (1997). *Volunteering and giving among teenagers 12 to 17 years of age.* Washington, DC: The Independent Sector.

Jenness, D. (1990). *Making sense of social studies.* New York: Macmillan.

Lutkus, A.D., Weiss, A.R., Campbell, J. R., Mazzeo, J., & Lazer, S. (1999). *NAEP 1998 civics report card for the nation.* Washington, DC: National Center for Education Statistics, U.S. Department of Education.

McNeil, L. (1986). *Contradictions of control: School structure and school knowledge.* New York: Routledge.

National Assessment of Educational Progress. (1990). *The civics report card.* Washington, DC: U. S. Department of Education.

National Center for Education Statistics. (1997). *1994 high school transcripts study.* Washington, DC: U. S. Department of Education.

Niemi, R.G., & Junn, J. (1998). *Civic education: What makes students learn.* New Haven, CT: Yale University Press.

Niemi, R.G., & Smith, J. (2001). Enrollments in high school government classes: Are we short changing both citizenship and political science training? *PS: Political Science and Politics, 34,* 281–288.

Nolin, M., Chaney, B., Chapman, C., & Chandler, K. (1997). *Student participation in community service activitiy.* Washington, DC: National Center for Education Statistics, U. S. Department of Education.

Parker, W.C. (1996). *Educating the democratic mind.* Albany: State University of New York Press.

Patrick, J., & Hoge, J. (1991). Teaching government, civics, and law. In J.P. Shaver (Ed.), *Handbook of research on social studies teaching and learning* (pp. 427–436). New York: Macmillan.

Rose, L., & Gallup, A. (2000). The 32nd annual Phi Delta Kappa/Gallup poll of the public's attitude toward the public schools. *Phi Delta Kappan, 82,* 41–66.

Tolo, K.W. (1999). *The civic education of American youth: From state policies to school district practices.* Austin: Lyndon B. Johnson School of Public Affairs, The University of Texas.

Torney-Purta, J., Hahn, C.L., & Amadeo, J.A. (2001). Principles of subject-specific instruction in education for citizenship. In J. Brophy (Ed.), *Subject specific instructional methods and activities* (pp. 371–408). Stamford, CT: JAI Press.

Torney-Purta, J., Schwille, J., & Amadeo, J.A. (Eds.). (1999). *Civic education across countries: Twenty four national case studies from the IEA civic education project.* Amsterdam: The International Association for the Evaluation of Educational Achievement.

Torney-Purta, J., Lehmann, R., Oswald, H., & Schulz, W. (2001). *Citizenship and education in twenty eight countries; Civic knowledge and engagement at age fourteen.* Amsterdam: The International Association for the Evaluation of Educational Achievement.

Wade, R. (1997). *Community service learning: A guide to including service in the public school curriculum.* Albany: State University of New York Press.

CHAPTER 5

ISSUE-CENTERED EDUCATION FOR DEMOCRACY THROUGH *PROJECT CITIZEN*

John J. Patrick, Thomas S. Vontz, and William A. Nixon

INTRODUCTION

There is broad consensus among social studies educators that the core mission of social studies is civic education. In a democracy, the need for a body of informed and responsible citizens capable of confronting, debating, and ultimately deciding current issues of public policy cannot be overstated. Civic education is a vital means by which our society transmits to the next generation the core knowledge, skills, and dispositions of democratic citizenship. It is what allows democratic societies to reproduce themselves across generations.

Of course, there is an appropriate place for civic education at every level of learning. It is increasingly recognized, however, that the middle school years are an especially crucial time in the development of civic roles and responsibilities. These are the formative years during which early-adolescent students are discovering their identities, their larger roles in their communities, and the values that they will hold throughout their lives. Educators, policymakers, parents, and concerned members of the community need to recognize civic education for democracy in the middle school as a prime concern.

Even where there is a commitment to providing a foundation in civic education, the pressing issue remains of exactly how democratic citizenship should be taught. On this point there has been considerable debate over the course of the twentieth century. A prominent part of this debate has addressed teaching and learning about public issues. Although several approaches to an issue-centered education for democracy have been advanced, most proponents agree on some common principles. Broadly speaking, issue-centered education for democracy examines social questions using the ideals of democracy as the criteria to judge competing responses to pressing social problems. The method can be used in either a discipline-based or an interdisciplinary curriculum. At the core of an issue-centered education for democratic citizenship are questions that can be answered variously, reflectively, and complexly. In the process of examining questions reflectively and reaching decisions deliberately, there is critical assessment of evidence, competing values, and alternative outcomes.

At its best, an issue-centered education for citizenship in a democracy promises a high level of integration and participation by students in the learning process. However, critics have correctly pointed to serious problems in its underlying conceptions and practical difficulties in its application in the classroom. As a result, issue-centered civic education has never been accepted or implemented extensively in American schools. Despite these criticisms and realities, educators should not dismiss issue-centered learning activities that may be effectively infused into the civics curriculum.

One issue-centered civics program that appears to be gaining support throughout the world is *We the People ... Project Citizen* (Center for Civic Education, 1998). First implemented in California in 1992, and expanded into a national program in 1995 by the Center for Civic Education and the National Conference of State Legislatures, *Project Citizen* represents a considered effort to take advantage of the benefits of an issue-centered education for democracy while resolving many of the problems that critics have found with that approach.

Project Citizen currently is used in schools throughout the United States and in 35 countries in different regions of the world. The materials have been translated from English to such languages as Albanian, Chinese, Croatian, Czech, Estonian, Hungarian, Latvian, Lithuanian, Mongolian, Polish, Romanian, Russian, Serbian, and Spanish. The international distribution and use of *Project Citizen* has been done through Civitas: An International Civic Education Exchange Program (Quigley & Hoar, 1999, pp. 137–138). The program's appeal around the world suggests that educators need to reconsider the positive benefits of an issue-centered approach in conjunction with other instructional strategies in forming the knowledge, dispositions, and skills of democratic citizenship.

Issue-Centered Education for Democracy through Project Citizen   95

This chapter has five sections. First, the philosophical and historical roots of the issue-centered approach are traced in order to demonstrate that *Project Citizen* represents a continuous strand of thinking in the United States that has been present at least since the inception of "social studies" in the schools. Second, the arguments for and against an issue-centered education are reviewed as a context for understanding how *Project Citizen* can be implemented in a way that avoids or reduces many of the problems that have been associated with this approach. Third, a closer look is taken at the structure, methods, and aims of *Project Citizen*. Fourth, methods and findings of a recent international inquiry about the instructional effectiveness of *Project Citizen* are summarized. Fifth, the chapter closes with recommendations about how *Project Citizen* can be implemented internationally using the countries of Latvia and Lithuania and the state of Indiana in the United States as examples of its effective implementation.

PHILOSOPHICAL AND HISTORICAL ROOTS OF ISSUE-CENTERED SOCIAL STUDIES

Issue-centered education has its ultimate roots in classical philosophy, and particularly the teachings of Socrates, as preserved in the dialogues written by Plato. As portrayed in the dialogues, Socrates, who was famous for claiming that he did not know anything, assumes the role of the critic drawing out ideas and opinions from others and subjecting them to rigorous scrutiny. The end result of this process was a new and genuine understanding. Contrary to some modern misconceptions about Socratic teaching, the method of inquiry associated with Socrates does not take the form of an adversarial contest or debate with potentially humiliating consequences for the participants; rather, it is a cooperative search for truth and understanding through the dialectical process (Sichel, 1996, p. 6). This classical focus on the process of inquiry as a way to gain knowledge parallels an issue-centered approach to teaching and learning of ideas.

Although issue-centered education can lay valid claim to this Socratic heritage, in the twentieth century it commonly is associated with the Progressive reform movement, and especially the philosopher and educator John Dewey. Dewey's instrumentalist philosophy centers on *inquiry* as both a means and an end. Whether looking at questions of morals, politics, or the sciences, Dewey called for the application of intelligent inquiry, understood as the self-correcting method of experimentally testing hypotheses created and refined from previous experience. In all cases, he insisted that inquiry take place in a social context that mediates both the terms of the initial problem and its solution, and that the social context is itself transformed through the process of inquiry. Dewey's epistemology was matched by his moral fallibilism and belief that no knowledge-claim, moral principle, or ideal can ever be assumed and treated as immune to possible criticism and revision (Hickman, 1996).

Dewey was interested in the processes of human thought and learning. In the Deweyan perspective, there are many different ways in which people think and learn. The better ways of thinking, labeled "reflective," lead to learning that is functional because it becomes part of a person's intellectual capital and basic approach to reality. In reflective thinking and learning, people learn as they think, and think best when confronted with problems that are real and relevant, and that pose meaningful questions (Dewey, 1933, pp. 3–16).

Reflective thinking, understood as a form of inquiry by Dewey, consists of five phases, outlined in his classic study, *How We Think* (Dewey, 1933, pp. 106–118). It is worth reviewing these stages because they are reflected, to a significant extent, in the underlying structure of *Project Citizen*.

The first phase is "suggestion," meaning a disturbed and perplexed situation that arrests a direct activity. This cannot be an artificial, ready-made problem, for such problems are merely tasks. In this phase there is no problem yet, but simply a perplexing situation. Such situations cause the mind, still committed to action, to formulate ideas about how to proceed.

Where more than one possible course exists, a state of suspense is created which leads to "intellectualization," the second phase of reflective thinking. In this phase, a difficulty or perplexity that has been felt and directly experienced is transformed into a problem to be solved, a question for which the answer must be sought.

The third phase, the "guiding idea," involves the use of one suggestion after another as the potential solution to the problem. This leads to the formulation of a working hypothesis to guide further observation and the collection of more data.

The fourth phase, "reasoning," is the process of mental elaboration by which our observations are transformed into an idea. This is the phase of great mental development. Through reasoning, solutions that seemed plausible at first sight might be rejected as unfit, and others that seemed implausible can be transformed into fruitful possibilities. The development of an idea through reasoning supplies the necessary intervening terms for linking elements of the problem that seemed in conflict with each other into a consistent whole. The ultimate product of reasoning is an idea about how the problem can be dealt with most expeditiously and effectively.

With such an idea comes the fifth and culminating stage, "testing" the hypothesis by overt or imaginary action. Testing can yield verification of the idea, or it can lead to a failure, or refutation, of the idea. The great advantage of reflective thinking is that neither outcome means an end to thinking. Through testing, the idea might become a conclusion, but it always remains subject to the possibility of contrary facts that indicate the advisability of revision. And the failure of an idea is itself highly instructive, suggesting what modifications could be introduced in the operating hypothesis, or perhaps bringing to light a new problem altogether. To a large extent Dewey's stages are evident in *Project Citizen*, which will be more fully discussed later in the chapter.

In Dewey's view, although reflective thinking broadly follows this five-phase course, the way in which these steps are managed and the amount of time each takes will depend upon the intellectual tact and sensitivity of the individual. Moreover, while Dewey argued that reflective thought was the best kind of thinking, he did not hold that prior information was of no use. On the contrary, Dewey was emphatic that there "must be *data* at command to supply the considerations required in dealing with the specific difficulty that has presented itself" (Dewey, 1916, p. 84). He strongly asserted that knowledge was "the working capital, the indispensable resource" of inquiry (Dewey, 1916, pp. 85–86).

Throughout his career Dewey was committed to finding ways to relate his philosophy to contemporary concerns, and no concern seemed more important to him that the problem of how to ensure the continuity and revitalization of democracy over the course of generations. Schools, he believed, must play a vital role in educating youth to become reflectively thinking participants in a democracy. Dewey's ideas about education for democratic citizenship found expression in the National Education Association's seminal *Report on the Social Studies in Secondary Education* (Committee on Social Studies, 1916). Although the *Report* is important for many reasons, not the least of which is its formal adoption of the term "social studies," what is most noteworthy here is its call for an eighth-grade community civics course that bears a striking similarity to *Project Citizen*, both in terms of its aims and its methods.

Because the *Report* stands as a crucial antecedent for *Project Citizen*, it is worthwhile to look closely at its goals and structure. In the view of the National Education Association (NEA), the aim of community civics was, broadly speaking, to help children to know and participate in their community. To accomplish its part in training for citizenship, community civics should aim primarily to lead students (1) to see the importance and significance of the elements of community welfare in their relations to themselves and to the communities of which they are a member; (2) to know the social agencies, governmental and voluntary, that exist to secure these elements of community welfare; and (3) to recognize their civic obligations, present and future, and to respond to them by appropriate action (Committee on Social Studies, 1916, pp. 21–22).

The emphasis on "elements of community welfare," was the lynchpin of the program. Rather than focus on the machinery of government, students were to look at their own community and consider typical categories of social concern during the Progressive era, such as health, protection of life and property, recreation, education, civic beauty, wealth, communication, transportation, migration, charities, and correction. Three steps were suggested in teaching about an aspect of community welfare:

1. *Approach to the topic.* In beginning the study of an element of welfare the teacher should lead the pupils to realize its importance to themselves, their neighborhood, and to the community, and to see the dependence of the individual upon social agencies. Much depends upon the method of approach. The planning of an approach appropriate to a given topic and applicable to a given class calls for ingenuity and resourcefulness. In this bulletin approaches to various topics are suggested by way of illustration, but the teacher should try to find another approach whenever he thinks the one suggested is not the best one for the class.

2. *Investigation of agencies.* The knowledge of the class should now be extended by a concrete and more or less detailed investigation of agencies, such as those suggested in the bulletin. These investigations should consist of first-hand observation and study of local conditions. The agencies suggested under each topic are so many that no attempt should be made to have the class as a whole study them all intensively. Such an attempt would result in superficiality, kill interest, and defeat the purpose of the course.

3. *Recognition of responsibility.* A lesson in community civics is not complete unless it leaves the pupil with a sense of his personal responsibility and results in direct action. To attain these ends is perhaps the most difficult and delicate task of the teacher. It is discussed here as the third step in teaching an element of welfare; in practice, however, it is a process coincident with the first two steps and resulting from them. If the work suggested in the foregoing paragraphs on "Approach" and "Investigation of Agencies" has been well done, the pupil's sense of responsibility, his desire to act, and his knowledge of how to act will thereby have been developed. Indeed, the extent to which they have been developed is in a measure a test of the effectiveness of the approach and the study of agencies (Committee on Social Studies, 1916, p. 23).

These aims and steps should be kept in mind as we describe *Project Citizen* later. While the areas of social concern and the terminology—not to mention the gendered language of the 1916 *Report*—have changed, the commitment to transmitting the skills and dispositions of democratic citizenship to early adolescent children through the examination of specific social problems has not changed significantly.

Since the *Report*, a significant and influential group of social studies educators, including Maurice Hunt, Lawrence E. Metcalf, Donald W. Oliver, James P. Shaver, Fred M. Newmann, Shirley H. Engle, Anna S. Ochoa, and Ronald W. Evans, to name only a few, have consistently pressed for application of the issue-centered approach to education for democracy (Engle & Ochoa, 1988; Evans, 1989; Hunt & Metcalf, 1955; Oliver & Shaver, 1966; Newman & Oliver, 1970; Shaver & Larkin, 1972). Moreover, advocates are now represented by the Issue-Centered Education Special Interest Group of the National Council for the Social Studies. Despite the tireless efforts of prominent leaders, the history of issue-centered civic education since 1916 has largely been the story of its non-implementation. This state of affairs, in which repeated and emphatic calls for the implementation of issue-centered civic education have, for the most part, been ignored in the schools, suggests that there are good arguments both for and against the approach (Gross, 1989; Hertzberg, 1981, pp. 80–81). In order to better understand these arguments and how *Project Citizen* balances these competing concerns, we now consider strengths and limitations of the issue-centered approach to curriculum and instruction.

THE STRENGTHS AND LIMITATIONS OF ISSUE-CENTERED EDUCATION

According to Hazel Whitman Hertzberg (1981, pp. 171–172), "nothing is clearer in the history of social studies reform than the central role assigned to the social studies in the education of citizens. This has been both a mainstay and a source of many of our problems.... The definition of the appropriate education of citizens has been one of the most vexing questions in social studies history." This is the contested terrain over which debates about the merits of an issue-centered civic education take place.

The standard arguments in favor of the issue-centered approach to education for democratic citizenship should not be surprising in view of the foregoing discussion. More than anything else, proponents rest on the arguments, reviewed above, about the benefits of learning through reflective thinking that have been in common currency since the Progressive era. This method directly ties students to problems in their communities in a direct and immediate way, and it engages them as active citizens, not merely as passive recipients of received knowledge. Most important, issue-centered civic education teaches the invaluable democratic practice of decision making. As Shirley H. Engle observed, "the mark of the good citizen is the quality of decisions which he reaches on public and private matters of social concern," and the best way to train good citizens is by an approach to civic education that is "reflective, speculative, thought provoking, and oriented to the process of reaching conclusions" (1968, p. 343).

Extreme proponents call for a comprehensive issue-centered social studies curriculum that subordinates systematic learning of academic subject matter to cognitive and participatory processes and skills. They claim that the main purpose of the school is not to teach a common core of knowledge but to provide the means for the learner to develop the intellectual skills related to critical thinking and problem solving (Barth, 1991). Others stress that knowledge is ephemeral and only cognitive processes are everlastingly valuable components of education for democratic citizenship. Thus, they oppose the very idea of a core curriculum anchored in subjects that should be commonly and systematically learned by students (Shor, 1992).

Promoters of a comprehensive issue-centered social studies curriculum claim that it greatly interests and motivates students, who view it as especially relevant and practical. They also claim that students are likely to learn as much knowledge, if not more, through the comprehensive issue-centered curriculum than they would through subject-based studies in history and the social sciences. Further, they believe that what students learn through their analyses of issues is likely to be most useful to them in their roles as citizens in a democracy.

The extreme advocates of an issue-centered social studies curriculum posit cognitive processes and skills as the constant and necessary elements of the curriculum. Content is to be organized flexibly and variously around current public issues or social problems of significance to the students' democratic society and government. These public issues or problems might vary among students in the same school and from one semester or year to the next. So subject matter would vary according to student interests and the changing public political and civic agenda (Shor, 1992).

Several criticisms have been made of comprehensive issue-centered education for democracy. The first pertains to the essential negativity of focusing on social problems. By directing students to social problems, too much emphasis is placed upon the negative aspects of society and not enough on the positive traditions and institutions that also characterize society. Another concern of some teachers, parents, and community groups is that persistent and pervasive emphasis on controversy in the classroom will lead to nihilism, or it might generate an unnecessarily adversarial climate in the classroom (Shaver, 1992, p. 83).

Another type of critique comes from proponents of a content-based civic education. Because an issue-centered approach requires a significant allocation of scarce classroom resources and curricular space, it effectively reduces the time that can be spent on content coverage, including development of deep conceptual understandings anchored in academic disciplines. This has made the comprehensive issue-centered approach unattractive to teachers who are committed to exposing students to a broad, well-structured content-based curriculum. Although most teachers are willing to trade breadth of knowledge for a greater depth of understanding, there is concern that by adopting a pervasive or comprehensive issue-centered curricular model, content will be sacrificed to the extent that students will lack the knowledge base that is a prerequisite for an informed examination of policy problems or public issues (Shanker, 1995, p. 5).

According to John T. Bruer, a leading cognitive scientist, "Expertise [development of intellectual capital] depends on highly organized, domain-specific knowledge that can arise only after extensive experience and practice in the domain [the academic discipline]. Strategies [and skills] can help us process knowledge, but first we have to have the knowledge to process" (1993, p. 15). Thus, well designed and delivered courses in civics/government, economics, geography, and history enable students to acquire a fund of knowledge they can use to comprehend the public issues of political and civic life and to cope with them. For example, concepts on the substance of democracy, such as constitutionalism, human rights, popular sovereignty, representative government, and civil society, are prerequisites or corequisites of effective inquiry on public issues. Without this kind of commonly held knowledge, which can be developed among students through common learning experiences in academic disciplines, citizens are unable to act together as a community of citizens to analyze public policy issues or problems, make cogent decisions about them, or participate intelligently to resolve them.

According to Alan Cromer in his acclaimed book, *Connected Knowledge* (1997), "The [effective] curriculum is concept driven. [And] all concepts are linked to experience through appropriate activities" (p. 178). This kind of education "provides a consistent, coherent, and universal framework of basic knowledge on which individuals can build their own understanding of the world" (p. 183). Thus, citizens would be prepared in schools to know and cogently respond to public issues through mastery of concepts in core subjects related to democratic citizenship, such as history, civics/government, economics, and geography.

Another key criticism of the comprehensive issue-centered curriculum is its extreme emphasis on processes and skills. However, development of intellectual capital through the school curriculum involves the conjoining of core content and cognitive processes, basic subject matter and skills of thinking that enable students to make sense of the world and thereby to act rationally and effectively within it. To elevate one over the other, core content over cognitive processes or vice versa, is a pedagogical flaw that impedes achievement of knowledge and its application to analysis and decision making about public issues (Gardner & Boix-Mansilla, 1994; Hirsch, 1996; Shanker, 1997). The kind of intellectual capital needed for responsible and effective citizenship includes knowledge about democracy, especially deep conceptual understandings anchored in the core academic subjects of history and the social sciences, and cognitive processes/skills needed to apply this knowledge to analysis and decisions about public issues (Hirsch, 1996, pp. 17–47; Nie, Junn, & Stehlik-Barry, 1996, pp. 14–38). The "most relevant cognitive ability in relation to democratic citizenship is verbal cognitive proficiency" that involves application of core concepts and principles about democracy to the challenges of political and civic life (Nie, Junn, & Stehlik-Barry, 1996, p. 41).

Warranted criticisms of an extreme or comprehensive issue-centered curricular model should not cause us to completely dismiss or ignore issue-centered civic education. Although a comprehensive issue-centered civics curriculum denies students the structure of discipline-based learning and will, in all likelihood, never receive broad-based support in the schools, the approach, properly conceived and utilized in the schools, has a great deal to offer. The challenge is how to take advantage of the benefits of issue-centered civic education without sacrificing student achievement of essential knowledge in the teaching and learning of the social studies. *Project Citizen* is the kind of issue-based civic education program that can meet this challenge for early adolescents.

A NEW KIND OF ISSUE-CENTERED EDUCATION FOR DEMOCRACY

Project Citizen is a new type of issue-centered civic education program. It fosters the democratic dispositions and skills that enable effective and responsible participation in government and civil society. The program asks students to become actively involved with governmental and civil society organizations to acquire the intellectual and social capital necessary for responsible democratic citizenship. The program rests on several theoretical underpinnings. First, democracy requires self-government and therefore active and informed citizen participation. Second, the essential component of citizen participation is the disposition and ability to monitor and influence decisions on public policy issues. Third, students learn this component best by actually engaging in the public policy process, while doing democratic citizenship. Fourth, the middle school years are an especially vital time to engage students in the democratic process and to foster democratic citizenship. And, fifth, civic education is at its best when young people study problems and issues that are important part of their lives in their schools or communities.

The purpose of *Project Citizen*, then, is to motivate and enable students to enjoy the rights and accept the responsibilities of democratic citizenship. The instructional materials are designed to foster the civic development of young people. Students are expected to (1) learn how to monitor and influence decisions on public policy issues in their communities; (2) learn about the public policy making processes in a democracy; (3) develop skills needed to become responsible participating citizens; (4) develop a propensity to participate responsibly and effectively in political and civic life; and (5) develop a sense of efficacy and confidence in exercising the rights and responsibilities of democratic citizenship (Center for Civic Education, 1998). Overall, *Project Citizen* gives to 10-to-15-year-olds the opportunity to participate in government and civil society while practicing critical thinking, dialogue and debate, negotiation, tolerance, decision-making, and political participation (Tolo, 1998, pp. 2–17).

Although designed for use by middle school students in social studies classrooms, the program has also been used at the upper elementary and high school levels in language arts, science, and interdisciplinary courses with students of all ability levels. Given 50 minute class periods, the program is approximately a six-week course of study. The teacher's role is primarily one of coach or facilitator, who guides students to new sources of information, helps them to arrange contacts, and provides them with other helpful suggestions during their inquiry. The teacher's guide succinctly explains each step of the inquiry process, provides many additional resources (e.g., suggested teaching strategies, guidelines for conducting a simulated hearing), and equips teachers with evaluation rubrics for both the students' written and oral performance. The program also provides certificates of achievement to be presented to students upon completion of the program. The student edition includes several innovative assignments to assist participants during each step of the program, specific criteria for completion of each assignment, a glossary of terms, and appendices to assist students in locating the resources needed for in-depth study of public policy issues.

For many students, the first step of *Project Citizen*, selecting the problem to study, is the most difficult (Tolo, 1998, p. xvii). Students are often so successful at brainstorming problems in their schools (e.g., trash in the school courtyard, attendance, grading scales, violence) and in their communities (e.g., "brown fields," lack of sidewalks, water pollution, or the discriminatory practices of local businesses) that they have a hard time selecting one problem to study. The program then asks students to investigate the significance of potential problems by interviewing community members and reviewing media resources for information about the problem (Center for Civic Education, 1998, pp. 11–15). Once the class is confident that it has obtained enough information about the problems under consideration to make an informed decision, the students vote on which problem to study. Although not a formal part of the curriculum, many teachers ask students to develop criteria to judge the worth of potential problems (e.g., importance of the problem, feasibility of study).

After selecting an important issue, the class is divided into research teams to gather information from multiple sources (e.g., libraries, newspapers, community members, community organizations, legislative offices, administrative agencies, and electronic sources). The class is again divided into cooperative teams for an in-depth focus on one of the stages of inquiry and engagement in the public policy making process:

1. *Explaining the problem.* This group is responsible for explaining the problem the class has chosen to study. The group also should explain why the problem is important and why that level of government or government agency should deal with it.
2. *Evaluating alternative policies to deal with the problem.* This group is responsible for explaining present and/or alternative policies designed to solve the problem.
3. *Developing a public policy that the class will support.* This group is responsible for developing and justifying a specific public policy that the majority of class agrees to support.
4. *Developing an action plan to get government to accept the class policy.* This group is responsible for developing an action plan showing how citizens can influence their government to adopt the policy the class supports (Center for Civic Education, 1998, pp. 24–25).

The efforts of each cooperative team are displayed in a four-part (one for each group) portfolio exhibit and documentation binder. The culminating activity for the program is a simulated legislative hearing where students demonstrate their knowledge by role-playing expert witnesses testifying before community members who represent members of a state legislature. During the hearing, each of the four portfolio groups prepares and presents a statement on its section of the portfolio. After each opening statement, the panel of community members asks the students questions and judges the quality of each team's work according to specific rubrics provided to each judge.

The format of the simulated hearing offers students an opportunity to demonstrate their knowledge and understanding of how public policy is formulated while providing teachers with an excellent means of assessing student performance. Knowing that they are studying a school or community problem that they selected and are part of a team that will make a public demonstration of their work, many students are more motivated to excel than they would be under other circumstances. In addition, the hearings are an opportunity for students to showcase their thorough understanding of a local public policy issue before parents and interested members of the community. Often, it is the community members involved in the simulated hearings that assist in expanding the program by attracting other teachers, further funding, and political support.

In the United States and in several other countries throughout the world, *Project Citizen* teachers and students are encouraged to participate in a local, regional, state, or national competition. Although not a requirement for participation in the program, the competitions serve to motivate student learning, reward student achievement, and highlight the program to members of the community and potential funding agencies (Tolo, 1998, p. xvii). Although not all states or countries have the resources to fund state or national competitions, most are working toward that goal or have developed innovative ways to reduce the costs associated with a competition (e.g., conduct a competition among the portfolios without the expense of bringing students to the site). In addition to funding concerns, many teachers choose not to participate because they dislike academic competitions generally, or because they feel pressured to quickly move on to other topics and concerns (Tolo, 1998, p. xviii). For many states and countries, one response to the aversion to competitions is to conduct a regional, state, or national "showcase" of student portfolios through simulated hearings without scoring the results. Without competing, a showcase retains many of the benefits of the competition (e.g., motivating students to excellence, exposure for the program) and has been successfully implemented in several locations throughout the world.

Project Citizen effectively responds to many of the criticisms that educators and others have directed against issue-centered education. Instead of injecting problems into the classroom merely for the sake of controversy, the program encourages students to examine important questions of policy that are relevant to them and their communities. The format of *Project Citizen* helps to ensure that when difficult questions are raised, as they so often are in civic and political life, the students think through the issues while remaining respectful of differences of opinion and other points of view. Moreover, the issues that are raised during a typical project are multifaceted and require that students carefully analyze the arguments and evidence on all sides of a given question.

Project Citizen is particularly well suited to effectively complement a well structured and content-based civics curriculum. Schools that use *Project Citizen* as one important component of their civic education program or social studies curriculum—contextualized by well-structured and disciplined-based courses in civics/government, history, economics, and geography—do not give up the positive benefits that go along with concept-based course content. *Project Citizen* becomes a vehicle for students to put ideas they have learned in the classroom into practice in the real world. Thus, *Project Citizen*, a promising example of an issue-centered program, can be used within the larger curricular framework of education for democracy through systematic study of academic disciplines in a core curriculum. Instead of bearing the full load of education for democratic citizenship, as would a stand-alone issue-centered program or comprehensive issue-centered curriculum, *Project Citizen* can be used in tandem with or infused into a well structured and academic discipline-based social studies curriculum.

AN INTERNATIONAL EVALUATION OF *PROJECT CITIZEN*

The instructional effectiveness of *Project Citizen* was evaluated recently through an international research project conducted at Indiana University by the Social Studies Development Center and the Indiana Center for Evaluation. The research design and results of this inquiry are reported in the monograph *Project Citizen and the Civic Development of Adolescent Students in Indiana, Latvia, and Lithuania* (Vontz, Metcalf, & Patrick, 2000).

Students and teachers selected to participate in this international inquiry were located in Indiana, Latvia, and Lithuania. *Project Citizen* has been implemented in Indiana schools since 1996 and since 1998 in schools in Latvia and Lithuania. In most of these schools, *Project Citizen* is incorporated into or connected with the academic subject-based core curriculum. Thus, it provides students with an opportunity to apply knowledge in the core curriculum to analysis and decision making about a public issue in their community. In none of these schools does *Project Citizen* constitute the singular or comprehensive approach to education for democratic citizenship.

Two sets of questions guided this inquiry:

1. What are the effects of *Project Citizen* on the civic development of adolescent students in Indiana, Latvia, and Lithuania?
    a. What are the effects of *Project Citizen* on the achievement by adolescent students in Indiana, Latvia, and Lithuania of particular kinds of civic knowledge?
    b. What are the effects of *Project Citizen* on the beliefs of adolescent students in Indiana, Latvia, and Lithuania about their achievement of particular civic skills?
    c. What are the effects of *Project Citizen* on the achievement by adolescent students in Indiana, Latvia, and Lithuania of particular civic dispositions?

2. What are the relationships between the effects of *Project Citizen* on the civic development of adolescent students in Indiana, Latvia, and Lithuania and particular contextual and personal factors?
   a. What are the relationships between the effects of *Project Citizen* on the civic development of adolescent students in Indiana, Latvia, and Lithuania and particular demographic factors?
   b. What are the relationships between the effects of *Project Citizen* on the civic development of adolescent students in Indiana, Latvia, and Lithuania and particular programmatic factors?
   c. What are the relationships between the effects of *Project Citizen* on the civic development of adolescent students in Indiana, Latvia, and Lithuania and particular instructional factors?
   d. What are the relationships between the effects of *Project Citizen* on the civic development of adolescent students in Indiana, Latvia, and Lithuania and particular school-type factors?

An instrument was developed, The Civic Development Inventory (CDI), to gather data in response to these questions. The CDI was conceptualized and developed in terms of three components of civic development: civic knowledge, civic skills, and civic dispositions. The research design involved 102 classroom groups and 1,412 students in three political units: Indiana in the United States, Latvia, and Lithuania. There were non-randomly selected treatment classes (51 with 712 students) and comparison classes (51 with 700 students). Indiana had 20 pairs of classes (275 treatment class students and 267 comparison class students); Latvia had 13 pairs of classes (139 and 126 students), and Lithuania had 18 pairs of classes (298 and 307 students). Every student responded to a pretest and a posttest, the Civic Development Inventory.

Personal and contextual data about students and teachers, gathered through responses to items of the Civic Development Inventory and a Teacher Questionnaire, were used to demonstrate comparability between treatment and comparison classes of students. This evidence for equivalence between pairs of classes warranted the claim that the treatment, *Project Citizen*, explained the positive differences in civic development between treatment and comparison groups, not existing differences in personal and contextual data associated with individuals in the paired classes. To ensure the preprogram similarity or comparability of treatment and comparison classes, multivariate analysis of variance was used. The results indicated that there were no significant differences between treatment and comparison classes across selected student, teacher, or school characteristics within each political unit—Indiana, Latvia, and Lithuania—or across the three political units of this inquiry.

In this study, the 102 classes of students (51 treatment and 51 comparison) were the units of analysis in order to avoid misleading claims about the positive and significant effects of *Project Citizen* on the civic development of students. For each class (in both the pretest and posttest), mean student performance on each of seven factors (civic knowledge, civic skills, and five civic dispositions) was calculated and aggregated by class. Differences in means between treatment groups and comparison groups were analyzed to determine statistical significance across political units.

The second set of research questions pertained to personal and contextual characteristics that might have contributed to explanations of *Project Citizen's* effects on students. The student, not the class, was the appropriate unit of analysis for this facet of the inquiry. Stepwise multiple regression techniques were applied to four sets of data pertaining to various personal and contextual factors.

The findings of this international study generally supported the instructional effectiveness of *Project Citizen*. This issue-centered program, for example, had a positive and statistically significant effect on the civic knowledge of students (i.e., conceptual understanding of democratic governance, public policy, and civil society) across the three political units of this inquiry: Indiana, Latvia, and Lithuania. *Project Citizen* also had a positive and statistically significant effect on the self-perceived civic skills of students in Indiana, Latvia, and Lithuania. After participating in the program, students in treatment classes perceived themselves to possess more civic skills than students in comparison classes, who were not exposed to *Project Citizen*. Finally, there was a statistically significant and positive effect of *Project Citizen* on one important civic disposition, students' propensity to participate in civic and political life. There was no such effect on the other four civic dispositions in this inquiry: political tolerance, political interest, commitment to constitutionalism and rights of citizenship, and commitment to responsibilities of citizenship.

The positive effects of *Project Citizen* on students' civic development were not dependent upon the political unit—Indiana, Latvia, or Lithuania—in which the instructional treatment was experienced. Effects were largely consistent across the three political units indicating that they were neither enhanced nor mediated by the political unit in which students experienced *Project Citizen*.

The statistically significant and positive effects of *Project Citizen* on the civic development of students were generally not related to or explained by various personal and contextual factors examined in this study. There were five exceptions: the student's perceived level of participation in *Project Citizen*, mother's level of education, type of issue selected for investigation, implementation of the proposed policy, and curricular implementation of *Project Citizen*. The student's self-perceived level of participation or involvement in *Project Citizen* was the variable most strongly related to gains in civic development. A higher level of the mother's educational attainment was also associated with greater gain in the student's civic development. Some of the differences in student gains in civic development could be attributed to the type of curricular implementation of *Project Citizen*; that is, use of the instructional treatment in a combination of curricular and extracurricular formats resulted in greater student gains in civic development than use of the program solely in the regular curriculum. Further, students gained more in civic development when they investigated an issue in the school instead of the larger community outside the school. Finally, attempted implementation of students' resolution of a community-based or school-based issue was associated with substantially more gain in civic development.

CONCLUDING RECOMMENDATIONS

The research-based evaluation of *Project Citizen* suggests that the program can be used to promote the civic development of adolescent students in various countries in different parts of the world (Vontz, Metcalf, & Patrick, 2000). These findings about the program's instructional effectiveness, however, are not definitive. More research is needed to investigate strengths and weaknesses of *Project Citizen*. In particular, curriculum developers, teachers, and researchers might collaboratively explore means to improve *Project Citizen's* impact on students' civic dispositions. The related-research literature indicates that civic dispositions tend to be resistant to change as a consequence of "one-shot" and short-term exposure to an instructional treatment. Thus, it is notable that *Project Citizen* had a positive impact on one civic disposition, propensity to participate. A broader impact on civic dispositions might be achieved through pointed, concept-based instruction about such factors as political tolerance, commitment to constitutionalism and rights of citizenship, commitment to responsibilities of citizenship, and political interest. It seems that long-term, in-depth instruction targeted directly to dispositional change is a key to improving *Project Citizen's* impact on a broad range of civic dispositions in addition to propensity to participate in civic and political life.

Findings of this inquiry suggest additional means to enhance *Project Citizen's* impact on students' civic development:

1. Involve all students in the class maximally as participants in all aspects of the program.

2. Emphasize school-based public policy issues, but not to the exclusion of community-based issues that strongly attract the attention and interest of students.
3. Encourage students to attempt implementation of the policy they proposed to resolve a public issue.
4. Implement the program through a combination of curricular and extracurricular activities.
5. Avoid brief and irregular involvement of students in *Project Citizen*; rather, integrate the program as fully as possible into the curricular foundations and extracurricular activities of the school.
6. Expand the civic knowledge component of *Project Citizen* and strengthen connections and interactions of civic knowledge, civic skills, and civic dispositions through instructional activities of the program.

In general, this study found *Project Citizen* to be worthy of continued use in various educational settings in different parts of the world. The continued implementation of the program as a means to students' civic development in a democracy should be investigated through subsequent research, which might be assisted by the conceptualization, instrumentation, design, and methods of inquiry reported in the research by Vontz, Metcalf & Patrick (2000). In the meantime, educators have ample justification for using *Project Citizen* to achieve positive instructional outcomes: significant gains in the civic development of adolescent students.

Although proponents of both issue-centered and content-based civic education will continue to disagree about the design and structure of the civic education curriculum, all can agree on the importance of education for democracy, particularly among adolescents. In the United States and abroad, *Project Citizen* appears to be the kind of issue-centered civic education program that could satisfy proponents of both views. If the question of curricular organization is not reduced to an either/or choice, then it is possible to appropriately place important issues or an entire issue-centered program into an existing well-structured civics or social studies curriculum. This approach minimizes many of the critiques of issue-centered education, preserves the benefits of well-organized content-based courses, and helps students to relate abstract political, historical, legal and economic concepts to real-world issues that have direct implications for their lives.

REFERENCES

Barth, J. (1991). Beliefs that discipline the social studies. *The International Journal of Social Education, 6*(2), 19–24.

Bruer, J.T. (1993). The mind's journey from novice to expert. *American Educator, 17*(2), 6–15, 38–46.

Center for Civic Education. (1998). *We the people... project citizen.* Calabasas: Center for Civic Education.

Committee on Social Studies. (1916). *The social studies in secondary education.* Washington, DC: U.S. Government Printing Office.

Cromer, A. (1997). *Connected knowledge.* New York: Oxford University Press.

Dewey, J. (1916). *Democracy and education.* New York: Macmillan.

Dewey, J. (1933/1910). *How we think.* Boston: D.C. Heath.

Engle, S.H. (1968). Decision making: The heart of social studies instruction. In J.P. Shaver & H. Berlak (Eds.), *Democracy, pluralism, and the social studies: An approach to curriculum decisions in the social studies* (pp. 342–348). Boston: Houghton Mifflin.

Engle, S.H., & Ochoa, A.S. (1988). *Education for democratic citizenship: Decision making in the social studies.* New York: Teachers College Press.

Evans, R.W. (1989). How should we direct present efforts to promote the issue-centered vision? *The Social Studies, 80*(5), 197–198.

Gardner, H., & Boix-Mansilla V. (1994). Teaching for understanding in the disciplines and beyond. *Teachers College Record, 96*, 198–218.

Gross, R.E. (1989). Reasons for the limited acceptance of the problems approach. *The Social Studies, 80*(5), 185–186.

Hertzberg, H.W. (1981). *Social studies reform: 1880–1980.* Boulder, CO: Social Science Education Consortium.

Hickman, L.A. (1996). John Dewey. In J.J. Chambliss (Ed.), *Philosophy of education: An encyclopedia* (pp. 146–153). New York: Garland.

Hirsch, E.D. Jr. (1996). *The schools we need and why we don't have them.* New York: Doubleday.

Hunt, M., & Metcalf, L.W. (1955). *Teaching high school social studies: Problems in reflective thinking and social understanding.* New York: Harper.

Nie, N.H., Junn, J., & Stehlik-Barry, K. (1996). *Education and democratic citizenship in America.* Chicago: University of Chicago Press.

Oliver, D.W., & Newmann, F.M. (1970). *Clarifying public controversy: An approach to teaching social studies.* Boston: Little, Brown.

Oliver, D.W., & Shaver, J.P. (1966). *Teaching public issues in the high schools.* Boston: Houghton Mifflin.

Quigley, C.N., & Hoar, J.N. (1999). Civitas: An international civic education exchange program. In J.J. Patrick & C.F. Bahmueller (Eds.), *Principles and practices of education for democratic citizenship: International perspectives and projects* (pp. 123–140). Bloomington, IN: ERIC Clearinghouse for Social Studies/Social Science Education.

Shanker, A. (1997). It's content, not process, that counts. *American Teacher, 81*(1), 5.

Shanker, A. (1995). The power of disciplinary learning. *American Teacher, 79*(4), 5.

Shaver, J.P. (1992). Rationales for issue-centered social studies education. *The Social Studies, 83*, 95–99.

Shaver, J.P., & Larkin, A.G. (1972). *The analysis of public issues: Concepts, materials, research.* Logan: Utah State University, Bureau of Educational Research.

Shor, I. (1992). *Empowering education: Critical teaching for social change.* Chicago: University of Chicago Press.
Sichel, B.A. (1996). Socrates. In J.J. Chambliss (Ed.), *Philosophy of education: An encyclopedia* (pp. 616–619). New York: Garland.
Tolo, K.W. (1998). *An assessment of we the people ... project citizen: Promoting citizenship in classrooms and communities.* Austin: Lyndon B. Johnson School of Public Affairs at the University of Texas.
Vontz, T.S., Metcalf, K.K., & Patrick, J.J. (2000). *Project citizen and the civic development of adolescent students in Indiana, Latvia, and Lithuania.* Bloomington, IN: ERIC Clearinghouse for Social Studies/Social Science Education.

CHAPTER 6

POLITICAL TOLERANCE, DEMOCRACY, AND ADOLESCENTS

Patricia G. Avery

INTRODUCTION

Political tolerance is the willingness to extend basic rights and civil liberties to those with whom you disagree. It sounds so simple, yet it is one of the most difficult and important tests of a pluralistic, liberal democracy. Almost all Americans have at least one group whose views deeply disturb their sensibilities: The Aryan Nation, the American Communist Party, Pro- Life or Pro-Choice advocates, the National Rifle Association, and the Gay- Lesbian Alliance are but a few of the groups that often evoke passionate opposition. In the face of ideas that violate our core beliefs, it is often difficult to demonstrate forbearance, to allow the "second sober thought" that restrains us from intolerant judgments.

In this chapter, I summarize the research on adult and adolescent political tolerance, with particular attention to the demographic, cognitive and psychological correlates of tolerance. I argue that because our "natural state" is to be intolerant, schools are particularly important institutions for developing young people's understanding of how tolerance promotes the democratic ideals of liberty, justice, freedom of expression, and minority rights. The obstacles to teaching for tolerance of diversity of belief are formidable, however, and to overcome them requires educators' strong commitment to developing an enlightened citizenry.

Before we examine the research on political tolerance, it may be worthwhile to explore the significance of tolerance to democracy. What difference does it make if we deny groups with whom we disagree, particularly those extremist groups that the majority of Americans find loathsome, basic civil liberties such as freedom of expression and assembly? If groups such as the Ku Klux Klan were prohibited from demonstrating in public places, wouldn't this alleviate some of the tensions in our society? It is to these questions that we now turn.

WHY TOLERANCE?

When thinking about the relationship between tolerance and democracy, it is important to recognize what tolerance is not. Tolerance is not approval of a group's ideas or actions. Recall the definition of tolerance: the willingness to extend basic civil liberties to those groups with whom one disagrees. By its very definition, tolerance assumes disapproval or dislike. A second common misconception about tolerance is that it connotes indifference. But it is not possible to demonstrate simultaneously tolerance and indifference toward a group, because again, the definition of tolerance assumes a negative—not a neutral—attitude toward the group. Further, an individual demonstrating tolerance toward the Aryan Nation's right to demonstrate, for example, may well be involved in a counter-demonstration, not to protest the Aryan Nation's right to demonstrate, but to show one's own disapproval for the group's ideas. The tolerant stance is neither one of approval nor indifference—it is an acknowledgment of everyone's right to basic civil liberties in a democracy.

Tolerance and democracy are linked in that one of our principal democratic tenets is "majority rule with respect for minority rights." Most schoolchildren quickly grasp the concept of "majority rule," but the idea of "respect for minority rights" is much more difficult to comprehend. What rights are inviolate? What rights are so basic to humanity that they cannot be taken away simply because of one's beliefs, no matter how loathsome those beliefs might be to the majority of the populace? The framers of the U.S. Constitution grappled with this issue, and although they were blinded by the prejudices of the times when it came to the rights of women and Blacks, they did establish certain rights as inalienable. Through a complex system of checks and balances, they provided many safeguards to prevent the will of the majority from denying these rights to the minority. There have been times in our history when the vagaries of the day have sanctioned intolerance—the McCarthy hearings of the 1950s that sought to blacklist or imprison American Communists, and the 1896 U.S. Supreme Court decision *Plessy v. Ferguson* that denied Blacks access to certain public facilities come to mind. This is precisely why support for minority rights cannot rest with government institutions, but must be supported by the general populace.

Democracy is predicated on the belief that the people as a whole can govern themselves—not the elite, a monarch, or a religious leader. Ideally, judgments about complex political and social issues are made after careful consideration of multiple perspectives, long- and short-term consequences, and competing values. Such deliberations can only take place if everyone is free to participate in the deliberation. When some views are silenced, important considerations are likely to be neglected. In other words, tolerance for diversity of belief enhances the quality of political discourse and decision-making. As Amy Gutmann (2000) puts it, "Voting is a far more valuable act if preceded by open-minded argument where different sides not only represent their own views but also listen to others" (p. 75).

Nie, Junn, and Stehlik-Barry (1996) offer a similar argument in their description of an engaged, enlightened citizenry. Engagement represents political behavior and skills, and enlightenment is composed of one's beliefs, values and understandings. The engaged citizen is actively involved in the political process: She votes regularly, is knowledgeable about current issues, knows who to contact and how to present her views to political decision-makers. The enlightened citizen understands and values basic democratic principles: equal rights, justice, liberty, freedom, and fairness. He knows that a fundamental principle of democracy is "majority rule with respect for minority rights," that certain rights are inalienable, and that the U.S. Constitution puts forth "rules of the game" that should prevent the majority from taking those rights away from the minority. He may find the views of some of his fellow citizens deplorable, and he may think the process of airing diverse viewpoints tedious, but he recognizes that all citizens have a legitimate right to be heard, and any abnegation of one group's rights places the rights of all in peril. He demonstrates a core democratic principle—tolerance—through his willingness to extend basic civil liberties to all persons, regardless of their views.

Self-interest drives the engaged citizen who is otherwise unenlightened. The enlightened though unengaged citizen, however, identifies injustice but does not do anything about it. Tolerance for diverse opinions is important because without the consideration of multiple perspectives, our decisions are likely to be motivated by self-interest. Hitler's adherents were engaged citizens, but they were hardly guided by democratic principles.

Finally, tolerance is about how we resolve conflict. Conflict is inevitable in a democratic, pluralistic society because of the myriad of perspectives that are likely to be present. Everyone is likely to find some viewpoints distasteful. So what do we do when we find a perspective that is abhorrent to us? We could try to censor the expression of that viewpoint, but then what shall we do when someone wants to silence our own viewpoint? A statement attributed to Pastor Martin Niemoeller, one of the earliest German Protestants to criticize the Nazi regime, famously illustrates this difficulty.

> First they came for the Communists, but I was not a Communist so I did not speak out. Then they came for the Socialists and the Trade Unionists, but I was neither, so I did not speak out. Then they came for the Jews, but I was not a Jew so I did not speak out. And when they came for me, there was no one left to speak out for me.

When we silence some viewpoints, we reduce our freedoms. Tolerance is the sacrifice we make for the many freedoms we enjoy. Political scientist Paul Vogt (1997) describes the need for tolerance as "a fact of life in societies that afford persons considerable individual liberty. . . .The only way to reduce the need for tolerance is to reduce liberty or diversity or both." (p. 26)

In summary, tolerance goes to the heart of a democracy; without "respect for minority rights," we risk the tyranny of the majority. Tolerance for a diversity of beliefs enhances our political discourse and decisions, and is one safeguard to our freedoms and liberties. Although the concept of political tolerance is embedded in our Constitutional framework, ultimately the strength of the democracy depends on the people's commitment to freedom and diversity. For an understanding of the status of that commitment, we turn now to a review of the research on political tolerance among adults.

RESEARCH ON POLITICAL TOLERANCE AND ADULTS

Since Stouffer's seminal work in 1955, political scientists have documented an interesting paradox in American politics. The vast majority of citizens strongly endorse the concept of "freedom of expression," but support drops dramatically when persons are asked whether they would extend the rights of free speech and assembly to extremist groups. Beginning with Stouffer's national survey, and continuing through the 1970s, political scientists tracked Americans' level of political tolerance by asking questions such as the following:

- Should an atheist be allowed to speak?
- Should an atheist be allowed to teach?
- Should a book written by an atheist be removed from the library?
- Should a communist be allowed to speak?
- Should a communist be allowed to teach?
- Should a book written by a communist be removed from the library?

When Stouffer asked these questions of citizens in 1954, only 37% and 27% would allow an atheist and a communist, respectively, to speak. Similar percentages of support were found for allowing books authored by the groups to remain in the library, but only 12% would allow an atheist and 6% a communist to teach in a public school. Given that the survey was conducted during the McCarthy Era, the results are not too surprising. Subsequent studies demonstrated a distinct trend toward higher levels of tolerance (Davis, 1975; Lawrence, 1976; McClosky, 1964; Nunn, Crockett, & Williams, 1978; Prothro & Grigg, 1960).

In the late 1970s a group of political scientists put forth a reconceptualization of political tolerance that had a significant impact on this area of research. Sullivan, Marcus, Piereson, and Feldman (1978–1979) suggested that political tolerance involves "a willingness to apply [democratic] norms without disfavor *to those whose ideas or interests one opposes*" [emphasis supplied] (p.116). Consider one of the items from the original Stouffer study: Should a communist be allowed to speak? Now imagine that two individuals respond affirmatively to the question, but the first one does so in spite of her disdain for the communist ideology because she believes that the right to speak is an inalienable right in a democracy. The second person supports the communist's right to speak, but does so because he is somewhat sympathetic to the communist philosophy, and does not perceive communism to be a threat to society. The first person is demonstrating political tolerance, but the second person's level of tolerance has not been tested because he has not been asked about a group whose views he finds objectionable. The decision is an easy one for him, but a much more difficult one for her.

Sullivan and his colleagues thus devised a "least-liked group" measure of political tolerance in which they would first ask respondents to identify their least-liked group, and then ask them whether they would be willing to extend certain civil liberties to the group. In a national survey conducted in the late 1970s (Sullivan, Piereson, & Marcus, 1982), people were asked to identify their least-liked group. Less than one-third (29%) mentioned communists, the group that had been the standard "target group" in previous surveys. Almost one-fourth mentioned the Ku Klux Klan (24%), followed by atheists (8%), the Symbionese Liberation Army (8%), and the Black Panthers (6%). When asked whether they would be willing to extend certain civil liberties to their least-liked group, respondents in the 1970s were only slightly more tolerant than persons surveyed in the 1950s. Sullivan et al. reasoned that the "targets of intolerance" may have changed, but the shift in the level of political tolerance, while positive, was not nearly as substantial as others had declared.

The work by Sullivan and his colleagues generated a lot of interest in this area of inquiry. Some scholars (Vogt, 1997) noted that the "content-controlled" method failed to take into account the range of a person's intolerance. That is, suppose one person denies civil liberties to only *one* group and another person denies civil liberties to *many* groups. Both individuals would be identified as intolerant according to the content-controlled method of measuring intolerance, with no recognition of the differences in the range of their intolerance. A second major criticism of the work was that it failed to differentiate between the type of groups that were the targets of people's intolerance. For example, some argued that to be intolerant of a group that was itself intolerant and would deny rights to others, such as Ku Klux Klan, is qualitatively different than to deny rights to groups that advocate greater tolerance, such as the Anti-Defamation League. Although the work by Sullivan and his colleagues has been criticized for these and other reasons (see, e.g., Weissberg, 1998), their research significantly changed the way in which political scientists conceptualized tolerance.

Over the past 50 years, scholars have offered different conceptualizations of political tolerance, have employed increasingly more complex research methodologies and more sophisticated statistical techniques in analyzing the concept. Initially, gender (male), social status (elite), income (high), residence (western or northeastern United States) and religiosity (more secular) were thought to be associated with higher levels of tolerance. Studies using more complex understandings of political tolerance, particularly the "least-liked group" conceptualization proposed by Sullivan and his colleagues, suggest that these demographic variables have much less impact on levels of political tolerance than previously thought, but do impact the choice of group one dislikes the most. Psychological characteristics, however, do appear to have a strong influence on levels of tolerance. High levels of intolerance are generally associated with those who are more dogmatic, more authoritarian, and have lower self-esteem. These individuals usually perceive a higher level of threat from the "target" group, and are less comfortable with the cognitive dissonance that may result from being exposed to viewpoints that are directly opposed to their own.

Throughout the research, one of the most powerful predictors of tolerance is education. The higher the level of education, the higher the level of political tolerance. For a long time, education has been considered to be something of a "black box"; no one knows exactly what happens in schools or universities, but somehow the more one progresses through school, the more likely one is to be tolerant. Scholars have offered different explanations for the transformation that takes place in the "black box." For example, exposure to people with different perspectives and backgrounds may engender an appreciation of diverse viewpoints and lessen the sense of threat associated with ideas opposed to one's own. Even when the student population is relatively homogenous, students usually talk with one another about course content, and they come to appreciate the different ways in which their peers approach problems. Formal education also gives people practice in applying abstract principles to concrete situations, a connection that almost certainly must be made if people are to choose tolerance responses.

Sullivan et al. (1982) demonstrated that education's effect on tolerance is primarily indirect. That is, education tends to reduce dogmatism and authoritarianism, increase self-esteem and strengthen support for democratic norms such as minority rights. Each of these characteristics is associated with higher levels of political tolerance. Studies of adults indicate that the greatest difference in levels of tolerance is between those who attend college and those who do not. In the next section, we examine the research on political tolerance among precollegiate students.

RESEARCH ON POLITICAL TOLERANCE AND ADOLESCENTS

Adolescents' emerging ability to apply abstract principles (e.g., minority rights) to concrete situations, their preoccupation with in-groups and out-groups, and their struggles with their own increasing rights and responsibilities in the adult world make adolescence a particularly important time for the development of political tolerance. The young person's search for self-understanding is marked by questions that lend themselves to personal and political identity formation. Who am I? What do I believe in? What am I for, and what am I against? Each of these questions provides opportunities for young people to explore the complexity of moral, social and political issues, and to test competing ideological perspectives and beliefs.

In his classic interviews with adolescents, Adelson (1971) noted that "the older adolescent . . . can move from the concrete to the abstract and back again. Having stated a principle, he illuminates it by a concrete instance, or having mentioned specific examples, he seeks and finds the abstract category that binds them" (p. 1015). This movement from concrete situations to abstract principles is prerequisite to the development and sustenance of political tolerance. Individuals must be able to see, for example, the relationship between a demonstration by the Ku Klux Klan and the principles of freedom of speech and association.

Studies of adolescent political tolerance are far fewer and more limited in scope than the research among adults. However, findings from surveys of adolescents have generally mirrored results from studies of adults: adolescents profess strong support for the abstract principles of democracy such as freedom of expression and freedom of assembly, but they are unlikely to afford their least-liked group these civil liberties (Conover &

Searing, 2000; Eyler, 1980; Owen & Dennis, 1987; Thalhammer, Wood, Bird, Avery, & Sullivan, 1994; Zellman & Sears, 1971); as the adolescent's perception of threat from the group increases, so too does his or her level of intolerance (Avery, 1988; Thalhammer et al., 1994). Additionally, age (older) and level of moral reasoning (higher) have consistently been found to be associated with higher levels of political tolerance (Avery, 1988; Patterson 1979).

Together with colleagues, I have interviewed adolescents about civil liberties issues, and tried to probe their understanding of selected democratic principles (Avery, 1992; Thalhammer et al., 1994). In general, we find that tolerant and intolerant students approach civil liberties issues differently. For example, tolerant students' conceptualizations of conflict and "outgroups" differ from those of their intolerant counterparts. When presented with situations involving the civil liberties of their "least-liked group," tolerant students envision a conflict that could be resolved through words, whereas intolerant students are more likely to foresee a conflict that involves physical violence. Tolerant students are cognizant of the *possibility* of a physical conflict, but intolerant students tend to be *certain* that physical violence will ensue. This is consistent with social psychological theories of intergroup relations which suggest that the [intolerant person's] perception of a "zero-sum game" between two groups, in which one group wins everything, is likely to result in overt conflict. On the other hand, when the relationship between two groups is not viewed in such competitive, absolutist terms, members of one group are more likely to be able to make accommodations to coexist with the other group (Dovidio, Maruyama, & Alexander, 1998).

Tolerant students are also likely to use the language of "rights" when confronted with civil liberties issues (e.g., "It's their right." "It's in the Constitution." "People have the right to express themselves."), whereas intolerant students tend to focus on the specifics of a situation and fail to make connections to underlying abstract principles (e.g., "I don't want to hear their opinions. I already know what they are about."). Tolerant students are more likely to see members of their least-liked group as having been influenced by outside forces, such as family socialization or peer group pressure. Intolerant students, on the other hand, are more likely to attribute members of their least-liked group's attitudes to some innate quality or characteristic (e.g., "He's just a bad person"). The different ways tolerant and intolerant students view the groups reflect, in part, their view of humanity. The negative outside influences tolerant students mention can be changed to positive outside influences, but the innate characteristics intolerant students attribute to members of their least-liked group are unlikely to change.

Similar to the more sophisticated students interviewed by Adelson in the early 1970s, tolerant students tend to display an understanding of the broader context of dissent, to think in terms of possibilities and probabilities instead of absolutes, and to link abstract democratic principles to concrete situations. There is reason to believe, however, that the tolerant students' responses are rarely grounded in an in-depth understanding of democratic principles. For example, although the tolerant students are more likely to invoke the principle of minority rights than are their counterparts, their conception of minority rights is still fragile and uncertain. When pressed to explain why freedom of expression is so important in a democracy, few students can provide more than simplistic, tautological reasons (e.g., "because it's one of our rights in a democracy"). And perhaps more disturbing, tolerant students are unlikely to protest if the right to assemble, for example, is denied their least-liked group, but intolerant students are quite likely to say they would protest if their least-liked group were *allowed* to gather for a rally. In other words, tolerant students are less likely to take action to support their views than are intolerant students.

There is ample evidence to suggest that intolerance is more our "natural state" than is tolerance (Aboud, 1988; Kawakimi, Dovidio, Moll, Hermsen, & Russin, 2000). That is, we are not born tolerant, but must learn to be tolerant. Intolerance is cognitively easier because we tend to categorize groups as "in groups" (our groups) and "out groups" (the other groups). In a revealing study by Devine (1989), the first response of individuals, regardless of whether they perceive themselves to hold prejudices against other groups, is to adopt the negative stereotypes they acquired through socialization. People need to actively work to override their natural impulse toward intolerance. Educational institutions could thus play a very important role in helping people to develop more tolerant orientations. As mentioned previously, however, while college tends to have a significant impact on students' level of tolerance, secondary schools' influence appears to be quite modest. Why doesn't the secondary school have a stronger impact on students' levels of tolerance? We focus on this question in the next section.

POLITICAL TOLERANCE AND THE SECONDARY SCHOOL

Learning about tolerance for diversity of belief means learning about conflict. An in-depth exploration of the role of tolerance in a democracy requires consideration of extremist political views, and the acknowledgment of some of the "darker sides" of U.S. history when ideas and opinions have been repressed. Unlike their college and university counterparts, however, elementary and secondary classrooms have typically not been places in which controversial issues have been explored in depth. Paul Vogt (1997) describes the situation precollegiate educators face:

> Schools have little incentive to go beyond sloganeering. Because tolerance involves not repressing "subversive" ideas, "disgusting" practices, and "evil" people, teaching tolerance is usually controversial. Educators are unlikely to enhance their careers by courting controversy and discussing the rights of unpopular minorities, to say nothing of advocating those rights. Prior to university-level studies, public education is usually too vulnerable to popular pressure to handle the conflict of values that can ensue from any serious attempt to deal directly with political tolerance. (p. 179)

I have written previously about how the norms of the student, school, and community cultures mitigate against the exploration of controversial issues (Avery, Johnson, Johnson, & Mitchell, 1999). For example, students are often concerned about "losing face" among their peers for expressing unpopular or dissenting views (Bickmore, 1993; Delpit, 1995). Many of their teachers fear "losing control" of the classroom if controversial issues are discussed in a substantive manner (McNeil, 1986). And indeed, facilitating in-depth discussions about controversial social and political issues requires complex skills that many educators have not developed (Parker, 2001). Add to these factors a society that places more value on teaching basic reading, writing and math skills than on teaching the habits of good citizenship (Wadsworth, 1997), and it is not surprising that so few students learn about political tolerance in school.

It is in civics and government classes that one would most expect to see young people analyzing and debating current political issues. But a number of studies suggest that the curriculum in these classes marginalizes the role of conflict and dissent in a democracy (Merelman, 1990; Niemi & Junn, 1998). Thoughtful class discussions about significant social and political issues, in which students engage in substantive conversation, challenge one another's thinking, and build a collective understanding of problems, alternatives, and consequences, are rare (Kahne, Rodriguez, Smith, & Thiede, 2000; McNeil, 1986; Newmann, 1990; Newmann & Associates, 1996). Although civics and government texts make frequent reference to the "slogans of democracy," such as "freedom of expression," and "freedom of assembly," concrete applications of these principles are generally avoided. It is through specific applications of these principles, however, that students come to understand their complexity. "Freedom of expression" has intuitive appeal until it is extended to groups whose views offend your core values. Most curriculum materials for the precollegiate level, however, tend to avoid discussion of controversial issues. One review of 18 standard civics textbooks described the texts as follows:

> The encyclopedic nature of these [civics and government] texts may be their greatest failing. Readers are led to conclude that what is most important to learn about government is facts, facts, and more facts. Dates, names and places abound, with little context to link them. What emerges is a portrait of government as lifeless institutions and mechanical processes, remote from politics and citizens.
>
> What is missing, in a word, is controversy. Eighty percent of the civics books and half of the government books minimize conflict and compromise. The dynamic sense of government and politics—the fierce debates, colorful characters, triumphs and tragedies—is lost. Controversies like school prayer and civil rights that have ignited passions at all points along the political spectrum are ignored or barely mentioned. The vitality of political involvement and the essential give and take between people and their elected officials is neglected. (Carroll et al., 1987, p. i)

More recent studies of history and civics texts reveal little change (Avery & Simmons, 2001; Loewen, 1995). Given that 87% of high school students report reading material from their civics textbooks at least once or twice a week (Niemi & Junn, 1998), it is safe to say that the textbook plays an important role in shaping the curriculum, and that it does not play a significant role in promoting an understanding of tolerance in a democracy.

INCREASING POLITICAL TOLERANCE AMONG ADOLESCENTS

Although most research indicates that secondary students do not learn about minority rights in more than a cursory fashion (Conover & Searing, 2000; Ehman, 1980; Patrick & Hoge, 1991; Zellman, 1975), some students and teachers do, of course, overcome formidable obstacles to explore civil liberties issues in a substantive manner. However, research indicates that if teachers are to address political and social issues in a meaningful way, they must depart from traditional curricula and classroom practices. In this section, we examine two areas of research: curriculum intervention studies designed to promote political tolerance, and research on the link between political tolerance and an open classroom climate.

At least three studies suggest that when curricula are specifically designed to teach young people about the role of tolerance in a democracy, levels of tolerance can increase. In the early 1990s, I worked with a team of scholars to conduct a quasi-experimental study designed to increase young people's level of political tolerance. We wrote a four-week curriculum unit, entitled *Tolerance for Diversity of Belief* (Avery et al., 1993), to help secondary students understand the historical, psychological, and sociological dimensions of tolerance. In developing the unit, we were cognizant of research indicating that civil liberties are often taught as abstractions or slogans with little reference to concrete situations. We called this phenomena "lip-synching to the tune of democracy." To move students beyond "lip-synching," we included a number of case studies of tolerance or intolerance at the national and international levels. Within each case study, students examine the role of the perpetrator as well as the victim: Why are some people or groups intolerant? What are the short and long-term effects of intolerance on the victim? On the perpetrator? On society? Students learn how minority rights are embedded in the U.S. Constitution, and how basic human rights are promoted in international documents such as the Universal Declaration of Human Rights. The curriculum emphasizes active learning strategies, such as role plays, simulations, structured discussions, journaling, and interviews. More important, the unit revolves around core questions about enduring issues in society: Why are ideas and opinions suppressed? Why is freedom of expression important in a democracy? Are there limits to freedom of expression? If one strongly disagrees with the beliefs of a group such as the Ku Klux Klan, does one have both a right and responsibility to express disagreement?

We thought it was important that students understand the fragile nature of civil liberties, and how they can be abrogated if the public is not sufficiently vigilant. Thus, students learn about instances of intolerance in the United States, such as the McCarthy Era and the Japanese-American internment during World War II. Lest students become cynical or feel powerless in the face of intolerance, they conduct an in-depth study of an individual or group that has fought intolerance, such as Raoul Wallenberg, Eleanor Roosevelt, Mothers of the Plaza, and Amnesty International. As a culminating activity, students write a "Class Declaration of Rights and Responsibilities."

In the early 1990s, we conducted two studies of more than 600 secondary students who participated in the curriculum (Avery, Bird, Johnstone, Sullivan & Thalhammer, 1992; Bird, Sullivan, Avery, Thalhammer, & Wood, 1994; Thalhammer et al., 1994; Wood et al., 1994). A comparison of pre- and posttests indicated that most of the students shifted from "moderate intolerance" to "moderate tolerance" as a result of participating in the curriculum. In both studies, students' self-esteem (high), authoritarianism (low), and perceived threat from disliked group (low) were important predictors of students' posttest tolerance. In the first study, a delayed posttest conducted four weeks after the conclusion of the unit indicated that the effects of the curriculum, though slightly attenuated, remained. In this study we also noted that a small group of students whose level of tolerance was fairly low prior to their participation in the curriculum, and either stayed the same or decreased further at the end of the unit of study. In the second study, we again noted a group of students whose level of tolerance decreased from the beginning to the end of the unit of study. When we looked at this group more closely, we found that the students tended to be male, to demonstrate a high level of authoritarianism, and low levels of empathy and self-esteem. We hypothesized that these students found the notion of supporting the expression of ideas that contradicted their own to be particularly threatening.

An earlier study by Goldenson (1978) examined the effects of a three-week curriculum specifically designed to help high school students link abstract civil libertarian principles to concrete situations. Similar to the *Tolerance for Diversity of Beliefs* curriculum unit, students studied relevant court cases, interviewed individuals likely to have differing perspectives on rights issues (e.g., members of the American Civil Liberties Union, persons involved in law enforcement) and participated in several simulations and role plays related to civil liberties. The teacher made a conscious effort to "minimize the rote memorizations of the 'right answers' supportive of U.S. civil liberties protections" (p. 50).

In comparison to a control class, the experimental class demonstrated significantly greater increases in support and concern for civil liberties than did the control group. Goldenson also found that the students' perception of the teacher's credibility (the extent to which the teacher was considered "fair," "knowledgeable," "concerned, "interesting," and "understandable") had a mediating effect on students' attitude change. The more credible the students perceived the teacher, the more likely they were to demonstrate increases in support for civil liberties. Students who did not perceive their teacher as very credible, however, expressed more negative attitudes toward civil liberties at the conclusion of the unit. Although Goldenson was not measuring classroom climate per se, the themes of fairness and respect in his measure of teacher credibility are often found in measures of classroom climate, a factor found in other studies to be associated with students' level of political tolerance.

In three international studies (Hahn, 1998; Nielson, 1977; Torney-Purta, Lehmann, Oswald, & Schulz, 2001), students' perception of an open classroom climate—one in which they feel free to express their ideas and opinions—has been linked to their level of political tolerance. There are several possible explanations for this association. First, teachers who foster an "open classroom climate" model respect for divergent views. Second, students who practice listening to different points of view may come to understand the way in which such discussions enhance their understanding of complex issues. Third, students may be less likely to feel threatened by unpopular views if they regularly engage in issues' discussions; they may come to see the expression of such views as part of the democratic process. Finally, Conover and Searing (2000) explain the connection between discussion and support for democratic ideals in terms of social capital theory.

Participation in regular class discussions strengthens students' skills in articulating their viewpoints, listening to others and analyzing issues—all valuable skills (i.e., social capital) in the formal political sphere. A particularly disturbing finding is that lower class, lower-achieving students are less likely to experience issues' discussions, and less likely to perceive their classroom climate as "open" (Baldi, Perie, Skidmore, Greenberg, & Hahn, 2001; Conover & Searing, 2000). These are, of course, the very students who tend to be the least empowered, and those who are least likely to engage in issues' discussions outside of the classroom. Rather than acting to "level the playing field," schools thus tend to enhance the disparity in students' "social capital."

Whether one thinks of teacher credibility as in the Goldenson study or of the open classroom climate research, it is clear that teachers play a role in determining how students interpret the curriculum. Teachers set the tone for their classrooms—if they place a high priority on respect and fairness, or if they model thoughtfulness and encourage students to share their ideas and opinions, the research indicates that they may be indirectly promoting more tolerant attitudes among young people.

The curriculum intervention studies (Avery et al., 1992; Bird et al., 1994; Goldenson, 1978; Thalhammer et al., 1994; Wood et al., 1994) are important because they demonstrate that tolerance *can* be taught, and that, by implication, the traditional curriculum does not engender greater tolerance among our youth. There is a caveat, however: A small group of students—those who see their teacher as lacking credibility, or those high in authoritarianism and low in self-esteem and empathy—may react against efforts to increase tolerance and actually become more intolerant.

The research that links political tolerance and an open classroom climate is significant because it suggests that new curricula are "necessary but not sufficient" to engender greater tolerance. Simply put, curricular content must provide concrete examples of complex civil liberties issues, instructional methods must encourage students to debate and discuss multiple perspectives on issues, and the classroom climate must support student expression of ideas and opinions. This is the meshing of conflictual content (e.g., students study complex civil liberties issues), conflictual pedagogy (e.g., students openly discuss differing perspectives on these issues), and classroom climate described by educational researchers Kathy Bickmore (1993) and Carole Hahn (1996). Bickmore examined the concepts of conflictual content and pedagogy in her observations of high school social studies classrooms. She noted that teachers could examine significant issues without encouraging students to express their opinions (conflictual content without conflictual pedagogy), and they could promote debate and discussion without reference to enduring social and political issues (conflictual pedagogy without conflictual content). The most powerful and transformative classes, however, combined conflictual content and pedagogy. Hahn (1996) later reviewed Bickmore's work, and argued that the interaction between conflictual content and pedagogy requires an open and supportive classroom climate in which students feel free to express their ideas and opinions, a contention supported by the research presented here. Although not extensive, the research on developing political tolerance among adolescents suggests that non-traditional curricula and instructional practices can promote increased tolerance among the majority of adolescents.

CONCLUSION

Most adolescents *can* develop an understanding of the role of tolerance in a democracy. Young people's developing ability to link abstract principles to concrete situations, their concern for "in-groups" and "out-groups," and their interest in their increasing rights and responsibilities suggest that this is an opportune time for them to grapple with civil liberties issues. The obstacles for both teachers and students are formidable, however, because student, teacher and community norms mitigate against the teaching of tolerance for diverse beliefs. Yet, tolerance goes to the heart of a democracy. Like the sustenance of other democratic principles, such as liberty, equality, and justice, tolerance requires much effort and ongoing commitment. The willingness to extend civil liberties to those groups whose ideas one finds abhorrent represents one of the enduring challenges of a liberal, pluralistic democracy.

REFERENCES

Aboud, F. (1988). *Children and prejudice*. Oxford: Blackwell.
Adelson, J. (1971). The political imagination of the young adolescent. *Daedalus, 100*, 1013–1050.
Avery, P.G. (1988). Political tolerance among adolescents. *Theory and Research in Social Education, 16*, 183–201.
Avery, P.G. (1992). Political tolerance: How adolescents deal with dissenting groups. In H. Haste & J. Torney-Purta (Eds.), *The development of political understanding* (pp. 39–51). San Francisco: Jossey-Bass.
Avery, P.G., Bird, K., Johnstone, S., Sullivan, J.L., & Thalhammer, K. (1992). Exploring political tolerance with adolescents: Do all of the people have all of the rights all of the time? *Theory and Research in Social Education, 20*, 386–420.
Avery, P.G., Hoffman, D., Sullivan, J.L., Theiss-Morse, E., Fried, A., Bird, K., Johnstone, S., & Thalhammer, K. (1993). *Tolerance for diversity of beliefs: A secondary curriculum unit*. Boulder, CO: Social Science Education Consortium.

Avery, P.G., Johnson, D.W., Johnson, R.T., & Mitchell, J.M. (1999). Teaching an understanding of war and peace through structured academic controversies. In A. Raviv, L. Oppenheimer, & D. Bar-Tal (Eds.), *How children understand war and peace* (pp. 260–280). San Francisco: Jossey-Bass.

Avery, P.G., & Simmons, A.M. (2000/2001, Fall/Winter). Civic life as conveyed in U.S. civics and history textbooks. *International Journal of Social Education, 15*, 105–130.

Baldi, S., Perie, M., Skidmore, D., Greenberg, E., & Hahn, C. (2001). *What democracy means to ninth-graders: U.S. results from the international IEA Civic Education Study* (NCES 2001–096). U.S. Department of Education, National Center for Education Statistics. Washington, DC: U.S. Government Printing Office.

Bickmore, K. (1993). Learning inclusion/inclusion in learning: Citizenship education for a pluralistic society. *Theory and Research in Social Education, 21*, 341–384.

Bird, K., Sullivan, J.L., Avery, P.G., Thalhammer, K., & Wood, S. (1994). Not just lip-synching anymore: Education and tolerance revisited. *The review of Education/Pedagogy/Cultural Studies, 16*(3–4), 373–386.

Carroll, J., Broadnex, W., Contreras, G., Mann, T., Orenstein, N., & Steihm, J. (1987). *We the people: A review of U.S. government and civics textbooks*. Washington, DC: People for the American Way.

Conover, P.J., & Searing, D.D. (2000). A political socialization perspective. In L.M. McDonnell, P.M. Timpane, & R. Benjamin (Eds.) *Rediscovering the Democratic Purposes of Education* (pp. 91–124). Lawrence: University of Kansas Press.

Davis, J.A. (1975). Communism, conformity, cohorts, and categories: American tolerance in 1954 and 1972–73. *American Journal of Sociology, 81*, 491–513.

Delpit, L. (1995). *Other people's children: Cultural conflict in the classroom*. New York: New York Press.

Devine, P.G. (1989). Stereotypes and prejudice: Their automatic and controlled components. *Journal of Personality and Social Psychology, 56*(1), 5–18.

Dovidio, J.F., Maruyama, G., & Alexander, M.G. (1998). A social psychology of national and international group relations. *Journal of Social Issues, 54*, 831–846.

Ehman, L.H. (1980). The American school in the political socialization process. *Review of Educational Research, 50*, 99–119.

Eyler, J. (1980). Citizenship education for conflict: An empirical assessment of the relationship between principled thinking and tolerance for conflict and diversity. *Theory and Research in Social Education, 8*, 11–26.

Goldenson, D.R. (1978). An alternative view about the role of the secondary school in political socialization: A field-experimental study of the development of civil liberties attitudes. *Theory and Research in Social Education, 6*, 44–72.

Guttman, A. (2000). Why should schools care about civic education? In L.M. McDonnell, P.M. Timpane, & R. Benjamin (Eds.), *Rediscovering the democratic purposes of education* (pp. 91–124). Lawrence: University of Kansas Press.

Hahn, C.L. (1996). Research on issues-centered social studies. In R. Evans & D. Saxe (Eds.), *Handbook on teaching social issues* (pp. 25–41). Washington, DC: National Council for the Social Studies.

Hahn, C.L. (1998). *Becoming political: Comparative perspectives on citizenship education*. Albany: State University of New York Press.

Kahne, J., Rodriguez, M., Smith, B., & Thiede, K. (2000). Developing citizens for democracy? Assessing opportunities to learn in Chicago's social studies classrooms. *Theory and Research in Social Education, 28,* 311–338.

Kawakami, K., Dovidio, J.F., Moll, J., Hermsen, S., & Russin, A. (2000). Just say no (to stereotyping): Effects of training in the negation of stereotypic associations on stereotype activation. *Journal of Personality and Social Psychology, 78,* 871–888.

Lawrence, D. (1976). Procedural norms and tolerance: A reassessment. *American Political Science Review, 70,* 80–100.

Loewen, J.W. (1995). *Lies my teacher told me: Everything your American history textbook got wrong.* New York: Touchstone.

McClosky, H. (1964). Consensus and ideology in American politics. *American Political Science Review, 58,* 361–382.

McNeil, L.M. (1986). *Contradictions of control: School structure and school knowledge.* New York: Routledge.

Merelman, R. (1990). The role of conflict in children's political learning. In O. Ichilov (Ed.), *Political socialization, citizenship education, and democracy* (pp. 47–65). New York: Teachers College Press.

Newmann, F.M. (1990). Qualities of thoughtful social studies classes: An empirical profile. *Journal of Curriculum Studies, 22,* 253–275.

Newmann, F.M., & Associates. (1996). *Authentic achievement: Restructuring schools for intellectual quality.* San Francisco: Jossey-Bass Publishers.

Nie, N.H., Junn, J., & Stehlik-Barry, K. (1996). *Education and democratic citizenship in America.* Chicago: University of Chicago Press.

Nielson, H.D. (1977). *Tolerating political dissent.* Stockholm: Almqvist & Wiksell International.

Niemi, R.G., & Junn, J. (1998). *Civic education: What makes students learn.* New Haven, CT: Yale University Press.

Nunn, C.Z., Crockett. H.J., & Williams, J.A. (1978). *Tolerance for nonconformity.* San Francisco: Jossey-Bass.

Owen, D., & Dennis, J. (1987). Preadult development of political tolerance. *Political Psychology, 8,* 547–561.

Parker, W.C. (2001). Classroom discussion: Models for leading seminars and deliberations. *Social Education, 65,* 111–115.

Patrick, J.J., & Hoge, J.D. (1991). Teaching government, civics, and law. In J.P. Shaver (Ed.), *Handbook of research on social studies teaching and learning* (pp. 427–436). New York: Macmillan.

Patterson, J.W. (1979). Moral development and political thinking: The case of freedom of speech. *Western Political Quarterly, 32,* 7–20.

Prothro, J.S., & Grigg, C.W. (1960). Fundamental principles of democracy: Bases of agreement and disagreement. *Journal of Politics, 22,* 276–294.

Stouffer, S. (1955). *Communism, conformity, and civil liberties.* New York: Doubleday.

Sullivan, J.L., Marcus, G.E., Piereson, J.E., & Feldman, S. (1978–1979). The development of political tolerance: The impact of social class, personality and cognition. *International Journal of Political Education, 2,* 115–139.

Sullivan, J.L., Piereson, J.E., & Marcus, G.E. (1982). *Political tolerance and American democracy.* Chicago: University of Chicago Press.

Thalhammer, K., Wood, S.L., Bird, K., Avery, P.G., & Sullivan, J.L. (1994). Adolescents and political tolerance: Lip-synching to the tune of democracy. *Review of Education, Pedagogy, and Cultural Studies, 16,* 325–347.

Torney-Purta, J., Lehmann, R., Oswald, H., & Schulz, W. (2001). *Citizenship and education in twenty-eight countries: Civic knowledge and engagement at age fourteen.* Amsterdam: IEA.

Vogt, W.P. (1997). *Tolerance and education: Learning to live with diversity and difference.* Thousand Oaks, CA: Sage.

Wadsworth, D. (1997). The public's view of public schools. *Educational Leadership, 54,* 44–48.

Weissberg, R. (1998). *Political tolerance: Balancing community and diversity.* Thousand Oaks, CA: Sage.

Wood, S.L., Thalhammer, K., Sullivan, J.L., Bird, K., Avery, P.G., & Klein, K. (1994). Tolerance for diversity of beliefs: Learning about tolerance and liking it too. *Review of Education, Pedagogy, and Cultural Studies, 16,* 349–372.

Zellman, G.L. (1975). Antidemocratic beliefs: A survey and some explanations. *Journal of Social Issues, 31,* 31–53.

Zellman, G.L., & Sears, D.O. (1971). Childhood origins of tolerance for dissent. *Journal of Social Issues, 27,* 109–135.

CHAPTER 7

TEACHING FOR DIVERSITY AND UNITY IN A DEMOCRATIC MULTICULTURAL SOCIETY

James A. Banks

INTRODUCTION

Most nation-states and societies throughout the world are characterized by cultural, ethnic, racial, language, and religious diversity (Eck, 2001). One of the challenges to pluralistic democratic nation-states is to provide opportunities for diverse groups to maintain components of their community cultures while at the same time constructing a nation-state in which these groups are structurally included and to which they feel allegiance. A delicate balance of diversity and unity should be an essential goal of democratic nation-states and of social studies teaching and learning in a democratic society (Banks et al., 2001).

The challenge of balancing diversity and unity is intensifying as democratic nation-states such as the United States, Canada, Australia, and the United Kingdom become more diversified and as racial and ethnic groups within these nations become involved in cultural and ethnic revitalization movements. The democratic ideologies institutionalized within the major democratic Western nations and the wide gap between these ideals and realities were major factors that resulted in the rise of ethnic revitalization movements in nation-states such as the United States, Canada, and the United Kingdom during the last four decades.

These nations share a democratic ideal, a major tenet of which is that the state should protect human rights and promote equality and the structural inclusion of diverse groups into the fabric of society. These societies are also characterized by widespread inequality and by racial, ethnic, and class stratification. The discrepancy between democratic ideals and societal realities and the rising expectations of structurally excluded racial, ethnic, language and social-class groups created protest and revival movements within the Western democratic nations.

DIVERSITY, UNITY, AND CITIZENSHIP EDUCATION

Because of growing ethnic, cultural, racial, language and religious diversity throughout the world, citizenship education needs to be changed in substantial ways to prepare students to function effectively in the 21st century (Banks, 1997). Citizens in this century need the knowledge, attitudes, and skills required to function in their ethnic and cultural communities and beyond their cultural borders. They should also be able and willing to participate in the construction of a national civic culture that is a moral and just community that embodies democratic ideals and values, such as those embodied in the Universal Declaration of Human Rights, the Declaration of Independence, the Constitution, and the Bill of Rights. Students also need to acquire the knowledge and skills required to become effective citizens in the global community.

Citizenship education in the past, in the United States as well as in many other nations, embraced an assimilationist ideology. In the United States, its aim was to educate students so they would fit into a mythical Anglo-Saxon Protestant conception of the "good citizen." Anglo conformity was the goal of citizenship education. One of its aims was to eradicate the community cultures and languages of students from diverse ethnic, cultural, racial, and language groups. One consequence of this assimilationist conception of citizenship education was that many students lost their first cultures, languages, and ethnic identities. Some students also became alienated from family and community. Another consequence was that many students became socially and politically alienated within the national civic culture.

Ethnic minorities of color often became marginalized in both their community cultures and in the national civic culture because they could function effectively in neither. When they acquired the language and culture of the

Anglo mainstream, they were denied structural inclusion and full participation into the civic culture because of their racial characteristics.

The U.S. Census Bureau (2000) projects that 47% of the U.S. population will consist of ethnic minorities of color by 2050. The percentage of ethnic minorities in nation-states throughout the world has increased significantly within the past 30 years. In many Western nations, the ethnic minority population is growing at significantly greater rates than the majority population. Institutionalized discrimination and racism are manifest by the significant gaps in the incomes, education, and health of minority and majority groups in many nation-states. Ethnic, racial, and religious minorities are also the victims of violence in many nation-states (Kymlicka, 2001).

Citizenship education must be transformed in the 21st century. Several worldwide developments make a new conception of citizenship education an imperative. They include the deepening ethnic texture of nations such as the United States and the United Kingdom, the large influx of immigrants who are now settling in nations throughout the world, the continuing existence of institutional racism and discrimination in various nations, and the widening gap between rich and poor nations (Castles & Davidson, 2000; Li, 1999).

Diversity, Unity and Cultural Communities

Citizens in a diverse democratic society should be able to maintain attachments to their cultural communities as well as participate effectively in the shared national culture. *Unity without diversity results in cultural repression and hegemony. Diversity without unity leads to Balkanization and the fracturing of the nation-state.* Diversity and unity should coexist in a delicate balance in a democratic multicultural nation-state. The attainment of the balance that is needed between diversity and unity is an ongoing process and ideal that is never fully attained. It is essential that both mainstream groups and groups on the margins of society participate in the formulation of societal goals related to diversity and unity. Both groups should also participate in action to attain these goals. Deliberation and the sharing of power by mainstream and marginalized groups are essential for the construction and perpetuation of a just, moral, and participatory democratic nation-state in a culturally diverse society.

Cultural and ethnic communities need to be respected and given legitimacy not only because they provide safe spaces for ethnic, cultural, and language groups on the margins of society, but also because they serve as a conscience for the nation-state. These communities take action to force the nation to live up to its democratic ideals when they are most seriously violated. It was the abolitionists and not the founding fathers in the United States who argued that freedom and equality should be extended to all Americans. African Americans led the civil rights movement of the 1960s and 1970s that forced the United States to eradicate its system of racial apartheid (Halberstam, 1998).

Okihiro (1994) points out that people and groups in the margins have been the conscience of the United States throughout its history. They have kept the United States committed to its democratic ideals as stated in its founding documents: the Declaration of Independence, the Constitution, and the Bill of Rights. He argues that the margins have been the main sites for keeping democracy and freedom alive in the United States. It was the groups in the margins that reminded and forced the United States to live up to its democratic ideals when they were most severely tested. Examples include: (a) slavery and the middle passage, (b) Indian removal in the 1830s, (c) the internment of Japanese Americans during World War II, and (d) segregation and apartheid in the South that crumbled during the 1960s and 1970s in response to the African American-led civil rights movement. In *The Story of American Freedom*, Foner (1998) makes an argument similar to Okihiro's:

> The authors of the notion of freedom as a universal birthright, a truly human ideal, were not so much the founding fathers who created a nation dedicated to liberty but resting in large measure on slavery, but abolitionists . . . and women. (p. xx)

Ethnic studies and multicultural education theorists and their supporters, and not mainstream educators, first called attention to and described the ways in which the school curriculum privileged students from some racial and cultural groups and made the cultures and histories of other students invisible. These scholars initiated an educational movement that resulted in substantial changes in the nation's school, college and university curriculum (Banks & Banks, 2001). The curriculum in the nation's educational institutions are now much more democratic and consistent with American Creed values (Myrdal, 1944) because of the reforms initiated by ethnic studies and multicultural education scholars.

Multicultural Citizenship and the Development of Cultural, National, and Global Identifications

A new kind of citizenship is needed for the 21st century, which Kymlicka (1995) calls *multicultural citizenship*. It recognizes and legitimizes the right and need of citizens to maintain commitments both to their cultural communities and to the national civic culture. Only when the national civic culture is transformed in ways that reflect and give voice to the diverse ethnic, racial, language, and religious communities that constitute it will it be viewed as legitimate by all of its citizens. Only then can they develop clarified commitments to the commonwealth and its ideals.

Citizenship education should help students to develop thoughtful and clarified identifications with their cultural communities and their nation-states. It should also help students to develop clarified global identifications and deep understandings of their roles in the world community (Diaz, Massialas, & Xanthopoulos, 1999). Students need to understand how life in their cultural communities and nations influences other nations and the cogent influence that international events have on their daily lives. Global education should have as major goals helping students to develop understandings of the interdependence among nations in the world today, clarified attitudes toward other nations, and reflective identifications with the world community.

Non-reflective and unexamined cultural attachments may prevent the development of a cohesive nation with clearly defined national goals and policies. Although we need to help students to develop reflective and clarified cultural identifications, they must also be helped to clarify and strengthen their identifications with their nation-states. However, blind nationalism will prevent students from developing reflective and positive global identifications. Nationalism and national attachments in most nations are strong and tenacious. An important aim of citizenship education should be to help students develop global identifications and a deep understanding of the need to take action as citizens of the global community to help solve the world's difficult global problems.

Cultural, national, and global experiences and identifications are interactive and interrelated in a dynamic way. Arnove (1999) writes:

> There is a dialect at work by which . . . global processes interact with national and local actors and contexts to be modified, and in some cases transformed. There is a process of give-and-take, an exchange by which international trends are reshaped to local ends. (pp. 2–3)

Students should develop a delicate balance of cultural, national, and global identifications; however, educators often try to help students develop strong national identifications by eradicating their ethnic and community cultures and making students ashamed of their families, community beliefs, languages, and behaviors. I believe that cultural, national, and global identifications are developmental, that individuals can attain healthy and reflective national identifications only when they have acquired healthy and reflective cultural identifications, and that individuals can develop reflective and positive global identifications only after they have realistic, reflective, and positive national identifications (Banks, 2001a). These identifications are dynamic and interactive, rather than discrete.

Individuals can develop a clarified commitment to and identification with a nation-state and the national culture only when they believe that they are a meaningful part of the nation-state and that it acknowledges, reflects, and values their culture and them as individuals. A nation-state that alienates and does not structurally include all cultural groups into the national culture runs the risk of creating alienation and causing groups to focus on specific concerns and issues rather than on the overarching goals and policies of the nation-state.

To develop reflective national and global identifications, students must acquire the knowledge, attitudes and skills needed to function within and across diverse racial, ethnic, cultural, language and religious groups. Teachers must undertake deliberate instruction in order to help students develop cross-cultural literacy skills and democratic racial and ethnic attitudes. Research indicates that during their early socialization students acquire stereotypes and misconceptions about racial groups such as African Americans (Aboud, 1988; Stephan, 1999). As early as age three children have internalized some of the stereotypes and attitudes toward racial groups that are institutionalized within American society (Aboud, 1988; Ramsey, 1998; Williams & Morland, 1976). White students as well as students of color internalize many of the negative racial attitudes toward ethnic minorities that are perpetuated within the media (Cortés, 2000), the family, and other institutions within society. Fortunately, research indicates that curriculum interventions can help students develop more positive attitudes toward marginalized racial and ethnic groups and have equal-status interactions with individuals who are members of these groups.

Diversity: An Opportunity and a Challenge

Diversity presents both opportunities and challenges to American society and to teachers. Diversity enriches our nation, communities, schools, and classrooms. Individuals from many different racial, ethnic, and cultural groups have made and continue to make significant contributions to American society. Diversity also provides our society with myriad and enriched ways to identify, describe, and solve social, economic, and political problems.

Diversity also poses serious challenges to our nation, to schools, and to social studies teachers. Research indicates that students come to school with many stereotypes, misconceptions, and negative attitudes toward outside racial, ethnic, and social-class groups (Aboud, 1988; Banks, 2001b; Stephan & Stephan, 1996; Tajfel, 1970). Without curriculum intervention by teachers, the racial attitudes and behaviors of students become more negative and harder to change as they grow older (Banks, 1993; Ramsey, 1998). An important aim of effective social studies teaching is to provide students with experiences and materials that will help them to become thoughtful and active citizens. In a diverse democratic society, effective citizens have positive attitudes and behaviors toward individuals from different racial, ethnic, social-class, and language groups, engage in deliberation with these individuals, and participate in equal-status contact situations with them (Banks, 1993, 2001b).

Figure 1 summarizes the characteristics of the effective citizen in a multicultural democratic society discussed in the first part of this chapter. The next part discusses theory and research that teachers can use to help students acquire more democratic attitudes, values, and behaviors and develop more thoughtful cultural, national and global identifications.

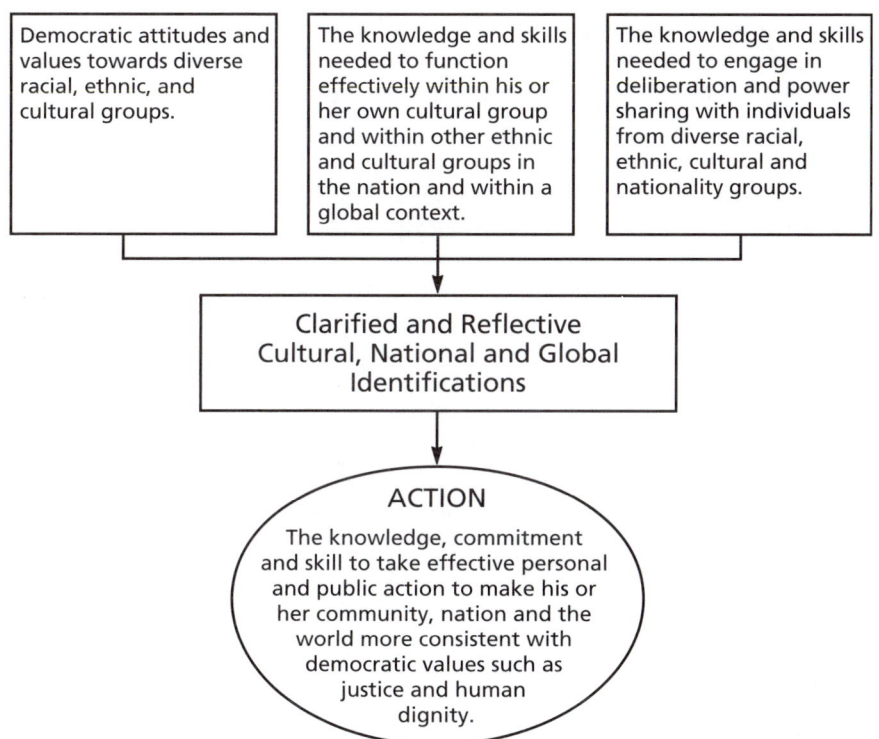

Figure 1. Characteristics of the effective citizen in a multicultural democratic society.

SOCIAL PSYCHOLOGICAL THEORY AND RESEARCH AND CITIZENSHIP EDUCATION

Whenever ingroups and outgroups form, stereotypes, prejudice and discrimination develops. Consequently, it becomes necessary for educators to design and implement strategies to improve intergroup relations. Social psychological theory and research known as the *minimal group paradigm* indicates that when mere categorization develops, individuals favor the ingroup over the outgroup and discriminates against the outgroup (Rothbart & John, 1993; Smith & Mackie, 1995). This can occur in situations without prior historical conflict and animosity, competition, physical differences, or any kind of important difference. Tajfel (1970) writes, "Whenever we are confronted with a situation to which some form of intergroup categorization appears directly relevant, we are likely to act in a manner that discriminates against the outgroup and favors the ingroup" (pp. 98–99).

It is beyond the scope of this chapter to examine closely the various theories that attempt to explain the genesis of social identity and the minimal group paradigm. Readers are referred to works by Tajfel and Turner (1986) and Sidanius and Pratto (1993) for detailed discussions of these theories.

One of the important causes of group distinctions is categorization itself. Categorization is both a cause and a perpetuator of group distinctions. When we categorize one group gifted and another as having a learning disability the basis for distinctions and discrimination has been constructed. Sidanius and Pratto (1993) have constructed a *social dominance theory* to explain the genesis of categorization and ingroup-outgroup distinctions. They argue that categorization and discrimination are based on group-based hierarchies. Their theory consists of several different propositions, including these:

> All human societies throughout recorded history have been hierarchically organized. Human social systems are predisposed to form group based social hierarchies. Social hierarchy is a survival strategy that has been selected by most if not all species of primates, including homo sapiens. (pp. 174–175)

In a series of studies, Tajfel and his colleagues (Billig & Tajfel, 1973; Tajfel, 1970) produced considerable evidence to support the postulate that individuals are likely to evaluate the ingroup more favorably than the outgroup and to treat the ingroup more favorably even when the differences between the groups are minimal, contrived and insignificant. This series of studies indicate the power of *categorization*. In one group of experiments Tajfel (1970) told a group of public school boys in Bristol that he had divided them into two groups based on whether they had under or overestimated the number of dots projected on a screen. The subjects were then given a series of tasks in which they could provide rewards to two anonymous students. When the students were in the same groups as the students giving the awards, they divided the awards equally. However, the students giving the rewards favored the ingroup when one student was an outgroup member and the other an ingroup member. The experimenter contrived the groups. The assignment of the groups was random and was not based on the estimation of the dots by the subjects.

The *minimal group paradigm*, also known as *social identity* theory, is in some ways more helpful in explaining the development of ingroup-outgroup boundaries than in suggesting practices to reduce them. One implication of social identity theory is that to increase positive intergroup contact the salience of group characteristics should be minimized and a superordinate group to which students from different cultural and language groups can become identified should be constructed. For example, in a classroom characterized by language diversity, group salience is likely to be reduced to the extent that all students become competent in the same languages. In a classroom with both Anglos and Mexican Americans, group salience is increased if only the Mexican American students speak Spanish. However, if both Mexican and Anglo American students become competent in English and Spanish, bilingual competency can be the basis for the formation of a superordinate group to which all of the students belong.

The Contact Hypothesis

Most of the work in social psychology related to race relations has been guided by the contact hypothesis and related research that emerged out of events surrounding World War II. The rise of Nazi anti-Semitism and its devastating consequences motivated social scientists in the postwar years to devote considerable attention to theory and research related to improving intergroup relations. The contact hypothesis that guides most of the research and theory in intergroup relations today emerged from the classic works by Williams (1947) and Allport (1954). Despite its significant influence on theory and practice, Pettigrew (1986), who was one of Allport's students, describes the contact hypothesis as a "middle-range theory of modest scope" (p. 171).

Pettigrew's characterization of the contact hypothesis indicates that it is consistent with most theories and explanations in the social sciences, including social identity theory. In his classic paper, "On Sociological Theories of the Middle Range," Merton (1968) points out that social scientists have not been successful in developing grand or all-inclusive theories, despite the efforts of social scientists such as Parsons (1990/1937). Merton argues that the best we can hope for in the social sciences are powerful middle-range theories that are empirically based. To improve intergroup relations in their classrooms, teachers can use the best available middle-range theories. The contact hypothesis is such a theory. This hypothesis, and the research and guidelines related to it, can help teachers improve intergroup relations in diverse classrooms.

Allport (1954) states that contact between groups will improve intergroup relations when the contract is characterized by these four conditions: (1) equal status; (2) common goals; (3) intergroup cooperation; and (4) support of authorities, law and custom. Allport (1954) writes:

> Prejudice (unless deeply rooted in the structure of the individual) may be reduced by equal status contact between majority and minority groups in the pursuit of common goals. The effect is greatly enhanced if this contact is sanctioned by institutionalized supports (i.e., by law, custom or local atmosphere), and provided it is of a sort that leads to the perception of common interests and common humanity between members of the two groups. (p. 281)

Cooperative Learning and Interracial Contact

Since the 1970s, a group of investigators has accumulated an impressive body of research on the effects of cooperative learning groups and activities on students' racial attitudes, friendship choices, and achievement. Much of this research has been conducted as well as reviewed by investigators such as Aronson and his colleagues (Aronson & Bridgeman, 1979; Aronson & Gonzalez, 1988), Cohen and her colleagues (Cohen, 1972, 1986; Cohen & Lotan, 1995; Cohen & Roper, 1972), Johnson and Johnson (1981, 1991), Slavin (1979, 1983, 1985), and Slavin and Madden (1979). Schofield (2001) has written an informative review of this research. Most of it has been conducted using elementary and high school students as subjects (Slavin, 1983, 1985).

The research on cooperative learning and interracial contact that has been conducted since 1970 is based on Allport's (1954) contact hypothesis. This research lends considerable support to the postulate that cooperative interracial contact situations in schools, if the conditions stated by Allport are present in the contact situations, have positive effects on both student interracial behavior and student academic achievement (Aronson & Gonzalez, 1988; Slavin, 1979, 1983). In his review of 19 studies of the effects of cooperative-learning methods, Slavin (1985) found that sixteen had positive effects on interracial friendships. In a more recent review

Slavin (2001) describes the positive effects of cooperative groups on cross-racial friendships, racial attitudes, and behavior.

Most of this research supports these postulates: (a) students of color and White students have a greater tendency to make cross-racial friendship choices after they have participated in interracial learning teams such as the jigsaw (Aronson & Bridgeman, 1979) and the Student Teams-Achievement Divisions (STAD) (Slavin, 1979); (b) the academic achievement of students of color such as African Americans and Mexican Americans is increased when cooperative learning activities are used; the academic achievement of White students remains about the same in both cooperative and competitive learning situations (Aronson & Gonzalez, 1988; Slavin, 1985). Investigators have also found that cooperative learning methods have increased student motivation and self-esteem (Slavin, 1985) and helped students to develop empathy (Aronson & Bridgeman, 1979).

An essential characteristic of effective cooperative learning groups and methods is that the students experience equal status in the contact situation (Allport, 1954). Cohen (1972) has pointed out that both African American and White students may expect and attribute higher status to Whites in an initial interracial contact situation that may perpetuate White dominance. Cohen and Roper (1972) designed an intervention to change this expectation. They taught African American children to build transistor radios and to teach this skill to White students. The Black children taught the White children to build the radios after the children watched a videotape showing the African American children building radios. When interracial work groups were structured, equal status was achieved only in those groups in which the African American children taught the White students to build radios. The White children dominated in the other groups.

The research by Cohen and Roper (1972) indicates that equal status between groups in interracial situations has to be constructed by teachers rather than assumed. If students from diverse racial, ethnic, and language groups are mixed without structured interventions that create equal-status conditions in the contact situation, racial and ethnic conflict and categorization is likely to increase. In a series of perceptive and carefully designed studies that span two decades, Cohen and her colleagues (Cohen, 1984a,b; Cohen & Roper, 1972; Cohen & Lotan, 1995) have consistently found that contact among different groups without deliberate interventions to increase equal status and positive interactions among them will increase rather than reduce intergroup tensions. Cohen (1994) has developed practical guidelines and strategies that can be used by teachers to create equal status within racially, culturally, and language diverse classrooms.

Curriculum Interventions

There is a great deal of discussion but little agreement about what constitutes equal status in intergroup contact situations. Some researchers interpret equal status to mean equal socioeconomic status. For example, in his summary of favorable and unfavorable conditions that influence interracial contact, Amir (quoted in Hewstone & Brown, 1986) describes this situation as an unfavorable condition: "In the case of contact between a majority and a minority group, when the members of the minority group are of lower status or are lower in any relevant characteristics than the members of the majority groups" (p. 7). Yet Cohen and Roper (1972) interpret equal status differently. Although the African Americans and White students in their study were from different social-class groups, they created equal role-status in the classroom by modifying the perceptions that students held of each racial group. They accomplished this task by assigning the African American students a task that increased their status in the classroom. Cohen and Roper had a social psychological, rather than an economic, view of equal status.

The representations of different ethnic, racial, and language groups that are embedded in curriculum materials and textbooks, and within the activities and teaching strategies of instructors, privileges some groups of students (thus increasing their classroom status), and erodes the status of other students by reinforcing their marginal status in the larger society. Studies of textbooks indicate that the images of groups in textbooks reflect those that are institutionalized within the larger society (Sleeter & Grant, 1991). If we view status from a social psychological perspective, as Cohen and Roper (1972) do, a multicultural curriculum that presents representations of diverse groups in realistic and complex ways can help to equalize the status of all groups within the classroom or school. Readers can see Stephan (1985) and Banks (1993, 2001) for comprehensive reviews of curriculum intervention studies.

Since the 1940s, a number of curriculum interventions studies have been conducted to determine the effects of teaching units and lessons, multiethnic materials, role playing, and other kinds of simulated experiences on the racial attitudes and perceptions of students. These studies, which have some important limitations and findings that are not always consistent, indicate that under certain conditions curriculum interventions can help students develop more positive racial and ethnic attitudes.

The limitations of curriculum studies in intergroup relations are similar to those that characterize most intergroup relations studies, such as those on categorization (Tajfel, 1970) and cooperative groups (Slavin, 1985). Most curriculum intervention studies have used African Americans and Whites as subjects, are of rather short duration, have little follow-up, are rarely related to the actual behavior of the subjects, use a variety of measures that have low intercorrelations, and have used interventions that are often not well defined, making it difficult for the studies to be replicated by other researchers (Banks, 2001b).

Despite the limitations of these studies, they provide guidelines that can help teachers improve intergroup relations in their classrooms and schools. Trager and Yarrow (1952) conducted one of the earliest curriculum studies. They examined the effects of a curriculum intervention on the racial attitudes of children in the first and second grades. In one experimental condition, the children experienced a democratic curriculum; in the other, non-democratic values were taught and perpetuated. No experimental condition was created in the control group. The democratic curriculum had a positive effect on the attitudes of both students and teachers.

White, second-grade children developed more positive racial attitudes after using multiethnic readers in a study conducted by Litcher and Johnson (1969). However, when Litcher, Johnson, and Ryan (1973) replicated this study using photographs instead of readers, the children's racial attitudes were not significantly changed. The investigators stated that the shorter length of the later study (one month compared to four), and the different racial compositions of the two communities in which the studies were conducted, may help to explain why no significant effects were produced on the children's racial attitudes in the second study. The community in which the second study was conducted had a much higher percentage of African American residents than did the community in which the first was conducted.

The longitudinal evaluation of the television program, *Sesame Street*, by Bogatz and Ball (1971) supports the hypothesis that multiethnic simulated materials and interventions can have a positive effect on the racial attitudes of young children. These investigators found that children who had watched the program for long periods had more positive racial attitudes toward outgroups than did children who had watched the show for shorter periods.

Weiner and Wright (1973) examined the effects of a simulation on the racial attitudes of third-grade children. They divided a class into Orange and Green people. The children wore colored armbands that designated their group status. On one day of the intervention the students who wore Orange armbands experienced discrimination. On the other day, the children who wrote Green armbands were the victims. On the third day and again two weeks later, the children expressed less prejudiced beliefs and attitudes.

In an intervention which has now attained the status of a classic, Jane Elliot (cited in Peters, 1987) used simulation to teach her students the pain of discrimination. One day she discriminated against the blue-eyed chil-

Blue Eyes/Brown eyes.

dren in her third-grade class; the next day she discriminated again the brown-eyed children. Elliot's intervention is described in the award-winning documentary, *The Eye of the Storm*. Eleven of Elliot's former students returned to Riceville, Iowa fourteen years later and shared their powerful memories of the simulation with their former teacher. This reunion is described in *A Class Divided*, a revealing and important documentary film.

Byrnes and Kiger (1990) conducted an experimental study to determine the effects of the kind of simulation for which Elliot had attained fame. They found that no experimental data existed on the effects of the blue-eyes-brown eyes simulation; and that all of the evidence on the effects of the intervention were anecdotal. The subjects in their study were university students preparing to become elementary students. Their simulation had positive effects on the attitudes of non-Black students toward Blacks, but had no effects on the subjects "stated level of comfort with Blacks in various social situations, as measured by the Social Distance scale" (p. 351).

Yawkey and Blackwell (1974) examined the effects of multiethnic social studies materials and related experiences on the racial attitudes of Black four-year-old children. The children were divided into three groups. The students in Group 1 read and discussed the materials. The Group 2 students read and discussed the materials as well as took a related field trip. The students in Group 3 experienced the traditional preschool curriculum. The interventions in Groups 1 and 2 had a significant, positive effect on the students' racial attitudes toward African Americans and Whites.

Research indicates that curriculum interventions such as plays, folk dances, music, role playing, exclusion from a group, discussion in dyads, and interracial contact can also have positive effects on the racial attitudes of students. A curriculum intervention that consisted of folk dances, music, crafts, and role-playing had a positive effect on the racial attitudes of elementary students in a study conducted by Ijaz and Ijaz (1981) in Canada. Four plays about African Americans, Chinese Americans, Jews, and Puerto Ricans increased racial acceptance and cultural knowledge among fourth, fifth, and sixth grade students in the New York City schools in a study conducted by Gimmestad and DeChiara (1982).

Ciullo and Troiani (1988) found that children who were excluded from a group exercise became more sensitive to the feelings of children from other ethnic groups. McGregor (1993) used meta-analysis to integrate findings and to examine the effects of role-playing and antiracist teaching on reducing prejudice in students. Twenty-six studies were located and examined. McGregor concluded that role-playing and antiracist teaching "significantly reduce racial prejudice, and do not differ from each other in their effectiveness" (p. 215).

Aboud and Doyle (1996) designed a study to determine how children's racial evaluations were affected by talking about racial issues with a friend who had a different level of prejudice than their own. The researchers found that "high-prejudice children became significantly less prejudiced in their evaluations after the discussion. Changes were greater in children whose low-prejudice partner made more statements about cross-racial similarity, along with more positive Black and negative White evaluations" (p.161). A study by Wood and Sonleitner (1996) indicates that childhood interracial contact has a positive, long-term influence on the racial attitudes and behavior of adults. They found that interracial contact in schools and neighborhoods has a direct and significant positive influence on adult racial attitudes toward African Americans.

Creating Cross-Cutting Superordinate Groups

Research indicates that creating salient superordinate and cross-cutting group memberships improves intergroup relations (Banks et al., 2001; Stephan, 1999). Banks et al. (2001) write: "When membership in superordinate groups is salient, other group differences become less important. Creating superordinate groups stimulates cohesion, which can mitigate pre-existing animosities." (p. 9)

Members of a sports team, Future Farmers of America, Girl Scouts, and Campfire are examples of cross-cutting or superordinate groups. Research and theory indicate that when students from diverse cultural, racial, and language groups share a superordinate identity such as Girl Scouts, cultural boundaries weaken. Students consequently are able to form friendships and to have positive interactions and relationships with students from different racial, cultural, language, and religious groups. Extra- and co-curricular activities, such as the drama club, the debating club, the basketball team, and the school chorus create rich possibilities for structuring superordinate groups and cross-cutting group memberships.

When teachers create cross-cutting or superordinate groups, they should make sure that the integrity of different cultures represented in the classroom are respected and given legitimacy within the framework of the superordinate group that is created. Superordinate groups that only reflect the norms and values of dominant and powerful groups within the school are not likely to improve intergroup relations among different groups in the school. If they are not carefully structured and monitored, cross-cutting groups can reproduce the dominant power relationships that exist within the school and the larger society.

IMPLICATIONS OF CURRICULUM INTERVENTION RESEARCH FOR TEACHING AND LEARNING

Teachers can use the insights and findings from social psychological research to help guide the development of curriculum and interventions that will help students in diverse classrooms to develop more positive intergroup attitudes and behaviors and, consequently, become more effective citizens in a multicultural democratic society. This theory and research indicate that students are likely to make categorizations that result in attitudes and behaviors that favor ingroups over outgroups. In experimental situations, these categorizations are often made on socially insignificant variables.

Because race, language, and religion are powerful forms of social identity, students make categorizations based on these factors. Research since the 1930s and 1940s has indicated that young children make categorizations based on race and that both children of color and White children often make racial preferences that indicate a White bias (Clark & Clark, 1939; Spencer, 1982). In a racially, culturally and language diverse classroom, students are likely to make categorizations and choices that reflect a bias toward the races, cultures and languages with high status.

Research indicates that teachers can improve intergroup relations by creating conditions in contact situations: (1) in which individuals from all groups experience equal status; (2) in which participants have common goals; (3) cooperation exits within the group; and (4) the contact is sanctioned by authorities such as teachers and principals. If these conditions do not exist in contact situations that include individuals from diverse racial, ethnic, language, and religious groups, categorization, stereotyping, and intergroup tension are likely to increase rather than decrease.

Teachers can use the theoretical and research guidelines described in this chapter to help students develop reflective cultural, national, and global identifications that are essential for effective citizenship in the diverse world society in which we live.

ACKNOWLEDGMENT

Parts of this chapter are adapted with permission of the publisher from: Banks, J.A. (2001). Citizenship education and diversity: Implications for teacher education. *Journal of Teacher Education, 52*(1), 5–16.

REFERENCES

Aboud, F.E. (1988). *Children and prejudice.* Cambridge: Basil Blackwell.
Aboud, F.E., & Doyle, A.B. (1996). Does talk foster prejudice or tolerance in children? *Canadian Journal of Behavioural Science, 28*(3), 161–171.
Allport, G.W. (1954). *The nature of prejudice.* Reading, MA: Addison-Wesley.
Arnove, R.F. (1999). Reframing comparative education: The dialectic of the global and the local. In R.F. Arnove & C.A. Torres (Eds.), *Comparative education: The dialectic of the global and the local* (pp. 1–23). New York: Rowman & Littlefield.
Aronson, E., & Bridgeman, D. (1979). Jigsaw groups and the desegregated classroom: In pursuit of common goals. *Personality and Social Psychology Bulletin, 5,* 438–446.
Aronson, E., & Gonzalez, A. (1988). Desegregation, jigsaw, and the Mexican-American experience. In P.A. Katz & D.A. Taylor (Eds.), *Eliminating racism: Profiles in controversy* (pp. 301–314). New York: Plenum Press.
Banks, J.A. (1993). Multicultural education for young children: Racial and ethnic attitudes and their modification. In B. Spodek (Ed.), *Handbook of research on the education of young children* (pp. 236–250). New York: Macmillan.
Banks, J.A. (1997). *Educating citizens in a multicultural society.* New York: Teachers College Press.
Banks, J.A. (2001a). *Cultural diversity and education: Foundations, curriculum and teaching* (4th ed.). Boston: Allyn & Bacon.
Banks, J.A. (2001b). Multicultural education: Its effects on students' racial and gender role attitudes. In J.A. Banks & C.A.M. Banks (Eds.), *Handbook of research on multicultural education* (pp. 617–627). San Francisco: Jossey-Bass.
Banks, J.A., & Banks, C.A.M. (Eds.). (2001). *Handbook of research on multicultural education.* San Francisco: Jossey-Bass.
Banks, J.A., Cookson, P., Gay, G., Hawley, W.D., Irvine, J.J., Nieto, S., Schofield, J.W. & Stephan, W.G. (2001). *Diversity within unity: Essential principles for teaching and learning in a multicultural society.* Seattle: Center for Multicultural Education, University of Washington.
Billig, M., & Tajfel, H. (1973). Social categorization and similarity in intergroup behaviour. *European Journal of Social Psychology, 3,* 27–52.
Bogatz, G.A., & Ball, S. (1971). *The second year of Sesame Street: A continuing evaluation.* Princeton, NJ: Educational Testing Service.
Byrnes, D.A. & Kiger, G. (1990). The effect of prejudice-reduction simulation on attitude change. *Journal of Applied Social Psychology, 20*(4), 341–356.
Castles, S., & Davidson, A. (2000). *Citizenship and migration: Globalization and the politics of belonging.* New York: The Guilford Press.
Ciullo, R., & Troiani, M.Y. (1988). Resolution of prejudice: Small group interaction and behavior of latency-age children. *Small Group Behavior, 19*(3), 386–394.
Clark, K.B., & Clark, M.P. (1939). The development of consciousness of self and the emergence of racial identification in Negro preschool children. *Journal of Social Psychology, 10,* 591–599.
Cohen, E. (1972). Interracial interaction disability. *Human Relations, 25,* 9–24.
Cohen. E.G. (1984a). Talking and working together: Status, interaction, and learning. In P. Peterson, L.C. Wilkinson, & M. Hallinan (Eds.), *The social context of instruction* (pp. 171–186). New York: Academic Press.

Cohen, E.G. (1984b). The desegregated school: Problems in status power and interethnic climate. In N. Miller & M.B. Brewer (Eds.), *Groups in contact: The psychology of desegregation* (pp. 77–96). New York: Academic Press.

Cohen, E.G. (1994). *Designing groupwork: Strategies for the heterogeneous classroom* (2nd ed.). New York: Teachers College Press.

Cohen, E.G., & Lotan, R.A. (1995). Producing equal-status interaction in the heterogeneous classroom. *American Educational Research Journal, 32,* 99–120.

Cohen, E.G., & Roper, S.S. (1972). Modification of interracial interaction disability: An application of status characteristic theory. *American Sociological Review, 37,* 643–657.

Cortés, C.E. (2000). *The children are watching: How the media teach about diversity.* New York: Teachers College Press.

Diaz, C.F., Massialas, B.G., & Xanthopoulos, J.A. (1999). *Global perspectives for educators.* Boston: Allyn and Bacon.

Eck, D.L. (2001). *A new religious America: How a "Christian Country" has become the world's most religiously diverse nation.* New York: HarperSanFrancisco.

Foner, E. (1998). *The story of American freedom.* New York: Norton.

Garcia, E.E. (1993). Language, culture, and education. In L. Daring-Hammond (Ed.). *Review of research in education* (Vol. 19, pp. 51–98). Washington, DC: American Educational Research Association.

Giles, H. (Ed.). (1977). *Language, ethnicity and intergroup relations.* New York: Academic Press.

Gimmestad, B.J., & DeChiara, E. (1982). Dramatic plays: A vehicle for prejudice reduction in the elementary school. *Journal of Educational Research, 76*(1), 45–49.

Halberstam, D. (1998). *The children.* New York: Random House.

Hewstone, M., & Brown, R. (1986). Contact is not enough: An intergroup perspective on the "contact hypothesis." In M. Hewstone & R. Brown (Eds.), *Contact and conflict in intergroup encounters* (pp. 1–44). New York: Basil Blackwell.

Ijaz, M.A., & Ijaz, I.H. (1981). A cultural program for changing racial attitudes. *History and Social Science Teacher, 17*(1), 17–20.

Johnson, D.W., & Johnson, R.T. (1981). Effects of cooperative and individualistic learning experiences on interethnic interaction. *Journal of Educational Psychology, 73,* 444–449.

Johnson, D.W., & Johnson, R.T. (1991). *Learning together and alone* (3rd ed.). Englewood Cliffs, NJ: Prentice-Hall.

Kymlicka, W. (1995). *Multicultural citizenship: A liberal theory of minority rights.* New York: Oxford University Press.

Kymlicka, W. (2001). *Politics in the vernacular: Nationalism, multiculturalism, and citizenship.* New York: Oxford University Press.

Lee, S.J. (1991). *Ethnic identification and social interaction: A study of Asian-American students at a Philadelphia High School.* Unpublished doctoral dissertation, University of Pennsylvania.

Li, P.S. (Ed.). (1999). *Race and ethnic relations in Canada* (2nd ed.). New York: Oxford University Press.

Litcher, J.H., & Johnson, D.W. (1969). Changes in attitudes toward Negroes of White elementary school students after use of multiethnic readers. *Journal of Educational Psychology, 60,* 148–152.

Litcher, J.H., Johnson, D.W., & Ryan, F.L. (1973). Use of pictures of multiethnic interaction to change attitudes of White elementary school students toward Blacks. *Psychological Reports, 33*, 367–372.

McGregor, J. (1993). Effectiveness of role playing and antiracist teaching in reducing student prejudice. *Journal of Educational Research, 86*(4), 215–226.

Merton, R.K. (1968). On sociological theories of the middle range. In R.K. Merton, *Social theory and social structure* (enlarged ed.) (pp. 39–72). New York: The Free Press.

Myrdal, G., with Sterner, R. & Rose, A. (1944). *An American dilemma: The Negro problem and modern democracy.* New York: Harper and Row.

Okihiro, G. (1994). *Margins and mainstreams: Asians in American history and culture.* Seattle: University of Washington Press.

Parsons, T. (1990/1937). *The structure of social action.* New York: Simon & Schuster (original work published 1937).

Peters, W. (1987). *A class divided: Then and now* (expanded ed.). New Haven: Yale University Press.

Pettigrew, T.P. (1986). The intergroup hypothesis reconsidered. In M. Hewstone & R. Brown (Eds.), *Contact and conflict in intergroup encounters* (pp. 169–195). New York: Basil Blackwell.

Ramsey, P.G. (1998). *Teaching and learning in a diverse world* (2nd ed.). New York: Teachers College Press.

Rothbart, M., & John, O.P. (1993). Intergroup relations and stereotype change: A social-cognitive analysis and some longitudinal findings. In P.M. Sniderman, P.E. Telock, & E.G. Carmines (Eds.), *Prejudice, politics, and the American dilemma* (pp. 32–59). Stanford, CA: Stanford University Press.

Ryan, E.B., & Carranza, M.A. (1977). Ingroup and outgroup reactions to Mexican American language varieties. In H. Giles (Ed.), *Language, ethnicity and intergroup relations* (pp. 59–82). New York: Academic Press.

Schofield, J.W. (2001). Improving intergroup relations. In J.A. Banks & C.A.M. Banks (Eds.), *Handbook of research on multicultural education* (pp. 635–646). San Francisco: Jossey-Bass.

Sidanius, J., & Pratto, F. (1993). The inevitability of oppression and the dynamics of social dominance. In P.M. Sniderman, P.E. Tetlock, & E.G. Carmines (Eds.), *Prejudice, politics, and the American dilemma* (pp. 173–211). Stanford, CA: Stanford University Press.

Slavin, R.E. (1979). Effects of biracial learning teams on cross-racial friendships. *Journal of Educational Psychology, 71*, 381–387.

Slavin, R.E. (1983). *Cooperative learning.* New York: Longman.

Slavin, R.E. (1985). Cooperative learning: Applying contact theory in desegregated schools. *Journal of Social Issues, 41*, 45–62.

Slavin, R.E. (2001). Cooperative learning and intergroup relations. In J.A. Banks & C.A.M. Banks (Eds.), *Handbook of research on multicultural education* (pp. 628–634). San Francisco: Jossey-Bass.

Slavin, R.E., & Madden, N.A. (1979). School practices that improve race relations. *American Educational Research Journal, 16*(2), 169–180.

Sleeter, C.E., & Grant, C.A. (1991). Race, class, gender, and disability in current textbooks. In M.W. Apple & L.K. Christian-Smith (Eds.), *The politics of the textbook* (pp. 78–110). New York: Routledge.

Smith, E.R., & Mackie, D.M. (1995). *Social psychology.* New York: Worth Publishers, Inc.

Spencer, M.B. (1982). Personal and group identity of Black children: An alternative synthesis. *Genetic Psychology Monographs, 106,* 59–84.

Stephan, W.G. (1985). Intergroup relations. In G. Lindzey & E. Aronson (Eds.), *The Handbook of social psychology* (vol. 2, 3rd ed., pp. 599–658). New York: Random House.

Stephan, W.G. (1999). *Reducing prejudice and stereotyping in schools.* New York: Teachers College Press.

Stephan, W.G., & Stephan, C.W. (1996). *Intergroup relations.* Madison: Brown & Benchmark.

Trager, H.G., & Yarrow, M.R. (1952). *They learn what they live: Prejudice in young children.* New York: Harper.

Tajfel, H. (1970). Experiments in intergroup discrimination. *Scientific American, 223*(5), 96–102.

Tajfel, H., & Turner, J.C. (1986). The social identity theory of intergroup behavior. In S. Worchel & W.G. Austin (Eds.), *Psychology of intergroup relations* (pp. 7–24). Chicago: Nelson-Hall Publishers.

U.S. Bureau of the Census (2000). *Statistical abstract of the United States: 2000* (120th ed.). Washington, DC: U. S. Government Printing Office.

Weiner, M.J., & Wright, F.E. (1973). Effects of undergoing arbitrary discrimination upon subsequent attitudes toward a minority group. *Journal of Applied Social Psychology, 3,* 94–102.

Williams, J.E., & Morland, J.K. (1976). *Race, color, and the young child.* Chapel Hill: University of North Carolina Press.

Williams, R.M. (1947). *Reduction of intergroup tensions.* New York: Social Science Research Council.

Wood, P.B., & Sonleitner, N. (1996). The effect of childhood interracial contact on adult anti-Black prejudice. *International Journal of Intercultural Relations, 20*(1), 1–17.

Yawkey, T.D., & Blackwell, J. (1974). Attitudes of 4-year old urban Black children toward themselves and Whites based upon multi-ethnic social studies materials and experiences. *The Journal of Educational Research, 67,* 373–377.

CHAPTER 8

EDUCATING "WORLD CITIZENS"

Toward Multinational Curriculum Development

Walter C. Parker, Akira Ninomiya, John J. Cogan

INTRODUCTION

On a rainy morning at a coffeehouse near campus, one of the authors was telling a colleague about the research we report here.[1] "Educators from nine nations in Asia, North America, and Europe have developed a set of school curriculum recommendations based on interviews and surveys with policy leaders in each of those nations," he began. "The world is changing, and the world studies curriculum in the schools needs to change with it." "Sure it does," replied the colleague, "but when hasn't the world been changing? And when haven't educators been revising the curriculum to keep up with it? Didn't you read *The Saber-Tooth Curriculum?*" She was referring to the famous satire on curricular entrenchment written by Harold Benjamin in 1939. Benjamin, under the pseudonym J. Abner Peddiwell, described a prehistoric society in which the major survival tasks were scaring away saber-toothed tigers with fire and catching fish with bare hands. The schools in this society had tailored a utilitarian curriculum to these tasks, teaching students to grab fish by hand and use fire to frighten away tigers. In time, the world changed: glaciers muddied the rivers and drove the tigers south. Fish nets were invented, since the fish couldn't be seen, let alone grabbed. Yet, the school curriculum continued to feature tiger scaring and fish grabbing. These had served society well in the past and were by now thought to be estimable human achievements in their own right. They were the things anyone with an ounce of intelligence knew how to do, and knowing how to do them well made one a well-educated person.

Benjamin's book both expressed and fueled the instrumentalist desire among educators in the United States in the 1920s and 30s to remake the curriculum, clearing it of what they believed were outdated subject matters tied to retrograde social aims and realities (e.g., Counts, 1932; Caswell & Campbell, 1935; Kilpatrick, 1936).[2] The destabilization of traditional communities by the modern forces of capitalism, industrialization, secularization, metropolitanism, rationality, democracy and immigration had loaded a buzzing array of topics and concerns onto the schools. Accordingly, "updating" the curriculum was the order of the day. Our colleague's point was that it is *still* the order of the day; she wondered what we were getting excited about. For better or worse, the rapid pace of change throughout this century in both "developed" (e.g., Canada, Japan) and "developing"[3] (e.g., Thailand, Hungary) societies has made instrumentalists, and therefore forecasters, of most educators. Educators are joined across the decades and across national and cultural boundaries with the belief that children should be educated for what is always a combination of existing and anticipated states of affairs. They are perennially trying to forecast and decipher social trends and develop the next in a long line of "next" curricula dating back to the saber-toothed curriculum and whatever preceded it.

This is no easy task. First, the rate and volatility of modern social change makes curriculum development an endless task. The job is never done. Second, the difficulty of forecasting makes curriculum development inevitably off-target. The job is never done "just right." Third, value conflicts within societies make the school curriculum a hotly contested social terrain. Stakeholders argue vehemently over aims and procedures. North Americans, for example, divide their loyalty between market-oriented and democracy-oriented curriculum reform. In Japan, educators struggle to internationalize the curriculum, which they are convinced has been insular and chauvinist; at the same time, nostalgia for homogeneity and exceptionalism runs strong. Hungarian educators debate the school curriculum in the same terms used to debate the social and political aims of the broader society, chief among which is the contest between social democracy and capitalist democracy. Everywhere, "relevance" is the watchword as educators attempt to tailor the curriculum to anticipated social needs.

Amid the perennial updating, however, curriculum renewal efforts have been largely national and local as distinct from regional or multinational. The tools and perspectives employed by curriculum workers in these nations thus have been limited in perspective and reach. The national and intranational cast of their work has accomplished important goals, among them nation-building, civic cohesion, employment training geared to the national and local political economy, and military-industrial competition and cooperation with other nations. Other goals, however, are removed from consideration or placed so far out on the periphery of curriculum deliberation as to be taken seriously by almost no one, even if they are included with some regularity in official curriculum documents (e.g., ". . . to prepare young people for citizenship in an interdependent world," Michigan State Board of Education, 1995, p. 1). Chief among these marginalized goals is civic education of a global kind—education for shared problem solving on messy international problems and, thereby, the cultivation of a global perspective on such problems (Case, 1993; Hanvey, 1978; Willinsky, 1992) and the eventual emergence of what Elise Boulding (1988) called a "global civic culture" in her book of that name.

Even reform efforts aimed ostensibly at "global education" or "international studies" or "world problems" proceed in ways that are heavily nation-bound; that is, supposedly international curricula are typically developed nationally. Exceptions can be found but typically there are *calls* for this sort of work[4] as distinct from *projects* that attempt it. National or local committees, along with textbook authors, do most of the actual curriculum theorizing and curriculum decision making, and, because they are no more superhuman than the rest of us in their capacity to transcend their vantage points, their work is constrained by local and/or national conceptual frameworks and representations of "the world." It could not be otherwise, for locus matters; there is no neutral ground. It matters where and with whom one is planning.

The study we report here shares one key similarity with the conventional approach to curriculum development: Our effort was a continuation (for better or worse) of the instrumentalist tradition of remaking curricula for the purpose of achieving "relevance" to extant and forecasted social realities. However, it was different in both locus and focus. As for locus, it was situated multinationally from the start. It was by purposes and procedures a multinational effort to develop both the forecast and the set of curriculum recommendations tailored to it. This will be detailed in the next section. As for focus, the object of our inquiry was education for *citizenship*, which has been predominantly a national and intranational concern in virtually every nation. By definition, modern citizenship is closely aligned to national borders and national identities (Beiner, 1995; Oommen, 1997) and, in federated nations, to states and provinces as well. By contrast, this study broached the subject of world or what we will call *multidimensional* citizenship as the aim of curriculum development. It rested on the view that the time has come for the "next curriculum" to be in some respects a shared world curriculum, developed at least in part by a multinational team, since the next world to which the curriculum must be made relevant is increasingly a shared world.

PURPOSE AND METHOD

Our purpose was to generate school curriculum recommendations that were multinational in origin, perspective, and aim and that were responsive to a crisis-laden, interconnected world. Such recommendations, we reasoned, would have to be developed by a multinational research team, the members of which would decide together which data to gather and what sense to make of it. Such a research team was drawn from nine nations in four geopolitical regions: East Asia (Japan), Southeast Asia (Thailand), Europe (United Kingdom, The Netherlands, Hungary, Germany, Greece), and North America (Canada, The United States).[5] Over a four-year period, this team, numbering twenty-six, collaboratively planned the study, gathered and analyzed data, deliberated the findings, and transformed them into a set of curriculum recommendations. To facilitate regional planning meetings between meetings of the entire research team, the researchers were divided among four smaller groups corresponding to the geopolitical regions; hence, there was a Japanese team (five members), a Thai team (six members), a European team (five members, each from a different nation), and a North American team (three Canadians, seven from the United States) adding up to twenty-six.

Data

First, we needed to apprehend this "crisis-laden, interconnected world." Accordingly, we identified a multinational panel of informants composed of 182 scholars, practitioners, and policy leaders selected from the fields of science and technology; health and education; politics and government; business, industry, and labor; and the arts in each of the nine nations above. Each of the four research sub-teams met to identify a pool of potential panelists. Many more were identified than could be included and so decisions were made for each category by the regional sub-teams. Four decision criteria were developed to guide this decision making, and each panelist had to meet each criterion. The criteria, as they eventually settled out from negotiations among research team members, were (as translated into English):

- *future orientation* as demonstrated by the ability to envision changes and opportunities in the future;
- *leadership* in one's field as demonstrated in speeches, writings, or their esteem among peers;
- *interest in civic affairs* as demonstrated in speeches, writings, policies implemented, or participation in civic groups;
- *knowledge of global trends and issues* as demonstrated in speeches, writings, and policies.

Additionally, the research team agreed that the selection of panelists by each sub-team would reflect as much as possible balance in gender, ethnicity, and between scholars and practitioners in the several categories.

Cross-cultural methods of data gathering and analysis were required. The research team selected a cross-cultural adaptation of the Ethnographic Delphi Futures Research model (Linstone & Turoff, 1975; Poolpatarachewin, 1980), which has been widely used to forecast future circumstances for the purpose of informing policy making in government, civil society, and industry. The adaptation, called Cultural Futures Delphi, begins with interviews of a subset of the panel and proceeds to iterative surveys of the entire panel. Our interview subset was large: 110 members of the 182-member panel participated in the interview round. These interviews were conducted for the purpose of developing a survey instrument, which was administered subsequently to the entire panel. We were seeking the panelists' agreement on global *trends* over the next twenty-five years, the desirable citizen *characteristics* they believed were needed for dealing with these changes, and the *strategies* likely to develop such citizens. Hence, the interview schedule had three main questions:

1. What are the major global trends likely to have a significant impact upon the lives of people during the next 25 years?
2. What will be the characteristics required of individuals in order to cope with and manage these trends?
3. How might these characteristics be developed? What approaches, strategies or innovations might best implement these characteristics?

Next, using the data gathered in the interviews, a survey was developed. This work was done by the entire research team meeting face-to-face in Minneapolis. The survey contained 106 items including sixty trend statements, twenty characteristics, and twenty-six strategies for achieving those characteristics. The entire panel (not only the subset that was interviewed) was asked to complete the survey. They were instructed to rate each of the *trends* on two six-point scales—one indicating the desirability of that trend, the other indicating the probability of it actually occurring during the next twenty-five years. They were instructed to rate each of the *strategies* on another six-point scale, this one indicating how strongly they would recommend that strategy (see Figures 1 and 2). With the twenty *characteristics*, they were asked to select five they judged to be most important. The instrument was translated into the relevant languages, then back-translated to assure validity.

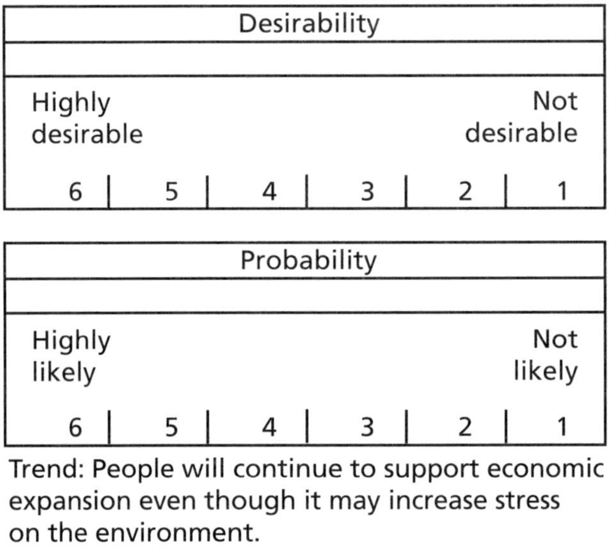

Desirability					
Highly desirable					Not desirable
6	5	4	3	2	1

Probability					
Highly likely					Not likely
6	5	4	3	2	1

Trend: People will continue to support economic expansion even though it may increase stress on the environment.

Figure 1. Rating a trend.

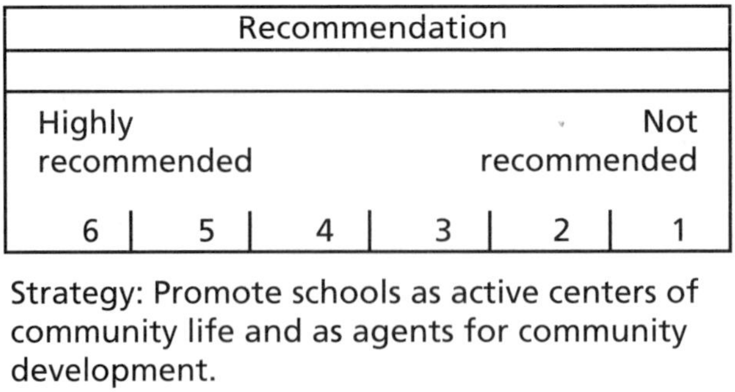

Recommendation					
Highly recommended					Not recommended
6	5	4	3	2	1

Strategy: Promote schools as active centers of community life and as agents for community development.

Figure 2. Recommending a strategy.

Educating "World Citizens" 157

After this survey was returned by the panelists, a second survey was created. It contained the same items as on the first survey, *except that it contained feedback*: Now panelists could see how one another had responded on the first survey. Alongside each trend and strategy statement was given the interquartile range and median value of the ratings on the first survey. Also given was with the individual panelist's own response (as a reminder). On the citizen characteristics statements, the feedback given was the percentage of panelists that had selected each characteristic for their priority list of five. In this way, a panelist was given aggregate international data in the light of which his or her own response could be reconsidered and changed if desired. Panelists thus were afforded an exchange of views—albeit a virtual exchange—which let them learn of one another's judgments, rethink their own response, and record any change of mind. This is the advantage of the Delphi survey method, all the more so given the multinational composition of the panel.

Analysis and Interpretation

Following the administration of the second survey, the research team analyzed the results first for the purpose of finding areas of consensus among the panelists, then for the purpose of formulating curriculum recommendations. Accordingly, the consensus trends, characteristics, and strategies were the first set of findings, and they are presented next. There was a second, interpretive set of findings as well, which is presented subsequently. These are the curriculum recommendations developed by the research team *using as a shared text the earlier analytic findings*. The interpretive method used to develop these recommendations was deliberation: face-to-face discussion for the purpose of decision making (Reid, 1981; Schwab, 1970). Team members together deliberated the trends, characteristics, and strategies and developed from them a set of education policy recommendations directed at educators in the nine nations. These recommendations fall into four categories: school-community interaction, classroom practice, teacher education, and curriculum. This report deals with the last of these: curriculum.[6] We present first the analytic findings.

ANALYTIC FINDINGS: CONSENSUS TRENDS, CHARACTERISTICS, AND STRATEGIES

We begin with the consensus findings of the Cultural Futures Delphi. The decision-rules for determining consensus were as follows: A *trend* or *strategy* was said to have achieved consensus if the mode minus the median on the six-point scale for that item was less than or equal to 1.0 and if the interquartile range was less than or equal to 1.5. A *characteristic* was said to have achieved consensus if the characteristic was selected by 25% or more of the panelists for inclusion in their list of the top five (of twenty) characteristics.[7]

Trends

The 182 members of the international panel reached consensus on 19 of 60 trends. These fell into three categories, which the research team named Increasingly Significant Challenges, Areas to Monitor, and Areas to Encourage (see Table 1). Each category represents a particular blend of desirability and probability and, thus, demands a particular level of consideration by citizens and policy makers so that policies are developed that might encourage desirable trends and discourage or manage undesirable trends.

Table 1. Trends

I. INCREASINGLY SIGNIFICANT CHALLENGES (Crises)

- The economic gap among countries and between people within countries will widen significantly.
- Information technologies will dramatically reduce the privacy of individuals.
- The inequalities between those who have access to information technologies and those who do not will increase dramatically.
- Conflict of interest between developing and developed nations will increase due to environmental deterioration.
- The cost of obtaining adequate water will rise dramatically due to population growth and environmental deterioration.
- Deforestation will dramatically affect diversity of life, air, soil, and water quality.
- In developing countries population growth will result in a dramatic increase in the percentage of people, especially children, living in poverty.

II. AREAS TO MONITOR

Undesirable but only moderately probable:

- Individuals, families, and communities will lose political influence due to the increased level of regulation and control by governments.
- It will be increasingly difficult to develop a shared belief of the common good.
- Drug-related crime will increasingly dominate social life in urban areas.
- People's sense of community and social responsibility will decline significantly.
- Consumerism will increasingly dominate social life.

Table 1. Trends (Cont.)

Very probable but only moderately desirable:

- Migration that flows from poor to rich areas, both within countries and between countries, will have a major impact on the internal and external order of nations.
- The increased use of genetic engineering will create more complex ethical questions.

III. AREAS TO ENCOURAGE

Highly desirable and highly probable:

- Economic growth will be fueled by knowledge (ideas, innovations, and inventions) more than by natural resources.

Very Highly desirable but only moderately probable:

- Corporations will increasingly adopt measures of environmental conservation in order to remain competitive.
- Systematic inequalities (e.g., racism, ethnocentrism, sexism) will decrease significantly.

Highly desirable and moderately probable:

- Previously marginalized groups of individuals (e.g., women, ethnic minorities) will occupy more positions of power.
- More regional alliances will be developed as a way of achieving peace and security.

The category Increasingly Significant Challenges contains seven trends that are undesirable but highly probable (i.e., crises). The dominant theme is increasing inequality coupled with increasing resource scarcity. The second category, Areas to Monitor, contains seven middle-ground trends identified by the panel as either undesirable but only moderately probable, or very probable but only moderately desirable. Not quite "crises," they deserve attention. An ominous theme in this group of trends is a general increase in undesirable life conditions, such as drug-related urban crime, combined with a decrease in citizens' ability to do anything about it. The third category, Areas to Encourage, contains five trends identified by panelists as highly or very highly desirable and highly to moderately probable. These trends provide some grounds for optimism; that is, they are good and they are likely.

Citizen Characteristics

The panel reached consensus on 8 of 20 competencies that citizens will need for dealing with the undesirable trends and encouraging the desirable ones. The eight are presented in descending order of importance as judged by the panelists. Note, in light of the trends above, that the most important characteristic of the eight is the ability to deal with serious worldwide problems as a member of a worldwide society. Easy to overlook or to dismiss as utopian, perhaps because of the national framework that is entrenched in thought and custom, this characteristic undergirds each of the others, and it powered the research team's curriculum recommendations (presented next).

- Ability to look at and approach problems as a member of a global society.
- Ability to work with others in a cooperative way and to take responsibility for one's roles/duties within society.
- Ability to understand, accept, appreciate and tolerate cultural differences.
- Capacity to think in a critical and systemic way.
- Willingness to resolve conflict in a nonviolent manner.
- Willingness and ability to participate in politics at local, national, and international levels.
- Willingness to change one's lifestyle and consumption habits to protect the environment.
- Ability to be sensitive toward and to defend human rights (e.g., rights of women, ethnic minorities).

Educational Strategies

The panel reached consensus on 16 of 26 strategies that are very highly or highly recommended for consideration and action by policy makers. Critical thinking is the most highly recommended strategy. Critical thinking[8] has been a favorite cause among educators for decades, of course, but here we have an international panel of scholars and practitioners, a minority of whom were educators, giving its strongest *joint* recommendation to it. The curriculum recommendations that are presented next will express this strategy recommendation directly: it is a question-driven (not answer-driven) curriculum with deliberation (not transmission) the pedagogy of choice. Note also in these consensus strategies the emphasis on multinational contacts and cooperation. *Critical thinking with different others on the crises named in the trends section* is how the research team summed up the consensus strategies.

Very highly recommended:

- Support the teaching of subject matter in a manner that encourages children to think critically.

- Emphasize students' ability to critically assess information in an increasingly media-based society.

Highly recommended:

- Establish a curriculum which uses the potential of information-based technologies.
- Establish extensive international links among educational institutions at all levels to support international studies, research, and curriculum development focusing on citizenship education.
- Cultivate a teaching population with international experience and cross-cultural sensitivity.
- Implement programs of international student exchange in order to promote mutual understandings among different cultures.
- Increase attention in the curriculum to global issues and international studies.
- Establish extensive liaisons and joint projects among schools and other social institutions (e.g., industry, NGOs, churches, community groups) to support education.
- Require that opportunities for community action and involvement be an important feature of the school curriculum.
- Promote schools as active centers of community life and as agents for community development.
- Decentralize decision making so that local communities and individual schools have considerable control of curriculum and educational administration.
- Increase opportunities for students to be involved in cooperative learning activities.
- Demand that the mass media act in a socially responsible, educative manner.
- Implement programs that effectively use the talents and skills of an aging population.
- Demand that all major social institutions and their officials set high standards of civic responsibility.
- Ensure that all social institutions have an abiding respect for the basic rights of children and contribute to their well-being.

INTERPRETIVE FINDINGS: CURRICULUM RECOMMENDATIONS

Now to the interpretive findings. Arriving at these was neither a matter of description nor analysis-by-decision-rules but, as Harry Wolcott (1994) describes the interpretive mode, an attempt to stretch beyond rule-bound analyses for broader and less constrained discussions about what is to be made of the data and the analysis for the purpose at hand.[9] Our purpose, recall, was to decide on a set of multinational curriculum recommendations that were derived from the panel's judgments on world trends, needed human characteristics, and strategies for developing them. Accordingly, research team members together examined the consensus findings, now using them as the shared text for a series of interpretive discussions with the aim to decide on curriculum recommendations. Discussion with an eye toward curriculum decision making is otherwise known as curriculum deliberation.[10] This was done across four days at a research team meeting in Hiroshima, Japan. Hiroshima is not just any modern city, of course; thus, it provided a historically unique and compelling locale for the interpretive work.

The set of recommendations that resulted is, in brief, a multinational, deliberation-based school curriculum focused on complex worldwide ethical problems. It is to be undertaken by students in each of the nine nations, and its goal is the development of multidimensional citizens. In this section we elaborate this recommendation. We begin by defining the terms *multidimensional, multinational,* and *deliberation,* then we describe the four components of the curriculum: (a) ethical questions for deliberation and (b) related concepts, (c) skills, and (d) attitudes.

Multidimensional Citizenship

Multidimensional citizens are men and women who possess the consensus characteristics described earlier and are thereby enabled (at least more than without them) to anticipate and grapple with the trends that make these characteristics necessary in the first place. We are well aware that these same men and women have numerous other characteristics as well, both cultural and individual. The citizen identity is surely not the only identity modern people have; they also have ethnic and gender identities, vocational and social class identities, religious and racial, regional and local; they have identities as individuals, memberships in faith communities and other associations, and avocations of all sorts. To the extent they have a citizen identity, they "have" it in widely varying degrees of elaboration and self-consciousness, and they value it, or do not, in many ways. One person may surmise legalistically, "I am a citizen of Canada; my grandparents are citizens of Japan." Another may think, "My citizenship is Canadian, and that refers to the laws and protections and obligations I have, but my culture is Japanese-Canadian, my faith is Catholic, my race is Asian, and I am first and foremost a mother."

By multidimensional citizenship, we mean to capture the personal, social, spatial, and temporal aspects of the citizen identity that are necessary for meeting the challenges of the early 21st century. The *personal* dimension involves mainly the personal commitment to nurture a citizen identity among one's other identities and with it a civic ethic characterized by socially responsible habits of mind, heart, and action. The *social* dimension involves the ability and willingness to work with other citizens in a variety of public settings, creating common ground, respectfully deliberating public problems with one another, especially those who are different culturally or politically from oneself. The *spatial* dimension refers to the modern requirement that citizens see themselves as members of multiple overlapping communities: local, regional, national, and global. The challenges of the 21st century transcend national boundaries—we could call them supranational or transnational challenges. Persons and groups who are going to face those challenges together, forging action in concert, must be able to think and act flexibly within multiple community affiliations. The *temporal* dimension means that citizens need to mount simultaneously a past-present-and-future outlook. Citizens cannot be so preoccupied with the present that they lose sight of the past and the future, nor can they be so preoccupied with the past that they undermine inventive thought in the present. Heritage and tradition matter tremendously in personal development, politics, and social relations, yet so does imaginative, future-oriented problem solving about the increasingly significant challenges of this new century. Citizens must be well informed by history, yet they cannot be trapped by the past in a way that prevents them from creating a good future.

This is a tall order. The personal, social, and temporal dimensions of contemporary citizenship are difficult enough, let alone the spatial. The intention to get along with others significantly different from oneself and the willingness to reason historically are long-standing human goals which appear to have barely taken hold in any society. Wishful thinkers are reminded by those who have seen history, whether in Hiroshima, Auschwitz, Bosnia, Cambodia, or Rwanda, that "the world was and is a charnel house" (Rieff, 1997, p. 2). Yet, the spatial dimension asks educators to aim still higher, for here is the requirement for divided sovereignty and multiply situated selves. Two millennia ago, Cicero argued for a similar kind of world citizenship in his *Duties* and *Commonwealth*, saying that humans owed recognition and respect to one another regardless of their immediate interests and affiliations—their being Romans or Greeks, for example. This line of reasoning made him and the Stoics famous—they were the West's first multiculturalists—but let us remember that he was beheaded and a needle stuck through his tongue for saying such things. Michael Sandel clarifies for our own time what Cicero was driving at in his:

Since the days of Aristotle's polis, the republican tradition has viewed self-government as an activity rooted in a particular place, carried out by citizens loyal to that place and the way of life it embodies. Self-government today, however, requires a politics that plays itself out in a multiplicity of settings, from neighborhoods to nations to the world as a whole. Such a politics requires citizens who can abide the ambiguity associated with divided sovereignty, who can think and act as multiply situated selves. The civic virtue distinctive to our time is the capacity to negotiate our way among the sometimes overlapping and sometimes conflicting obligations that claim us, to live with the tension to which multiple loyalties give rise. (1996, p. 350)

Is the notion of "multiple loyalties" utopian? Are those who espouse it doomed to mockery and having needles stuck through their tongues by cultural nationalists and other patriots? The research team believes not, as there already are so many movements in this direction. Multiple loyalties are a well-established necessity in many, perhaps most, modern societies; kinship, ethnic, racial, occupational, gender, and class affiliations, to name a few, are experienced simultaneously. Furthermore, migrations within and between societies require the assumption and abandonment of political and national identities. Abdullahi Ahmed An-Na'im (1992) captures the pluralization of identity in his examination of human rights from a cross-cultural perspective. Culture itself is dynamic, recall, not the fixed and intensely homogeneous entity we are inclined to make it when we stereotype the members of a particular cultural group (Tibetans are . . . Ibo are . . . non-Westerners are . . . Women are . . . My people are . . .). "Internal cultural discourse," as An-Na'im calls it, is usually more common within a cultural boundary than outsiders are wont to notice; it is the chief means by which disadvantaged individuals and groups within a culture press the entrenched powers for negotiation of the societal norms to which members are held. This internal cultural discourse, along with cross-cultural dialogue (e.g., Catholics and Buddhists sitting together on a village council in Japan), indicates that multiple identities are increasingly a fact of modern life. This in turn provides a foundation for widening the identity array to include that of global citizen.[11]

Multinational

The curriculum we propose is multinational in two ways. First, its core subject matter is explicitly organized around pressing and complex problems that affect persons across national boundaries. The primary subject matter of the curriculum is a set of six ethical questions that the research team derived from the consensus trends, characteristics, and strategies. The ethical questions are:

1. What should be done in order to promote equity and fairness within and among societies?
2. What should be the balance between the right to privacy and free and open access to information in information-based societies?
3. What should be the balance between protecting the environment and meeting human needs?
4. What should be done to cope with population growth, genetic engineering, and children in poverty?
5. What should be done to develop shared (universal; global) values while respecting local values?
6. What should be done to secure an ethically based distribution of power for deciding policy and action on the above issues?

These questions are augmented by a set of related concepts, skills, and attitudes. Each is pertinent to considering the six ethical questions knowledgeably, critically, cooperatively—as members of a *global public.* (Recall the top-ranked characteristic above. We will have more to say about this concept shortly.)

Second, the curriculum is multinational by virtue of the fact that its implementation is intended to occur across national boundaries. The research team recommends that curriculum committees in the nine nations specify primary and secondary grade course experiences that have students join these questions, form these concepts, and develop these skills and attitudes over a number of years. It recommends, further, that specific courses be designed as capstone experiences in which students address this subject matter squarely as the core focus of the course. A common syllabus dealing with these four components could unite sections of a high-school Contemporary World Problems course *in each nation.* This course could share a broad syllabus that is elaborated locally and shared by electronic or other means with course participants in other nations. Students' work on the questions could be shared and discussed multinationally.

Deliberation

The proposed curriculum is "deliberation-based." This means that the core practice in the curriculum is discussion of the ethical questions themselves with the intention of recommending suitable public action. The English word deliberation derives from the Latin "libra" for "scale." Deliberation means "to weigh," as in weighing which actions will best address a problem. Here, deliberation means making choices about what to do about problems a group is facing in common. Neither negotiation nor debate, deliberation is making decisions together about the kind of world a "we" wants to forge.

The research team understands that goals are transformed right within the process of public discourse. For this reason, deliberation is not only an instructional means but a curriculum outcome itself, for it creates a particular kind of democratic public culture among the deliberators: listening as well as talking, sharing resources, forging decisions together rather than only advocating positions taken earlier, coming to disagreement. Because the issues being deliberated in the curriculum are multinational issues, and because students are conjoining in some way (e.g., face-to-face; electronic) on these common problems, this curriculum has the potential to contribute to the development what Boulding (1988) called a "global civic culture" or what today might be called a transnational civil society.[12] That is, by moving purposefully toward a multinational perspective on "citizenship" and citizenship education, this project loosens somewhat the conventional meaning of *citizen* as one who has membership in a political entity, such as a nation or province, and raises the concept *world citizen*. There is no world political entity (a world state) in which an individual might have membership, of course, and the participants in this study—the panelists and the researchers alike—were not interested in advocating such an entity; rather, *world citizen* comes to mean, as in the spatial dimension of citizenship discussed earlier, one for whom the commonwealth is not only a local or national political community, but alongside these a transnational civic culture concerned with global problems and global problem solving.

Ethical Questions

We are not recommending an "international relations" curriculum. Our goal is different: a multinational problems curriculum featuring six ethical questions as the core subject matter. Each question is built around ideas and tensions that were judged to be central to understanding and acting on the trends identified by the panel: equity and fairness, privacy and access to information, environmental stewardship and human prosperity, population growth and child care, universalism and particularism, and power relations.

But why *ethical* questions? The research team was struck by the ethical mandates embedded in the consensus characteristics and strategies. The Thai and Japanese members of the research team repeatedly returned the team's attention to one of the consensus educational strategies: "Ensure that all social institutions (including the family, and educational religious institutions) have an abiding respect for the basic rights of children and contribute to their well-being." Keeping children uppermost in mind—not just "our" children but all children—keeps the global responsibilities of citizenship in the foreground, and focusing on children's well-being requires the continual enactment of an ethical imagination—seeing what can be done that is not now being done, anticipating conflict and preventing it, planning ahead for coming crises (e.g., water shortage), and, most of all, paying close and continual attention to the lives of children. We look more closely now at why the team decided on questions and why deliberation was selected as the pedagogic vehicle for the curriculum.

First, why *questions*? There were two reasons. A consensus item on the *strategies* list, "Support the teaching of subject matter in a manner that encourages children to think critically," suggests that students should be helped to join questions rather than merely learn answers. More basic than this pedagogical reason, however, is a substantive one: the team did not believe that "answers" were available. The consensus trends identified by the multinational panel pose extraordinarily complex social, cultural, and environmental problems. These are messy, real problems of the sort that, in John Dewey's words, are "set by actual social situations which are themselves conflicting and confused" (1939, p. 498). "Actual" problems, particularly world civic problems, are inherently woolly and controversial. They do not fit easily into disciplinary frameworks taken from the inventories of knowledge amassed in each academic field. Such frameworks are important to problem-solving, to be sure, and are one of the four components of the recommended curriculum, but they are *resources* to the problem-solving activity and no substitute for it. In fact, such frameworks are revised during the activity of problem solving.

Accordingly, the six questions confront students with what psychologists call "ill-structured" problem arenas.[13] Scholars and citizens are barely able to define let alone understand or solve them. Consider the trend, "Conflicts of interest between developing and developed nations will increase due to environmental deterioration." Much of the information that would be helpful in an attempt, first, to understand this problem and then to reason toward a course of action is absent from the presentation of the problem, and competing perspectives and value orientations can and will be brought to bear on it. Numerous solutions are possible, assuming one ever grasps the problem itself, and citizens are bound to disagree on the best course of action. In brief, these are both serious and difficult problems. Our recommendation is that students in diverse nations be taught to tackle them together, striving to forge policy recommendations together *and* to communicate with one another and officials their understanding of the problems.

Moreover, why *deliberation*? When a group deliberates, it is trying to decide on "the best" course of action from among the alternatives. Deliberation ends, therefore, not in action itself but in a decision to take a particular course of action. Forging that decision together, reasoning together, generating and weighing alternatives, is the main activity of deliberation. It is, practically speaking, discussion with an eye toward decision making. It is thus a prudential, moral, and circumstantial activity. Before it begins, the parties to it have experienced a problematic situation together which motivates the deliberation in the first place. Of course, in heterogeneous societies, deliberation is done with persons who are more or less different from one another (in political views, religion, language, gender, race, ethnicity, social status, income and power); we recommend for pedagogical purposes, therefore, that the deliberative groups—schools and classrooms—be as diverse as possible in these ways. What the participants have in common are the problems they experience together and must work out together. It is a problematic situation that has brought them together in the first place; this is the common ground that makes of them a single public, a "we the people," at least for the time being.

In addition to the problems themselves, what brings the participants together is dialogue itself:

> Dialogue is not a matter of two isolated persons who simply decide to start talking with one another . . . Once constituted as a relation, the dialogical encounter engages the participants in a process at once symbiotic and synergistic; beyond a particular point, no one may be consciously guiding or directing it, and the order and flow of the communicative exchange itself take over. The participants are *caught up*, they are *absorbed*. (Burbules, 1993, p. 21)

There are ways other than deliberation for publics to decide the question "What should we do?" *Voting* is one way. In a plurality, the alternative that receives the most votes wins; in a majority system, a decision is not reached until one of the options wins at least 51% of the votes. Either way, the give-and-take of discussion is not required. In the electronic at-home systems being considered in numerous nations, the decision could be made by individuals having utterly no interaction with one another. *Debate* is another way for groups to make a decision without discussion. The proposals being debated were not themselves forged by the group that is debating them, but by subsets of the group (e.g., debate "teams") or by parties outside the group. Either way, it is an adversarial process; one proposal wins and another loses. *Negotiation* is a third way. Here discussion is involved, certainly, but the group is assuming competing interests and the discussion is guided by calculating constantly the gains and losses of each interest. As in debate, there is not actually one group, but at least two groups present in the same forum engaged in a contest. Deliberation, by contrast, involves everyone in the group forging together the alternatives and making a decision.[14]

Of course, "everyone in the group forging together the alternatives" is hugely problematic in actually existing societies where power and status control participation in deliberation as well as the topics considered appropriate for deliberation. The poor, women, and subordinate ethnic, religious, and racial minorities are the first to suffer de facto exclusion from ostensibly "open forums" in most societies. And, by virtue of this exclusion, the issues they would raise for discussion are never placed on the table. Measures to increase equity of access must be in place, therefore, before any pretense to deliberation can be taken seriously. Numerous political theorists have made helpful suggestions, including the idea that *multiple* deliberative forums are desirable because they allow a range of access points and deliberative styles (Benhabib, 1996; Fraser, 1995; Mansbridge, 1991). A church basement, a parliament, a union hall, a rural health center, a farmers' cooperative, and a classroom, for example, each affords a particular context for public talk. None of them assures that all voices and topics are welcome; certainly, for *within* them status and power are at work (e.g., within a women's study group in the Netherlands, race still matters; within an African-American church in urban America, gender still counts; within a farmer's cooperative in the hill country of Thailand, ethnic tensions can shape most interactions). Expanding the array of forums, however, seems likely to foster the diversity of persons speaking and listening, the communicative practices that are admitted (e.g., storytelling in addition to critical argument[15]) and, in general, the depth and breadth of public space formation and public problem solving. Let us summarize now the several reasons why deliberation was selected.

First, deliberation is a democratic way for a diverse group to grapple with shared problems and to try to reach a shared decision about what to do. It is thus an authentic democratic activity and arguably the single most important activity in which democratic citizens must engage. Second, deliberation is a form of pedagogy that is bound up with the problems being deliberated. In fact, it is absolutely meaningless when separated from problems worth deliberating; therefore, it cannot be linked—not logically at least—to the process-without-content pedagogies roundly criticized by cognitive psychologists, educational researchers, and parent groups worried about lowered expectations for their children in the name of "progressive education." Third, disciplined deliberation by students on pressing multinational problems should produce two socially valued results. On the one hand, students are learning by experience the democratic problem-solving ability at which they are expected to be skilled as adult citizens of their various communities. This is an important curriculum outcome. On the other hand, they are helping actually to sort out and solve, or at least think about, the pressing global problems they are asked to deliberate. This is an important local and world community service. Fourth, deliberation on common problems is a public-building activity. "Publics" are groups that come together to decide what to do about common problems (e.g., Dewey, 1927; Mathews, 1994; Parker, 1996). Within a nation's public schools, deliberation helps bring students together in relations as public citizens for public purposes, tackling public problems. When students within classrooms in several nations are deliberating roughly the same set of cross-culturally felt problems, then a larger multinational relation—a global civil society—emerges. This strikes us as the major contribution of our curriculum recommendations.

Ancillary Components

Deliberation on shared ethical problems is the primary component of the curriculum, and there are three ancillary components: concepts, skill, and attitudes. We regard each of these as instrumental to the achievement of right deliberation on the ethical questions and, in turn, right action. Together these enable students to bring knowledge, know-how, and favorable dispositions to the ethical questions. (Deliberation should not be confused with blather.)

The first are generative ideas or *concepts*. Instruction on well-chosen concepts related to the six ethical questions is recommended for two reasons: so that deliberation is enriched by knowledge and so that the knowledge fund in turn can be revised and refined by the deliberation. Conceptual clarity is sorely needed for transnational deliberation, and its pursuit is a major purpose of that deliberation. T.K. Oommen (1997, pp. 3–4) notes that even a quick perusal of social science writing "unfolds a widespread prevailing ambiguity. For example, *nationalism* is qualified by the following terms: autonomist, anti-colonial, bureaucratic, black, bourgeois, civic, colonial . . . , linguistic, liberal, mass, Marxist . . . , separatist, sub-, supra-, sacred, socialist, secessionis. . . . " The same goes for *citizenship*:

> (T)oday we have advocates of active, democratic, cultural, communitarian, earth, European, ecological, environmental, gender-neutral, global, individualistic, liberal, participatory, race-neutral, republican, neo-republican, and world citizenship, to list a few. (Oommen, p. 224)

Concepts for study should be decided locally and shared eventually with course participants in other nations. Examples drawn directly from the six ethical questions might be *equity, fairness, privacy, access to information, population growth, genetic engineering, children in poverty, distribution of power and wealth,* as well as tensions such as that between protecting the environment and meeting human needs, between privacy and access to information, and between universal and local values. There are also concepts that undergird these but are not specifically stated in the questions themselves; for example, *citizen, citizenship, nationality, ethnicity, human rights, democracy, social class, status, culture, pluralism, political economy, ecosystem,* and *sustainable future.*

We recommend, further, that only a small group of concepts be targeted for intensive study so that meaningful learning might occur (e.g., in-depth, sustained study on a limited number of topics) and so that faculty can focus limited resources on key instructional objectives. Over and above these instructional reasons, to push for a limited set of key concepts is to encourage consideration of the all-important curricular question, Which concepts are of most worth? Curriculum decision making among students, faculty, and community members on this question is precisely the dialogue we hope to achieve. Such deliberation could well lead to a revision of the set of ethical questions. The revisions and the rationale for them can be shared with course participants in other nations, thus contributing substantively to the overall multinational public-building project.

In addition to instruction on key ideas, the research team recommends instruction on *skills*. Specifically, the team recommends instruction on skills related to *researching* and *deliberating* the six issues. By research, the team means scientific inquiry or critical thinking: that cluster of activities centering on finding and framing worthy problems, making and testing hypotheses, evaluating the quality of evidence, judging the strength of arguments, and exposing one's conclusions to the criticism of peers. By deliberation, as defined above, we mean cooperative discussion with an eye toward decision. Related skills include data-gathering and -analysis procedures, participating in and moderating discussions of controversial issues, seeking opposing points of view, expressing positions and the reasoning that supports them, searching for missing voices and perspectives, weighing alternatives, and predicting consequences of alternatives.

Particular *attitudes* should be singled out for cultivation as well. Key are those that support inquiry and deliberation on ill-structured ethical questions and development of a global perspective. Not merely tolerating diversity, but respecting it, is one attitude. Respecting evidence over prejudice and disciplining oneself to form tentative conclusions are others. The willingness actually to listen to opposing points of view and to be skeptical of one's own position are two more.

DISCUSSION

Historical study has enjoyed considerable attention in the United States. Still, most American historians are Americanists doing research and teaching on matters relating principally or exclusively to the United States (Graubard, 1997). Scholarly parochialism may or may not be exceptional among modern nations (it probably is not—think of Japan or England), but clearly it has had its costs. Leaving aside United States foreign policy, one glaring cost is the American school curriculum's limited attention to world studies. Two courses are the mainstays in the United States: world geography in the junior high school and world history in the senior high school (Woyach & Remy, 1989). Most school districts in the United States require the world geography course; less than half requires the world history course. By contrast, to give just one example, world history (and a second language, too) is required in Japan *even in the vocational track.*

But this is a curriculum matter, and popular fashion in educational research today does not permit much attention to the school curriculum. The field of educational psychology is preeminent still, and it is interested mainly in questions of knowing and learning. Driven by its cognitive revolution and, recently, the constructivism craze, this field skirts the myriad questions of curriculum planning, particularly the mundane on-the-ground questions of scope and sequence: *Which* subject matter should be learned, when, in relation to what other subject matter, by whom, with whom, in what sorts of activity settings, and why? A required world geography course in the seventh grade and an elective world history course in the 10th grade have been better than nothing, certainly, but presently they function as place holders for curriculum deliberation about the proper education of citizens for anticipated world situations. Are they saber-toothed curricula? Only curriculum deliberation will tell; that is, a diverse group of teachers—and scholars, parents, students, and other stakeholders—needs to engage in shared inquiry and decision making about what in the world is worth knowing and learning and, therefore, teaching. This activity mirrors the broader scholarly challenge today: "to know which areas of the world merit particular study and whether the national frameworks, so useful in the past, still retain some validity" (Graubard, p. xix).

We doubt whether the national framework "so useful in the past" retains its validity as the driving paradigm for curriculum development in the schools today. The study reported here was a foray into an alternative paradigm: multinational curriculum development. By interviewing and surveying a multinational panel drawn from an array of fields, then identifying consensus concerns among the panelists, the research team was able to construct an empirical platform for multinational curriculum deliberation. Certainly this is not the only valid platform, but it served a key purpose in relation to the alternative, multinational paradigm we are exploring: The consensus findings became a shared text—a *multinational* shared text—which was the focal point of the multinational research team's curriculum deliberation. This text grounded our deliberation, linking our curriculum decision making to a common set of data that propelled us outside our own heads and locales into one another's heads and locales—not fully, of course, but at least to some meaningful extent. The research team at this point took the role of a curriculum development committee—a multinational one—that was intent on deliberating rather than negotiating. The research team then decided on deliberation as the driving pedagogy for a world problems curriculum. By this route, not only would key world problems be studied but, through deliberation, a new kind of public—a global public—and with it an expanded civic identity might be encouraged. The pivotal assumption here is that students' study of world subject matter must go hand in hand with a mode of study that is geared to building multinational publics.

Deliberation, then, played multiple roles in the study. The nine-nation research team agreed *through* deliberation *on* deliberation as the pedagogy of choice for addressing the set of ethical questions. That is, deliberation was the interpretive method used by the research team to transform the findings from the multinational panel into a set of policy recommendations, and it was the teaching-learning method recommended for the six ethical questions that are the core of the recommended curriculum. Deliberation also will be relevant in subsequent research, for it may well be the method used locally as school policy makers set about examining these recommendations and deciding how and whether to implement any portion of them. Follow-up studies on this next phase of deliberation should contribute a needed multinational perspective to the literature concerned with local curriculum development (e.g., Ben-Peretz, 1990; Schwab, 1970).

Limitations

Clearly, this study is only a beginning, and a limited one at that. It counts *at least* as a beginning because it is, most important, a multinational attempt to develop a multinational curriculum geared to multinational problems. Such an effort counters a pervasive, taken-for-granted norm, which is to undertake such work only provincially (i.e., nationally or intranationally). Still, the study is *only* a beginning on a number of counts.

It should be clear by now that the consensus findings and curriculum recommendations are multinational in origin and intent; however, they do not speak for or to all persons in all nations. "Multi" means in this study *not world wide* by any stretch of the imagination but *beyond the provincial*, involving cross-national discussions of cross-national problems. We do not pretend to have a world wide panel or research team. Quite the contrary we have only a small multinational panel and research team, and both were drawn from only nine nations. These nine do not represent the people and nations of Earth; they are skewed to the "first world"—to the industrialized, democratized, and secularized world—and, generally speaking, to the colonizers, not the colonized.[16] We are in no position to generalize either the analytic or interpretive findings to other societies, therefore; doing so was never our intent and would constitute a serious misreading of the results. We feel confident that the involvement of panelists from Latin America, the Middle East, South Asia, and Africa would challenge the present findings—both the consensus findings and the curriculum recommendations—in interesting and no doubt surprising ways. Wealth distribution *within* societies, for example, which is only implied somewhat in the first and sixth ethical questions, may emerge fully and sharply as a matter for deliberation (or it may not); the themes of decolonization and resistance—long prevalent in the literature (e.g., Fanon, 1963; Ngugi wa Thiong'o, 1986)—may be emphasized (or not).

In other words, the multinational curriculum we recommend here cannot be confused with the curriculum recommendations that would emerge from other groups of deliberators, whether poor people in these same societies or panelists and researchers from other world regions. The findings of the present study, then, are open to comparison with other data sets, particularly from contrasting data sets, and we welcome them. Using grounded theory research procedures, the findings presented here—both analytic and interpretive—can be treated as hypotheses to be tested with data gathered from additional samples that are selected because they are thought likely to challenge the present conclusions.[17] Better, other approaches can be taken up that intentionally privilege views and viewpoints that counter the findings and interpretations of the present study (see Eisner & Peshkin, 1990; Kincheloe, 1991). The advantage of subsequent investigations of this sort is straightforward: an enlarged understanding of multinational problems, as identified and described from diverse subject positions, and another multinational curriculum recommendation that could be developed to address those problems.

Let us move to a limitation of a different sort. This study was constrained by the spotty conceptual frameworks within which our effort had to take place. Forecasting the future, then employing that forecast in deciding which action to take in the present, is a notoriously unreliable enterprise. This doesn't mean that it cannot be attempted; it is commonplace in ordinary life, happening daily around the world in pubs, markets, board rooms, faculty clubs, and legislatures. But to do it well, to attempt in a disciplined and reflective way to utilize forecasts in curriculum decision making, is bounded on one side by the complexity of the task, on another by the unpredictability of social and natural events, and on another by the necessarily partial and biased knowledge of the forecasters and the curriculum developers.

More generally, there was the weak theoretical base in precisely those literatures on which this kind of work should rely: citizenship, citizenship education, globalization, and global education. Let us exemplify the weak theoretical base by considering two of these: globalization and global education. Following Anthony Giddens (1990), let us agree that globalization concerns the intensification of something that has been happening for some time already; specifically, "the intensification of worldwide social relations which link distant localities in such a way that local happenings are shaped by events occurring many miles away and vice versa" (p. 64). Indeed, the world appears to be "in the midst of a deep sea change in the ways people experience, understand, negotiate, and represent global relationships" (Buell, 1994, p. 6). *Everyone* seems cognizant of this shift. Concern with "the world" and its anticipated transformation has become "a central hermeneutic" (Robertson, 1990, p. 19); that is, across the fields of politics, health, business, art, anthropology, education, and so on, it is increasingly the norm to try to make sense of social phenomena with reference to "globalization." However, the sheer trendiness of the idea and the highly exercised way in which it often is invoked act as serious threats to thinking about it. To wit: Ideas such as "the global economy," "the third world," and "developing nations" are wielded confidently as though they were referential terms pointing to something positively "out there" when they are instead rough working tools that serve mainly the arguments and purposes of their wielders. For example, it is not uncommon in some quarters to believe that nations of the "third world" are defective versions of the genuine article. "Things are filthy there and nothing works," goes this complaint. Not surprisingly, this view is held by many people in the "first" world. On the other side of the same coin (the side popular among multiculturalists, anthropologists, and some members of third world societies) one often finds the veneration of "the third world" as sacred ground—as an untainted realm of cultural integrity and human authenticity.[18]

A second example of inadequate theorizing on globalization is the paucity of work on the fate of the nation-state framework during this intensification of transnational relations. "It is striking," writes David Held, "that there has been no systematic and coherent attempt within contemporary political theory to theorize the changing form of the modern polity in its global setting" (1991, p. 9). Perhaps some sort of transnational legal system and transnational norms of justice are needed just now as transnational corporations and popular culture wield increasing power over daily life. But this has scarcely been examined. The national framework holds social theorists (including educators) rather firmly in its grasp.[19] This is ironic, given the hermeneutic centrality of "globalization," and the situation may be changing. "As is often the case in periods of momentous transformations such as the ones we have been living through since 1989, old and new definitions, presuppositions, currents of thought, assumptions, and values mix, mingle, and clash in inchoate ways," observes Seyla Benhabib (1996, p. 5). This stepped-up mixing, mingling, and clashing may press social theorists to extend their reach.

Moving now from "globalization" theory to "global education" theory, consider the manner in which multinational curriculum development efforts might proceed. As we have said, the practice of curriculum development typically is done nationally and intra-nationally. Even "global education" curricula, ironically, usually are developed nationally and intra-nationally. Our move in this study was to attempt this development activity in a multinational milieu. This was an important move, we believe, but still the findings and recommendations are not "global"—not "world-wide." They are (always and already) limited by the commitments, knowledge, and experiences of the participants—now a multinational group rather than a national group, but still only a partially multinational group that possesses the biases and interests one might expect. Is *im*partiality possible? Certainly not from mortals. Accordingly, the road ahead is very much a practical, on-the-ground one that includes varied efforts at multinational curriculum theorizing and development, always reflecting the authors' positions. These efforts might eventually be cobbled together into something more elegant than the sum of the parts, or they may remain an array of alternatives that local curriculum planners can consider. Either way, a multinational curriculum move has been made, which we believe is needed, yet it is made—returning now to the point of the limitation under discussion—on thin theoretical ice.

We turn now to limitations in our method. An adaptation of Ethnographic Delphi Futures Research (Linstone & Turoff, 1975; Poolpatarachewin, 1980) was employed. We caution readers on three points. First, the consensus trends, characteristics, and strategies that form the analytic platform for the research team's interpretive curriculum deliberation were the product of a set of quantitative decision-rules. For example, panelists were said to have achieved consensus on a trend if the mode minus the median on the six-point scale for that trend was less than or equal to 1.0 and if the interquartile range was less than or equal to 1.5. A somewhat different set of consensus findings could be produced, therefore, with a strategic turn of the quantitative dial. The term "consensus" functions rhetorically to belie this fact and suggest a more nuanced and dialogic agreement than was the case in these findings. Second, ours was a methodological search for consensus, not an informal one, and for this reason we were attracted to the Delphi procedure. This choice, however, turned our attention away from *dis*agreement, which can be just as informative a resource as agreement. As one reviewer of a prior version of this article gently asked, "Can 'consensus' be used to rationalize differing opinions based on empirical evidence?" Indeed it can and for this reason the contingent origin of a consensus finding in the Delphi procedure generally and our decision-rules particularly needs to be remembered when examining both the consensus findings themselves and the curriculum decisions that were derived from them. Third, research methods themselves are without exception social constructs. The Delphi method, like other methods, is contingent on historical forces and relations. Named after the ancient Greek town that housed a renowned oracle, this forecasting method was developed in the cold-war 1950s by the RAND Corporation, on contract with the U.S. Air Force, to ascertain U.S. military preparedness. The irony of meeting in Hiroshima to interpret the Delphi findings did not escape the members of the research team and, in fact, shaped our decision to meet there and, no doubt, the deliberations we conducted there.

Finally, there was the recognition that curriculum "updating" itself is loaded with pitfalls. The instrumentalist bias for "relevance" carries, we recognize, viral strains of presentism, vocationalism, and anti-intellectualism (DuBois, 1903) which contribute to the long-standing suspicion, at least in North America, of theorizing and reflection. A sober comprehension of this danger and an abiding respect for liberal studies—learning for its own sake—undergirded the research team's deliberations. Nonetheless, the presence of grave world problems requiring increased multinational attention, together with the widespread comprehension that yesterday's "answers" (e.g., the nation-state curriculum development framework) are not fruitfully focusing this attention, motivated the research team to conduct a study and recommend a curriculum that was capable of paying attention to these problems. To do less, to flee the practical realm of decision, action and consequence, would be irresponsible and, as several Thai and Japanese members of the research team emphasized repeatedly, irresponsible particularly to *children* who must inhabit a world fashioned by their elders.[20]

The project will have achieved its aim if it sparks discussions of the multinational consensus findings, the curriculum recommendations, and most of all, the desirability of the trajectory we support: multinational curriculum-development efforts geared to creating and educating a world public for world problem solving.

CONCLUSION

Consensus views on world trends, citizen characteristics, and education strategies were developed in interviews and surveys of a multinational panel composed of opinion makers, scholars, and practitioners in the arts, health, education, science, technology, politics, religion, business, industry, and labor. With these findings in hand, the research team, also multinational in composition, deliberated a set of school curriculum recommendations. The recommendations consist of a goal (multidimensional citizenship), subject matter (a set of ethical questions, plus related concepts, skills, and attitudes), and a global civic culture-building pedagogy (inquiry and deliberation). We can imagine a set of primary and secondary course experiences in which students across nations join a common set of complex ethical questions that address problems—some of them crises—which increasingly are confronting the world's people. Through inquiry, students will search for and interpret data that are pertinent to the questions. Through deliberation, they will clarify the problems, weigh solutions, and in so doing constitute a different kind of public—an international public—and an additional identity: "world citizen." This identity will not replace the others (that would be no gain) but run alongside them. A Contemporary World Problems course for high school seniors could serve as the capstone experience of this curriculum. Offered simultaneously in various nations, with communication among project sites, it could sponsor a kind of relating that may deserve, at least somewhat, the name *global civic culture*.

Motivating this project was a prior question. It rested on the knowledge that school curricula everywhere are sociopolitical artifacts and are virtually everywhere, therefore, developed nationally and intranationally—by national or local curriculum committees. Even the portion of the curriculum that involves world study (e.g., courses in World History; World Geography; Contemporary World Problems) is developed within nations. Has the time not come to create multinationally some portions of the school curriculum? Would it not be wise and prudent especially to develop multinationally a curriculum concerned to teach young people to grapple with multinational issues together and to seek one another's counsel? We believe that such inclinations (versus tiger scaring or fish-grabbing by hand) will mark the well-educated world citizen of tomorrow.

ACKNOWLEDGMENT

This chapter is a slightly revised version of an article of the same name that appeared in *American Educational Research Journal*, Summer 1999, Vol. 36, No. 2, pp. 117–145. Copyright 1999 by the American Educational Research Association. Adapted with permission of the publisher.

NOTES

1. This research was supported by the Sasakawa Peace Foundation, Tokyo. The authors are grateful to Somwung Pitiyanuwat (Chulalongkorn University, Thailand), Ken Osborne (University of Manitoba, Canada), and anonymous reviewers at *American Educational Research Journal* for helpful comments on earlier drafts of this chapter.
2. Our audience probably is mainly North American. We reference, therefore, mainly North American educational literature. This creates the problem of casting the project further in North American terms and viewpoints (further than is already the case with two of three authors being positioned in that milieu). For present purposes, we accept the trade-off.
3. These are problematic terms, which we discuss under "Limitations."
4. Some of these are quite helpful. See Lynch (1989) and reviews of Carson, Willinsky, Gutek, Wilson, Thelin and others in chapter 14 of *Understanding Curriculum* (Pinar, Reynolds, Slattery, & Taubman, 1995).
5. The nine member nations were selected because of already-existing relationships on other projects (comparative educational research; university student exchanges). They were selected purposively, then, to deepen existing multinational relationships while affording an array of societies from four world regions—Southeast Asia, East Asia, North America, and Europe. Funding from the supporting foundation (in Japan) was limited, which prohibited the involvement in this phase of researchers and panelists from additional world regions (the Middle East, South Asia, Latin America, Africa). Whether and in what direction involvement from other regions would change the analytic or interpretive findings of the present study—we assume it would—is both a theoretical and an empirical question. It can be investigated by deploying the present findings as hypotheses to be disconfirmed or refined per the grounded theory tradition (see Strauss & Corbin, 1990), or by setting aside the present findings altogether (de-privileging them) and beginning anew with a panel thought to hold sharply different views (see McCarthy, 1990). We welcome such studies.
6. For reports on the other categories see Cogan and Derricott (1998).
7. "Consensus findings" can be a misleading term as consenses were not so much "found" as constructed. In other words, they were artifacts of our decision rules. We discuss this further under "limitations."
8. On critical thinking: Through a psychological lens see Perkins (1981) and Chipman, Segal, amd Glaser (1985); through a philosophical lens, see Paul (1990) and Toulmin (1958).
9. In this sense, interpretation is even more transparently tied to researchers' interests and commitments than analysis.
10. See Reid (1981) and the collection by Dillon (1994).
11. On the necessity and associated problems of divided sovereignty and multiple identities, see Habermas, (1997), Young (1989), and Kymlicka and Norman (1995).
12. Civil society is a different public realm from government. It counterbalances government and is important, therefore, in preventing state tyranny. See Jeffrey Alexander's (1997) sociological (versus economic) account of civil society as a realm of nongovernmental solidarity.
13. On the informal reasoning needed for addressing ill-structured problems, see Perkins (1985).
14. This typology is from Dillon (1994).

15. Iris Marion Young (1996) distinguishes three discursive modes in addition to critical argument: storytelling, greeting, and rhetoric.

16. Nor do the panelists or researchers represent the populations of the nations from which they/we were drawn. To the contrary, they are skewed sharply to the moderately affluent, professional-class symbol managers of these societies.

17. See the discussion of "theoretical sampling" in Glaser and Strauss (1967).

18. That the latter view is not widely held *within* these societies is explained by Buell (1994).

19. Exceptions include An-Na'im (1992), Beiner (1995), Boulding (1988), Habermas (1997), Ong (1999), Oomen (1997), and Said (1993).

20. See Joseph Schwab's (1970) account of such flights.

REFERENCES

Alexander, J.C. (1997). The paradoxes of civil society. *International Sociology, 12*(2), 115–133.

An-Na'im, A.A. (Ed.). (1992). *Human rights in cross-cultural perspectives: A quest for consensus.* Philadelphia: University Pennsylvania.

Beiner, R. (Ed.). (1995). *Theorizing citizenship.* Albany: State University of New York Press.

Ben-Peretz, M. (1990). *The teacher-curriculum encounter.* Albany: State University of New York Press.

Benhabib, S. (Ed.). (1996). *Democracy and difference: Contesting the boundaries of the political.* Princeton, NJ: Princeton University Press.

Benjamin, H. (1939). *The saber tooth curriculum.* New York: McGraw-Hill.

Boulding, E. (1988). *Building a global civic culture: Education for an interdependent world.* New York: Teachers College Press.

Buell, F. (1994). *National culture and the new global system.* Baltimore, MD: Johns Hopkins University Press.

Burbules, N.C. (1993). *Dialogue in Teaching.* New York: Teachers College Press.

Case, R. (1993). Key elements of a global perspective. *Social Education, 57,* 318–325.

Caswell, H.L., & Campbell, D.S. (1935). *Curriculum development.* New York: American Book Company.

Chipman, S.F., Segal, J.W., & Glaser, R. (Eds.). (1985). *Thinking and learning skills* (Vol. II). Hillsdale, NJ: Erlbaum.

Cogan, J.J., & Derricott, R. (Eds.). (1998). *Citizenship for the 21st century: An international perspective on education.* London: Kogan-Page.

Counts, G.S. (1932). *Dare the school build a new social order?* New York: John Day.

Dewey, J. (1927). *The public and its problems.* Chicago: Swallow.

Dewey, J. (1939). *Logic: The theory of inquiry.* New York: Holt.

Dillon, J.T. (Ed.). (1994). *Deliberation in education and society.* Norwood: Ablex.

DuBois, W.E.B. (1903/1990). *The souls of black folk.* New York: Vintage.

Eisner, E., & Peshkin, A. (Eds.). (1990). *Qualitative inquiry in education.* New York: Teachers College Press.

Fanon, F. (1963). *The wretched of the earth.* New York: Grove Press.

Fraser, N. (1995). Politics, culture, and the public space: Toward a post-modern conception. In L. Nicholson & S. Seidman (Eds.), *Social postmodernism: Beyond identity politics*, (pp. 287–312). Cambridge: Cambridge University Press.
Giddens, A. (1990). *The consequences of modernity.* Cambridge: Polity.
Glaser, B.G., & Strauss, A.L. (1967). *The discovery of grounded theory.* New York: Aldine.
Graubard, S. (1997) Preface. *Daedalus, 126*(2), v-xxii.
Habermas, J. (1997). *A Berlin republic.* Lincoln: University of Nebraska.
Hanvey, R. (1978). *An attainable global perspective.* New York: Center for Global Perspectives.
Held, D. (Ed.). (1991). *Political theory today.* Stanford: Stanford University Press.
Kilpatrick, W.H. (1936). *Remaking the curriculum.* New York: Newson and Company.
Kincheloe, J. (1991). *Teachers as researchers: Qualitative inquiry as a path to empowerment.* London: Falmer.
Kymlicka, W., & Norman, W. (1995). Return of the citizen. In R. Beiner (Ed.), *Theorizing citizenship*, (pp. 283–322). Albany: State University of New York Press.
Linstone, H.A., & Turoff, M. (1975). *The Delphi method: Techniques and applications.* Reading, MA: Addison-Wesley.
Lynch, J. (1989). *Multicultural education in a global society.* London: Falmer.
Mansbridge, J. (1991). Democracy, deliberation, and the experience of women. In B. Murchland (Ed.), *Higher education and the practice of democratic politics*, (pp. 122–135). Dayton, OH: Kettering Foundation.
Mathews, D. (1994). *Politics for people: Finding a responsible public voice.* Urbana: University of Illinois Press.
McCarthy, C. (1990). *Race and curriculum.* London: Falmer.
Michigan State Board of Education. (1995). *Michigan framework for social studies education—Content standards.* No city: Author.
Ngugi wa Thiong'o. (1986). *Decolonizing the mind: The politics of language in African literature.* Portsmouth, NH: Heinemann.
Ong, A. (1999). *Flexible citizenship: The cultural logics of transnationality.* Durham, NC: Duke University Press.
Oomen, T.K. (1997). *Citizenship, nationality, and ethnicity.* Cambridge: Polity.
Parker, W.C. (Ed.). (1996). *Educating the democratic mind.* Albany: State University of New York Press.
Paul, R. (1990). *Critical thinking.* Sonoma: Center for Critical Thinking.
Perkins, D.N. (1981). *The mind's best work.* Cambridge, MA: Harvard University Press.
Perkins, D.N. (1985). Reasoning as imagination. *Interchange, 16*(1), 14–26.
Pinar, W.F., Reynolds, W.M., Slattery, P., & Taubman, P.M. (1995). *Understanding Curriculum: An introduction to the study of historical and contemporary curriculum discourses.* New York: Peter Lang.
Poolpatarachewin, C. (1980). Ethnographic Delphi Futures Research: Thai University Pilot Project. *Journal of Cultural and Educational Futures, 2*(4), 11–19.
Reid, W. (1981). The deliberative approach to the study of the curriculum and its relation to critical pluralism. In M. Lawn & L. Barton (Eds.), *Rethinking curriculum studies* (pp. 160–187). London: Croom Helm.
Rieff, D. (1997, July 7). Rieff replies. *The Nation*, p. 2.

Robertson, R. (1990). Mapping the global condition: Globalization as the central concept. *Theory, Culture & Society, 7*(2–3), 20–30.
Said, E.W. (1993). *Culture and imperialism.* New York: Knopf.
Sandel, M.J. (1996). *Democracy's discontent: America in search of a public philosophy.* Cambridge, MA: Harvard University Press.
Schwab, J. (1970). *The practical: A language for curriculum.* Washington, DC: National Education Association.
Strauss, A., & Corbin, J. (1990). *Basics of qualitative research: Grounded theory procedures and techniques.* Newbury Park, CA: Sage.
Toulmin, S.E. (1958). *The uses of argument.* New York: Cambridge University Press.
Willinsky, J. (1992). Towards a Pacific cultural literacy. *Pacific-Asian Education, 4*(1), 1–10.
Wolcott, H.F. (1994). *Transforming qualitative data: Description, analysis, and interpretation.* Thousand Oaks, CA: Sage.
Woyach, R.B., & Remy, R.C. (1989). *Approaches to world studies.* Boston: Allyn and Bacon.
Young, I.M. (1989). Polity and group difference: A critique of the ideal of universal citizenship. *Ethics, 99,* 250–274.
Young, I.M. (1996). Communication and the other: Beyond deliberative democracy. In S. Benhabib (Ed.), *Democracy and difference,* (pp. 120–135). Princeton, NJ: Princeton University Press.

Part III

ASSESSMENTS

CHAPTER 9

AN ASSESSMENT OF WHAT FOURTEEN-YEAR-OLDS KNOW AND BELIEVE ABOUT DEMOCRACY IN TWENTY-EIGHT COUNTRIES

Judith Torney-Purta and Wendy Klandl Richardson

INTRODUCTION

The assessment of educational programs is of increasing importance for teachers and policy makers in the United States and other countries in their efforts to monitor and improve education. The development of meaningful, valid, and reliable assessments of students' understanding of social studies topics, including civic education, is especially challenging. The learning objectives in this area include beliefs and skills as well as factual knowledge. Further, the effects on achievement in these areas extend far beyond the school curriculum and are influenced by cultural and institutional contexts such as the family and community. Overcoming many of these challenges, the International Association for the Evaluation of Educational Achievement (IEA) has conducted the most extensive and comprehensive study of civic education to date.[1] Approximately 90,000 14-year-olds from 28 countries were surveyed on topics ranging from their knowledge of democratic principles and attitudes toward government and media, to opportunities for political activities in school. About 10,000 teachers in the participating countries were also surveyed about their beliefs about citizenship education, as well as the content presented and methods used in their classrooms. The magnitude of the sample and research quality of this study offer opportunities for understanding the outcomes of various models of civic education across different democracies and cultural contexts.

The IEA Civic Education Study began in 1993 with the preparation of twenty-four national case studies (published in Torney-Purta, Schwille, & Amadeo, 1999). These case studies pointed to the ways in which education for citizenship takes place as part of social studies or history classes and sometimes as a separate subject area. They also provided an outline of the expectations in different countries about the knowledge and beliefs of 14-year-olds, a first step in preparing a content framework on which a test and survey were built.

A major milestone for the study was the release of the international report of the large-scale assessment results (Torney-Purta, Lehmann, Oswald, & Schulz, 2001). This represents a culmination of collaborative efforts that produced a way of conceptualizing, understanding, and measuring the content outcomes and processes of civic education internationally in a way judged to be fair by national experts. These cross-national researchers used commonality among these countries concerning important concepts and principles of democracy to construct an instrument that met high psychometric standards that could be used across democratic countries.

This research offers educators the opportunity to learn about how students are being prepared to take on the role of citizen in different contexts. It allows teachers to turn the lens on practices within their school and through comparison with other countries see directions for improving the policies, programs, and everyday interactions that influence students' preparation for citizenship. It has lessons as well for teachers' understanding of the results and methods of assessments.

This chapter presents international findings from the IEA Civic Education Study about student knowledge, attitudes, and engagement, and about teachers' beliefs and practices. This includes summaries of the ways in which young people respond across countries (international averages), cross-country comparisons (with specific examples from the United States), and analyses of gender differences. Comparisons among sub-populations (e.g., ethnic groups) cannot be made internationally, since the particular subgroups are different across countries (defined by race in some countries, by language, immigrant status or religion in others). These analyses will be found in national reports authored by National Research Coordinators in each country.[2]

An overview of the study and questionnaire is given first, providing context for understanding the results. A cross-country comparison of student performance on the knowledge and skills portion of the assessment is presented second. The third section of the chapter focuses on descriptive findings about students' concepts of democracy and good citizenship, trust in government and media, and attitudes toward immigrants and women. The engagement of students in school activities and expected political participation of students as adults is described in the fourth section. Section five presents an exploration of potential factors influencing knowledge and engagement. The sixth section describes teacher beliefs and practices with regard to citizenship education. The chapter closes by drawing together some implications of the study for curriculum, instructional methods, and assessment.

OVERVIEW

The IEA Civic Education Study was conducted in two phases. In the first, each participating country prepared an extensive case study about the context, content, and process of citizenship education, including responses to 18 framing questions about specific civic-related topics (Torney-Purta et al., 1999). National Research Coordinators and the International Steering Committee then collaborated to identify a common core of topics from these case studies that could be used as the basis for a valid and reliable test and survey of civic knowledge and attitudes. These topics were organized into three domains to frame the development of the testing instruments. Domain I, Democracy, consists of three sub-domains: defining characteristics of democracy, institutions and practices in democracy, and the rights and duties of citizens. The case studies emphasized this domain, and so it received the most emphasis on the test. Another area identified as important was national identity, regional and international relationships (Domain II). Social cohesion and diversity was Domain III. Domains II and III were more difficult to assess cross-nationally, since national identity and diversity have many unique within-country facets. Other issues such as the media or economics were included, but not covered as extensively in the test and survey as the three core domains.

The assessment used in the IEA Civic Education Study consisted of a two-part instrument. The first part of the assessment was a multiple-choice test of civic content knowledge (25 items) and skills (13 items) designed to have correct and incorrect answers. The test did not include any items about the political structures or situations particular to a single country, for example, how many members comprise the national legislature or the steps by which a law is passed. Each item on the test was pilot tested, reviewed by international and national groups, and revised if necessary. The test meets high psychometric standards. The second part of the assessment was a 136-question survey without right and wrong answers, covering students' concepts of democracy, attitudes about the political rights of women and immigrants, and expected future political participation. Instruments were translated and the translations independently verified.

Questions were also asked about how free students felt to express opinions in class, the emphasis given to various civic-related topics, and student background information. In addition, school administrators and teachers completed questionnaires to provide information about school characteristics and the implementation of civic education.

Items Included in the Assessment

The student instrument contained five types of items. Type 1 items were designed to assess students' knowledge of content. Type 2 items assessed skills such as interpreting a political leaflet, a mock newspaper article, or a political cartoon. Students' understanding of concepts was tapped with Type 3 items. Type 4 items assessed student attitudes and Type 5 items assessed current and expected participation in activities associated with politics. The Type 1 and 2 items form the test portion of the instrument. Examples of these item types provided in figures in the next section include the average percentage correct across all countries, which provide information about the difficulty of the item.

Sampling of Students

Approximately 90,000 14-year-olds from 28 countries responded to the instrument during 1999. The age of 14 was selected as the target population because compulsory education ceases at 15 in some participating countries. This choice also was consistent with the population tested in the first IEA Civic Education Study (Torney, Oppenheim, & Farnen, 1975). The grade tested was the one that contained the largest proportion of 14-year-olds. Within each country, schools containing that grade were sampled using a probability proportional to size. Then one classroom per school was randomly selected. It was specified that this class was not to be in a subject tracked by ability and if possible was to be a civic-related subject (such as history or social studies). All respondents had full confidentiality; no names, either of individuals or schools districts, are attached to scores. The purpose of most IEA tests, including this one, is to assess group and country differences not to assess individuals or schools.

STUDENTS' KNOWLEDGE, ATTITUDES, AND ENGAGEMENT

Knowledge

Figure 1 displays the results of the international test of civic knowledge (Torney-Purta, Lehman, et al., 2001). The table presents the international average and organizes the countries according to their mean; significantly above the international mean of 100, below the mean or at the mean. Interestingly, there are no obvious regional differences in knowledge scores. Countries scoring above the international mean include Western European, North American and post-Communist countries. Note that within each of the three groups, country scores are not necessarily significantly different from each other. For example, Poland had the highest average score of 111 but this was not significantly different from most of the other countries in the highest scoring group.

Looking at performance on individual items shows that the majority of students in the participating countries appear to have a basic understanding of the principles, institutions, processes, and values important in democracies. While it is promising that the majority of students demonstrate this basic knowledge, there are still a number of students (a substantial number in some countries) who have not attained that level.

In general the ninth graders in the United States performed well, with a score above the international mean on the total civic knowledge test. An interesting difference was observed, however, between performance on the items about democratic principles and concepts and those measuring skills in interpreting political communication (Type 1 and Type 2 items referred to previously). For example, students in the United States performed on average better than the students in other countries when asked to interpret the message of a political leaflet (example in Figure 2, 83% correct for the United States compared to 65% internationally) and in interpreting the main message of a cartoon about history (example in Figure 3, 79% correct for the United States compared to 57% internationally). The thirteen skill items formed the sub-scale measuring skills in understanding political communication.

In contrast, the students in the United States performed at a level very close to the international mean when they were asked to demonstrate their understanding of the importance of having many organizations available for people who wish to join them, the possible negative effects if one publisher was to buy many newspapers, the characteristics of a non-democratic government, and the function of having more than one political party. Twenty-five knowledge items formed the sub-score measuring civic content knowledge.

Country	Mean Scale Score		Tested Grade*	Mean Age**
Poland	111	(1.7)	8	15.0
Finland	109	(0.7)	8	14.8
Cyprus	108	(0.5)	9	14.8
Greece	108	(0.8)	9	14.7
Hong Kong (SAR)[3]	107	(1.1)	9	15.3
United States[1]	106	(1.2)	9	14.7
Italy	105	(0.8)	9	15.0
Slovak Republic	105	(0.7)	8	14.3
Norway[4]	103	(0.5)	8	14.8
Czech Republic	103	(0.8)	8	14.4
Australia	102	(0.8)	9	14.6
Hungary	102	(0.6)	8	14.4
Slovenia	101	(0.5)	8	14.8
Denmark[4]	100	(0.5)	8	14.8
International sample	100	(0.2)	8/9	14.7
Germany[2]	100	(0.5)	8	n.a.
Russian Federation[3]	100	(1.3)	9	15.1
England[1]	99	(0.6)	9	14.7
Sweden[1]	99	(0.8)	8	14.3
Switzerland	98	(0.8)	8/9	15.0
Bulgaria	98	(1.3)	8	14.9
Portugal[5]	96	(0.7)	8	14.5
Belgium (French)[4]	95	(0.9)	8	14.1
Estonia	94	(0.5)	8	14.7
Lithuania	94	(0.7)	8	14.8
Romania	92	(0.9)	8	14.8
Latvia	92	(0.9)	8	14.5
Chile	88	(0.7)	8	14.3
Colombia	86	(0.9)	8	14.6

▨ Country mean significantly higher than international mean.
☐ No statistically significant difference between country mean and international mean.
▨ Country mean significantly lower than international mean.

1 Countries with testing date at beginning of school year.
2 National Desired Population does not cover all International Desired Population.
3 Countries did not meet age/grade specification.
4 Countries' overall participation rate after replacement less than 85 percent.
5 In Portugal grade 8 selected instead of grade 9 due to average age. Mean scale score for grade 9 was 106.
* In Switzerland grade 8 was tested mainly in German cantons, grade 9 mainly in French and Italian cantons. In Russia students in grade 9 have 8 or 9 years of schooling depending on the duration of the primary school they finished. In 1999 about 70% of Russian students tested had 8 years of schooling at the end of grade 9.
**Information on age was not available for Germany. International mean age based on 27 countries only.

Source: IEA Civic Education Study, Standard Population of 14-year-olds tested in 1999.

Figure 1. Distributions of civic knowledge.

Assessment of What Fourteen-Year-Olds Know and Believe About Democracy   191

Country	Correct Answers (in %)	Example 1 (Item #23) Type 2: Skills in interpretation
Australia	78 (1.3)	**We citizens have had enough!** A vote for the Silver Party means a vote for higher taxes. It means an end to economic growth and a waste of our nation's resources. Vote instead for economic growth and free enterprise. Vote for more money left in everyone's wallet! Let's not waste another 4 years! VOTE FOR THE GOLD PARTY. 23. **This is an election leaflet which has probably been issued by…** A. the Silver Party. B. a party or group in opposition to the Silver Party. * C. a group which tries to be sure elections are fair. D. the Silver Party and the Gold Party together.
Belgium (French)	56 (1.8)	
Bulgaria	47 (2.4)	
Chile	54 (1.5)	
Colombia	40 (2.4)	
Cyprus	81 (0.9)	
Czech Republic	66 (1.6)	
Denmark	49 (1.1)	
England	75 (1.2)	
Estonia	54 (1.4)	
Finland	85 (0.8)	
Germany	81 (0.9)	
Greece	73 (1.3)	
Hong Kong (SAR)	76 (1.4)	
Hungary	78 (1.2)	
Italy	85 (1.2)	
Latvia	44 (1.9)	
Lithuania	55 (1.6)	
Norway	57 (0.9)	
Poland	58 (2.0)	
Portugal	55 (1.3)	
Romania	46 (2.0)	
Russian Federation	45 (1.9)	
Slovak Republic	66 (1.6)	
Slovenia	75 (1.0)	
Sweden	73 (1.5)	
Switzerland	77 (1.3)	
United States	83 (1.4)	
International Sample	65 (0.3)	

( ) Standard errors appear in parentheses.
* Correct answer.

Source: IEA Civic Education Study, Standard Population of 14-year-olds tested in 1999.

Figure 2.   Item Example: This is an election leaflet.

Country	Correct Answers (in %)	Example 2 (Item #36) Type 2: Skills in interpretation
Australia	75 (1.2)	
Belgium (French)	66 (2.1)	
Bulgaria	47 (2.3)	
Chile	49 (1.5)	
Colombia	48 (2.3)	
Cyprus	53 (1.1)	
Czech Republic	54 (1.5)	
Denmark	60 (1.0)	
England	76 (1.2)	
Estonia	39 (1.2)	
Finland	65 (1.3)	
Germany	61 (0.9)	
Greece	56 (1.3)	36. What is the message or main point of this cartoon? History textbooks…
Hong Kong (SAR)	76 (1.4)	
Hungary	67 (1.3)	
Italy	61 (1.3)	A. are sometimes changed to avoid mentioning problematic events from the past.*
Latvia	48 (1.7)	
Lithuania	48 (1.4)	
Norway	49 (1.0)	
Poland	64 (2.1)	B. for children must be shorter than books written for adults.
Portugal	49 (1.1)	
Romania	26 (1.7)	
Russian Federation	45 (2.1)	C. are full of information that is not interesting.
Slovak Republic	72 (1.5)	
Slovenia	56 (1.1)	D. should be written using a computer and not a pencil.
Sweden	52 (1.5)	
Switzerland	67 (1.4)	
United States	79 (1.4)	
International Sample	57 (0.3)	

( ) Standard errors appear in parentheses.
* Correct answer.

Source: IEA Civic Education Study, Standard Population of 14-year-olds tested in 1999.

Figure 3. Item Example: This is the way history textbooks are sometimes written.

Studies conducted by IEA do not set specific standards for performance on items (as does the U.S. National Assessment of Educational Progress [NAEP] with its basic, proficient, and advanced categories of achievement). There is no set number of items that is required to "pass" the IEA test (as in some district and state tests). But the group differences indicate some cause for concern. If, for example, we look at the distributions from the IEA study in the United States, it is clear that there is a group of about 25% of students who do not perform well on the test (estimates indicate that they answer fewer than one third of the questions correctly). Their performance is weak when they are asked to demonstrate an understanding of some principles of democracy or a market economy. Many of these low-performing students also have difficulty answering questions about the positions favored by political parties in an election leaflet, materials describing contrasting opinions in news stories, and distinctions between facts and opinions about taxes or the environment. These are skills especially important for informed participation in democracies.

This lowest one quarter of students in the United States is disproportionately composed of individuals who report few books in their homes (a measure of home literacy resources), individuals whose parents did not graduate from high school, individuals who themselves do not expect to graduate from high school, and individuals who attend schools where a majority of the student body is eligible for free lunch (home literacy and expected education results from Torney-Purta, Lehman, et al., 2001; other results from Baldi, Perie, Skidmore, Greenberg, & Hahn, 2001). These findings, which are similar to those in many other subject areas, show that civic education is like general education in that it is also heavily influenced by socioeconomic contexts. A later section of this chapter will demonstrate, however, that there also appear to be educational factors of special importance in civic education. (On the point that poverty and lack of political information are associated in adults, creating a disadvantage for individuals who could use such information to develop more effective political participation see Delli Carpini & Keeter, 1996).

The issue of gender as it relates to political knowledge is also important. Gender differences are not as large in the 1999 IEA study as in earlier studies. When male and female students were compared without holding other factors constant, there was a sizable difference in only one of the 28 countries. And even when other factors were held constant, female students scored lower than males in slightly less than half the countries. There were, for example, no significant gender differences in the United States, Australia, or England. Over the last decade gender differences appear to be lessening in this area.

Attitudes

An important part of the IEA study was its recognition that civic education is about more than learning the principles, processes, and laws of democracy and skills to interpret information. The study moved beyond assessing civic knowledge and tried to gain insight into student attitudes and concepts related to democracy.

Enabling students to understand concepts underlying democracy was identified as an expectation for civic education in the national case studies. Therefore the survey assessed students' concepts of what was good or bad for sustaining a democracy and what qualities were necessary for a good citizen. Group and country analyses were made by identifying areas of consensus across countries and ranking mean scores.

It is noteworthy that many of the attributes of a strong democracy reported by students are consistent with descriptions in the national case studies about the focus of school curriculum. There were seven items with strong consensus across countries including three items referring to attributes of a strong democracy such as the importance of free elections and the right to express political opinions, and four attributes judged to be bad for democracy such as limits on free speech and special influence on policy by the wealthy. Concepts of political parties were an area where there were country differences and not consensus. Students in some countries believed that democracy is strengthened when political parties have different opinions on important issues and when people participate in political parties to influence government, while those in other countries were much more negative (Torney-Purta, Lehman, et al., 2001).

There appears to be relatively little consensus across countries about what constitutes good citizenship. Only obeying the law was identified as an important characteristic of a good citizen across countries. Knowing the country's history, being willing to serve in the military, and showing respect for government representatives were concepts of good citizenship that were endorsed in some countries but not in others.

Students in the United States were somewhat more likely than the average student internationally to endorse the idea that the good citizens should vote in every election, show respect for government leaders, follow political issues in the media, and engage in political discussion. They were considerably more likely to endorse these activities by citizens than were the students in Australia, England, Germany, or the Nordic countries (Denmark, Finland, Norway, and Sweden), for example.

The results show that most adolescents are already part of the political culture of their country. Many of their beliefs about government responsibilities are consistent with previous research on adults' attitudes toward government. For example, in general adolescents were quite likely to believe the government should play a role in supporting society by providing free basic education and guaranteeing peace and order in the country. They were considerably less likely to believe that the government should undertake economic responsibilities such as reducing differences in income and wealth or guaranteeing a job for everyone who wants one. The school curricula and instruction described by many countries in the national case studies emphasized social rather than economic responsibilities.

Where there were differences between 14-year-olds from the participating countries, student attitudes paralleled the specific political-socioeconomic context of their own country. Students from post-Communist countries such as Bulgaria or the Russian Federation, had higher expectations for government involvement in the economy, for example, whereas countries with strong free-market traditions like the United States were considerably less likely to have a concept of government that included responsibility for the economy.

Confidence in democratic institutions is considered by many to be a prerequisite for a strong democracy. Trust in government institutions was an area of concern identified in the national case study phase of the study. In general, the attitudes of 14-year-olds match those reported in other studies of adults. Young people across countries have relatively high levels of trust in police and courts and moderate levels of trust in other government institutions. However, none of these levels is above 65% for trusting the institutions "always" or "most of time." The lowest level of trust is in political parties; they are trusted "always" or "most of the time" by only 28% (Torney-Purta, Lehman et al., 2001). The pattern in the United States was slightly different, with the largest proportion of students trusting the local or town government, followed by the courts, Congress, the police, and the national government. The level of trust in political parties was also low relative to other institutions among U.S. students, however (Baldi et al., 2001).

Trust in the mass media, as a source of news is also an important factor in democracies. Television news is trusted more than radio or the press in every country except the United States, where newspapers are trusted more than television news. Not surprisingly, in all countries students watch more television news than they listen to the radio or read the newspaper. Adolescents' understanding about mass media appears shallow in terms of the role of news media in preserving or enhancing democracy. While there is consensus that a monopoly of newspaper ownership is bad for democracy, several other concepts are supported less fully, perhaps indicating somewhat superficial student understanding. To take one example, in a number of countries, although students would be concerned about a reduction of differences in opinion among newspapers, they seem to be relatively unconcerned about having all the TV stations present the same viewpoints on politics.

Another important component of citizenship education identified in the national case studies was the area of social cohesion and diversity. Problems of discrimination were mentioned by many of the countries in the case studies. Although in many cases there are country differences in the group or groups subject to discrimination, there was consensus among National Research Coordinators on the appropriateness of asking about attitudes toward the political rights of immigrants and of women. A large majority of 14-year-olds indicated a positive attitude toward the rights of both immigrants and women in 1999. More than 75% of the students across countries "agreed" or "strongly agreed" that immigrants should have the right to vote, keep their own language, customs and lifestyle, and have the same rights as other citizens. Comparable percentages of students "agree" or "strongly agree" that women should run for public office, be involved in politics, have equal rights to a job and equal pay, and are qualified to be political leaders. Students in the United States scored relatively high on these two scales (above the international mean).

Interestingly, responses to these two attitude scales revealed the largest gender differences in the instrument. Females were significantly more supportive than males of immigrants' rights in 23 countries. The gender difference in support for women's political rights was significant and large in all 28 countries. Females were more supportive of women's political rights than males. As one might expect, in countries with substantial numbers of immigrants (such as the United States) students who themselves were immigrants were more likely to support immigrants' rights than students born in the country. These differences are important to teachers because they demonstrate the role of identity groups in students' attitudes and beliefs. These identities may condition responses to topics discussed in class (see Merryfield's qualitative research, 1994, 1998).

Engagement

Learning about participation in democracies is an important component of citizenship identified in the case studies. Many countries expressed concern about low levels of civic engagement among youth. The IEA Civic Education Study attempted to gauge adolescent participation in two ways. First, the study asked students in which political activities they expected to participate as adults. Second, the study developed several measures of participation in the school context including perceptions of classroom climate, sense of confidence in the value of participating at school, and actual participation in civic-related organizations.

Expected participation was measured regarding both conventional forms of activities such as voting and writing letters to a newspaper and more unconventional activities such as participating in a nonviolent demonstration. The most common type of conventional political participation in which students expect to engage is voting. Although this finding only represents an intention to vote, it is interesting nonetheless since in some countries (including the United States) the percent of young voters has been shown to be considerably lower than the voting rate in older populations. In general, students across countries hold low expectations for participation through conventional political avenues apart from voting. Only around one-fifth of the students believe they will join a political party, be a candidate for local or city office, or write letters to a newspaper about social or political concerns.

This does not mean that students fail to see any role for themselves in politics. Rather they appear to have a vision about the nature of political engagement that involves more support for social-movement related participation. They believe that adult citizens should join human rights and environmental organizations or participate in groups acting to benefit the community. More than half of the students say they would be willing to collect money for a social cause and nearly one half of the students expect that they will "probably" or "definitely" collect signatures for a petition or participate in a nonviolent protest march. Students differ across countries in the types of political engagement they anticipate being involved in. For example, two-thirds of the students in Colombia, Cyprus, Greece, and Italy are likely to participate in nonviolent protests, whereas fewer than one-third of the students in the Czech Republic, England, and Finland intend to take such action. An emphasis on social-movement related activities may dilute students' willingness to participate in conventional politics. Students may fail to connect such activities with particular government policies, thereby weakening a sense of membership in the larger democratic system (Niemi, 2000).

Since 14-year-olds cannot vote and are usually not welcomed into other adult-like participatory roles in these democracies, the study attempted to assess the degree to which schools serve as a context for the development of confidence in participation in groups and as models of democratic processes. Further, it was important to know to what degree school experience in democratic structures influences civic knowledge and expected engagement. Many previous studies of political attitudes have attempted to measure attitudes about how influential citizens are in the shaping government decisions. Rather than measure such an abstract principle of political efficacy with 14-year-olds, the IEA Civic Education Study developed a measure of confidence in the effectiveness of student participation at school. The resulting scale asked four questions dealing with confidence that groups of students who participate in school-based groups can have an impact on solving school problems. More than 84% of the students across countries "agreed" or "strongly agreed" that participation in student groups at school is an effective way to achieve change within the school. Students in the United States were quite close to the international mean on this scale. Relatively high levels of this confidence in student participation at school were expressed by students in Cyprus, Greece, and Portugal.

Students also reported the degree to which they had opportunities to learn various skills and topics in their classes. Learning to cooperate in groups was the area in which students felt most emphasis was placed, with more than 80% of the students in all countries agreeing. In contrast, fewer than 55% of the students across countries reported that they learned about the importance of voting in national and local elections. In some countries, such as Denmark, Finland, Germany, and Slovenia this figure was below 40%. Although elections are certainly not regular events, they are vitally important to strong democracies. This study also shows that explicit teaching about elections and voting in school makes a difference to students' intended participation. It is associated with students saying that as adults they are likely to vote (see the description of the predictor model in the next section).

One important finding of the earlier IEA Civic Education Study (Torney et al., 1975) was that students' belief that their classroom offered opportunities to speak openly was positively associated with civic knowledge and support for democratic values. More recent studies have also found related positive correlations between open classroom climate and political interest and trust (Hahn, 1998), as well as a sense of political efficacy (Ichilov, 1991). The 1999 IEA Civic Education Study developed a 6-item scale asking about students' perception of the openness in their classrooms to discuss issues and express their opinions.

Like the first IEA Civic Education Study (Torney et al., 1975), the results of the 1999 study found that open classroom climate is a predictor of both civic knowledge and likelihood to vote (see the description of the predictor model in the next section). However, the majority of students do not report such opportunities for open discussion in their classrooms. Across all countries, between 27 and 39% of the students say that they are "often" encouraged to make up their own minds, encouraged to express their opinions, free to express opinions that differ from those of other students and of the teacher, and are likely to hear several sides of an issue. An even smaller percent, 16%, of students have teachers who encourage them to discuss issues about which people have different opinions. On average, fewer students in the post-Communist countries report opportunities for open classroom discussions than in the older democracies participating in the study. In a study of regional differences in the United States, Conover and Searing (2000) found that students in suburban and rural communities had more opportunities to discuss political issues than did students from urban or immigrant areas. Parallel comparisons have not yet been made with the IEA data, but further analyses of within country regional or school-type differences is expected to provide important additional insights.

Participation in voluntary organizations has long been considered an important component of a strong democracy. Recent longitudinal studies in the U.S. have linked participation in school organizations to later involvement in communities (Verba, Schlozman, & Brady, 1995; Youniss, McLellan, & Yates, 1997). The role of such organizational membership was cited as an important area in the national case studies. The study coordinators, together with the National Research Coordinators, developed a list of 15 organizations to which students might belong that would be applicable across countries.

Collecting money for a social cause and participating in student council engage the largest number of students across countries. However, in only a few countries is the percent of engaged students above 50% for the more civic-related organizations. In Cyprus and Greece more than 55% participate in student council, 50% of students in the United States report participation in volunteer activities to help the community, and more than 50% of students in Denmark, England, Greece, and Norway report collecting money for a social cause. There are also a number of countries where participation in all types of organizations is low: Bulgaria, the Czech Republic, Estonia, Finland, Germany, Italy, Latvia, Lithuania, Poland, and the Slovak Republic. These are predominately but not exclusively post-Communist countries.

FACTORS THAT PREDICT CIVIC KNOWLEDGE AND ENGAGEMENT

While differences between countries provide a useful perspective on civic education, exploring how various other factors in the school, community, and home are related to such knowledge and engagement offers even more information to educators interested in ways of improving the process of civic education. Statistical modeling cannot prove that one factor causes a particular outcome. However, it can demonstrate how certain factors and outcomes are related especially within each country. Therefore a simple path model was constructed to explore factors in the school and home that might relate to selected outcomes in civic education. These analyses were conducted for a composite sample of 14,000 students (500 randomly selected from each of the 28 countries). They were also conducted separately for each country using the entire sample for that country (Torney-Purta, Lehman, et al., 2001).

To summarize the method of analysis, the total score on the civic knowledge test and the students' stated expectation that they will vote when adults were used as dependent variables. Eight family and school variables were selected as possible predictors of the knowledge score and likelihood to vote. A model was constructed that tested the strength of the association between the family and school factors and the two dependent variables (see Figure 4).

Gender and home literacy resources (number of books in the home) were selected as basic background variables. Four variables were included from the section of the instrument about school experiences: number of years of expected further education; the students' reports of the extent to which there is an open climate for discussion in their classrooms; the students' reports of opportunities they have had to learn about voting in school; and the students' reports that they have participated in school councils or parliaments. In order to consider the influence of factors outside school two variables were included that measured students' out-of-school activities: evenings spent outside home with peers and frequency of watching television news. The choice of potential predictors to explore was made in light of previous studies in this area in the United States and other countries (Niemi & Junn, 1998; Torney et al., 1975).

The numbers (standardized regression coefficients) presented in the model indicate strength of the relationship between each factor and the two outcome variables (holding other factors constant). The figures for r-squared indicate how much of the differences between student scores is explained by the predictors. In this model, the most important variable in explaining civic knowledge is expected years of further education (.26). This variable reflects the future educational aspirations of the individual student, in many cases influenced by parents, peers, or type of school program in which the student is enrolled. The second largest predictor is home literacy resources (.19). The more books that students report having in their homes, the higher their level of civic knowledge. Students' perception of an open classroom climate for discussion is another variable that is positively related to the civic knowledge score (.13). This variable reflects the individual's perception of the atmosphere in class. Perceptions may vary within a class. However, in this area, an individual's view of whether it is a good idea to express an opinion is one factor that is important in determining the extent of involvement in class discussion.

Predictors with significant but smaller positive effects on civic knowledge in this model are reported participation in a school council or parliament and the frequency of watching television news. Gender has a relatively small effect on civic knowledge. Spending evenings outside home

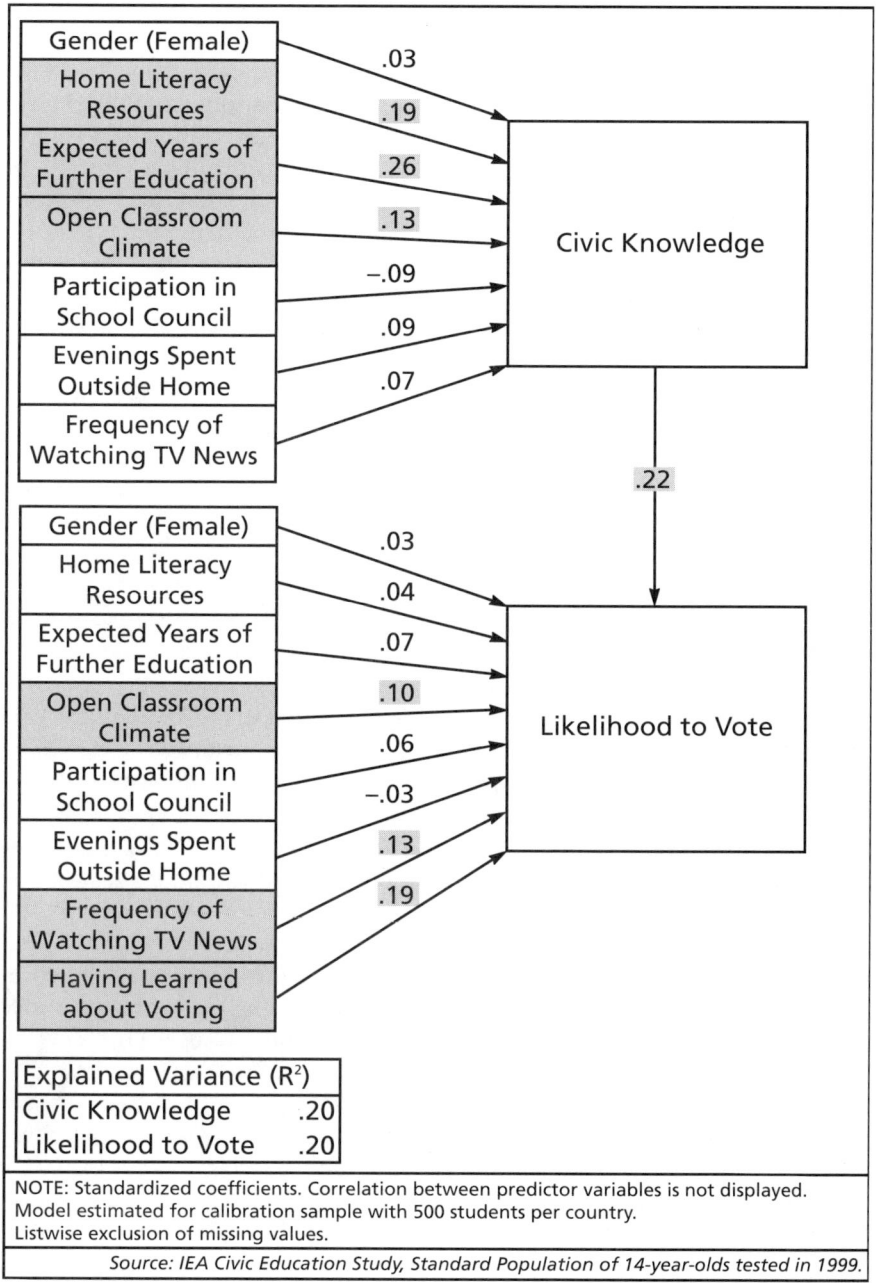

Figure 4. Path model for predicting civic knowledge and likelihood to vote using home, school, peer, and media characteristics.

is the only independent variable negatively related to civic knowledge. Those students who report that they spend most evenings with peers outside the home have lower test scores than others.

The model was also computed for a second dependent variable, the students' statement about how likely they are to vote as adults. The biggest predictor here is civic knowledge (.22). This demonstrates a strong relationship between what students know and expectations for future political participation. The more young people know about democracy and the higher their skills in interpreting political information, the more they expect to exercise their right to vote. The second most important predictor in this model is the student's report of whether he or she has learned in school about the importance of voting (.19). Explicit emphasis on elections and on the importance of voting can make a difference. Frequency of watching television news also has a considerable positive relation to the expectation to vote (.13). Perception of an open classroom climate (.10) has a positive effect, as it did also as a predictor of civic knowledge. Expected years of further education, and reported participation in a school council or parliament have small positive effects. The effect of the home background factor of literacy resources is small overall but important in some countries, especially Germany, Sweden, Switzerland, and the United States. The effects of gender and students' reports of spending evenings outside their homes with peers are almost negligible.

These analyses suggest a number of educational components that have particular importance in civic education. Of clear importance is the connection between knowledge and participation. Since higher levels of civic knowledge and learning about voting in school are both associated with likelihood of voting, explicit instruction in civics seems likely to increase participation. Another component unique to civic education is the opportunity to engage in inquiry and discourse and other processes that model democratic principles, including the chance to explore one's political identity. An open classroom climate and issue-centered instruction are teaching techniques that seem especially influential in providing these opportunities. Expected further education and home literacy resources have a direct effect on knowledge but appear to be less related to future political participation. Special efforts should be made to ensure civic education reaches all socioeconomic groups. The influence of TV news, especially on anticipated voting, suggests that additional opportunities for schools to enhance civic education might be to connect media resources more closely to school learning. Additionally the positive, albeit small, influence of participation in student council or parliament suggests that these activities need more explicit connections to civic knowledge and participation, perhaps through reflection activities as have been noted by researchers in the area of service learning (Billig, 2000; Torney-Purta, Hahn, & Amadeo, 2001).

TEACHER BELIEFS AND PRACTICES

Although the focus of the IEA Civic Education Study was on 14-year-olds, data from the teacher questionnaire offers additional insight into the school context of civic education. Input from teachers is particularly important in citizenship education since the topic is interdisciplinary and often a subject where teachers play a large role in determining the content and nature of instruction.

Sampling of Teachers

In many countries civic education is embedded in other social science courses or history. This made the identification of civic education teachers difficult. The selection procedure for teachers was dependent in part on students chosen for participation. The sampled schools were asked to select three teachers of civic education-related subjects who were teaching the tested class of students. Thus the sampled teachers do not necessarily represent all teachers from civic-related subjects in a country, but are linked to the representative sample of students used for this study. In Colombia and the United States there were problems at the country level in confirming the linkage between teachers and classes of students. Therefore, the data from only twenty-six countries are included in these tables.

Content and Objectives for Civic Education

The national case studies indicated a variety of patterns in the offering of civic education content to 14-year-olds, sometimes in a separate course but quite frequently as part of other courses. In this survey, across countries most teachers felt that civic education should be integrated into courses such as social studies or history. However, having civic education as a specific subject was appealing to teachers in a number of the post-Communist countries, perhaps as a way of ensuring at least a minimum amount of time spent on it.

It was also important to get a sense of which content topics were emphasized. From a list of 20 topics teachers were asked to identify those they thought were the most important, those they felt most confident to teach, and those they were most likely to cover with students. Not surprisingly the topics teachers thought most important and where they reported the most confidence were those they were most likely to cover with students. Teachers across countries rated national history, citizens' rights, human rights, and the environment as the most important topics. International affairs and economics were rated less important and received less coverage by the teachers in their classes.

One set of identical questions was included asking about what teachers and students believe is taught (learned) in school. The student responses were described in general in a previous section on engagement. A comparison between results from teachers and students shows agreement that students learn how to cooperate in groups with other students, to understand people who have different ideas, to be patriotic and loyal citizens of their country, and to contribute to solving social problems in the community.

It is interesting that across countries the proportion of teachers who believed that students learned about voting in school was much higher than the proportion of students who believed they had actually learned this. The model presented in a previous section showed the clear importance of emphasis on voting in school as a correlate of enhanced likelihood of voting on the part of students. This suggests that if learning about voting and election processes were a more explicit part of the school curriculum, students might be more likely to expect to vote. The potential importance of this topic is enhanced because many students reported in the survey that they have not had opportunities in their classes to learn about the debate and discussion that is part of election campaigns.

Curricular guidelines are very influential in determining what is taught in any subject area. Teachers may be teaching in ways that they professionally do not believe to be ideal. An important finding from this study was the discrepancy between the way civic education instruction actually occurs according to teachers, and the vision that they hold for the subject. In most countries teachers report that their instruction emphasizes knowledge transmission (the light gray part of the top bar for each country in Figure 5). However, many teachers have a vision of civic education that emphasizes critical thinking, values or political participation (see the white, dark gray and black of the bottom bar for each country graphs in Figure 5).

The discrepancy appears to be the largest in countries that report knowledge transmission as the most common emphasis of instruction. For example, in Italy where teachers of 82% of the Italian students think that knowledge transmission is emphasized, only 2% of these teachers feel that this is the most desirable focus. In comparison countries such as Belgium (French), Bulgaria, Chile, England, Lithuania, and Slovenia where teachers of more than 30% of the students report that values are currently emphasized, the gap between reality and vision is not as wide. The dissatisfaction with a knowledge emphasis found here is similar to that reported in other studies, for example Davies, Gregory, and Riley (1999) who surveyed British teachers.

Assessment of What Fourteen-Year-Olds Know and Believe About Democracy

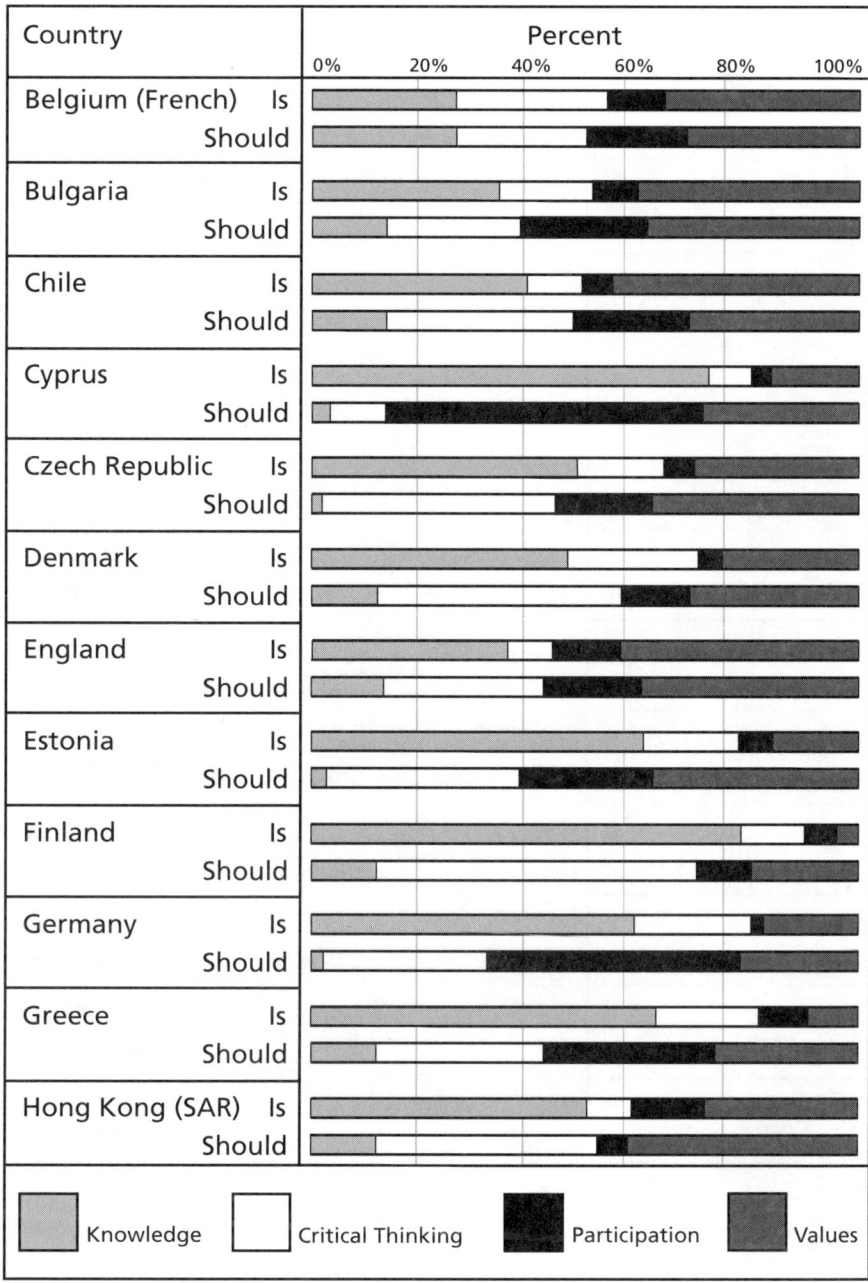

Figure 5. Where teachers think the emphasis of civic education is and should be placed.

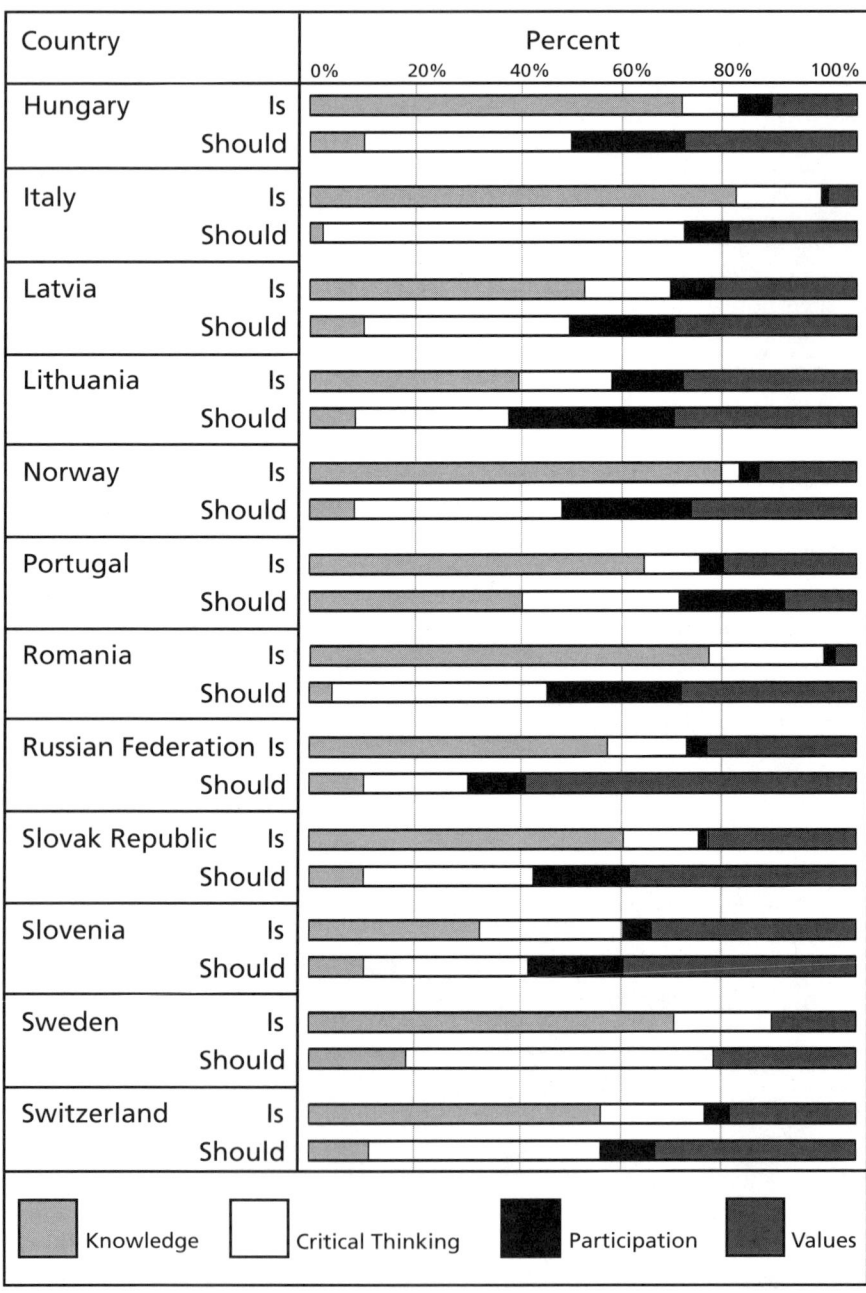

Figure 5. Where teachers think the emphasis of civic education is and should be placed. (cont.)

The vision of civic education that teachers appear to hold is consistent with many components of the vision laid out by educational specialists in the national case studies. Specifically, they believed that civic education should be participative, interactive and related to life in school and community. Different countries are in different positions relative to curricular reform. Many would argue that change in teaching practice requires helping teachers to meet their own goals for improvement rather than orienting themselves only to goals set by others. This gap between current practice and teachers' perceptions of the ideal form of civic education suggests an important starting point.

Instructional Methods

The instructional methods teachers report appear to reflect their view that knowledge transmission is the current emphasis in most of their classrooms. Across countries teacher-centered methods such as use of textbooks and recitation predominate. Discussion of controversial topics seems to occur with some degree of frequency as well. Role-playing exercises and projects are techniques that are not used as often.

Although the teacher data is not available from the United States, there is data from students who were asked about the instructional methods used in their classrooms. This provides corroborating information about the prevalence of teacher-centered methods. Baldi et al. (2001) indicate in the U.S. national report that reading from the textbook and filling out worksheets are the most frequent activities, with role-playing, debates, discussions, and more interactive activities much less frequent according to students.

The national case studies led to the expectation that no single mode of assessing students would predominate. This is also what the teacher survey shows. Written composition and oral participation are the most often cited forms of assessments. However, multiple-choice tests are mentioned in many places, including the post-Communist countries. No category of assessment was selected by a large majority of teachers in any country, as might have been expected if a formal national assessment were part of the civic education program.

Teachers across countries also have relatively definite opinions when it comes to ways in which civic education might be improved. The top-ranked need is for better materials and textbooks, followed by additional training in content and more time for instruction. Assistance with planning special projects is less important. Teachers across countries express relatively little need for enhanced autonomy in decision making, an area that many educational advocates emphasize. According the these teachers, improvements are needed that have an impact on daily classroom experience by enhancing subject-matter expertise, the quality of materials students can use, and the amount of classroom time devoted to civic education. Such improvements could capitalize on the grasp of basic principles of democracy that students in many countries appear to have according to the IEA student results.

CONCLUSIONS

Civic education is a rich topic for reflection in terms of the content of the curriculum, the instructional practices of teachers, and processes of assessment. At the curricular level it is clear that having an explicit civic-related content focus is important, though the instruction can be contextualized within social studies or history. Results from both the student and teacher surveys indicate that the goals of civic education extend beyond knowledge transmission. Optimally, curriculum in civic education includes links to practices and environments outside of the school community. Values, critical thinking, participation, and issues of identity are important components of civic education. Finally, the existence of a low performing group of students with low educational expectations from home backgrounds with limited resources suggests that excellence in civic teaching must be spread across socioeconomic status groups if the democratic promise of education is to be fulfilled.

In the area of instructional practices, one of the best ways to strengthen civic education would be through enhancing the climate for open and respectful discussion in the classroom. This would require extensive efforts in teacher training, and communication with parents to explain the purpose for these approaches. Likewise teachers need assistance in adapting instruction to meet the needs of specific groups, referred to here as identity groups. Integrating participation (such as service learning) into the curriculum also remains a promising avenue for improving civic education, especially when it includes opportunities to reflect on the connections between principles and practice.

In the area of assessment, the IEA Civic Education Study provides a standard and model of rigorous assessment,[3] as well as indicating that there is a body of cross-nationally valid content knowledge about principles of democracy and skills in interpreting political communication that can be assessed. The identification of a body of content knowledge provides a framework that can also be used to create and evaluate civic education programs. Although the IEA assessment emphasizes group and country differences largely in a quantitative fashion, it does provide some insight into meanings students construct about democracies. It also suggests some preliminary connections between teachers' beliefs and practices in civic education and student outcomes that should be explored in future research.

In summary, the IEA Civic Education Study has provided extensive insight into a variety of areas of importance to the design of programs and practices to improve education for citizenship.

NOTES

1. IEA is best known for its international assessments in the fields of mathematics and science (TIMSS). This cooperative effort of research institutes has members in more than 50 countries and has conducted more than 20 studies over the past 30 years.

2. Summaries of these reports may be found on www.wam.umd.edu/~iea/.

3. The majority of the instrument used in the study can be found at www.wam.umd.edu/~iea/.

REFERENCES

Baldi, S., Perie, M., Skidmore, D., Greenberg, E., & Hahn, C. (2001). *What democracy means to ninth-graders: U.S. results from the international IEA Civic Education Study (NCES 2001–096)*. U.S. Department of Education, National Center for Education Statistics. Washington, DC: U.S. Government Printing Office.

Billig, S.H. (2000, May). Research on k-12 school-based service-learning: The evidence builds. *Phi Delta Kappan*.

Conover, P.J., & Searing, D.D. (2000). A political socialization perspective. In L.M. McDonnell, P.M. Timpane, & R. Benjamin (Eds.), *Rediscovering the democratic purposes of education* (pp. 91–124). Lawrence: University Press of Kansas.

Davies, I., Gregory, I., & Riley, S. (1999). *Good citizenship and educational provision*. London: Falmer Press.

Delli Carpini, M., & Keeter, S. (1996). *What Americans know about politics and why it matters*. New Haven, CT: Yale University Press.

Hahn, C. (1998). *Becoming political: Comparative perspectives on citizenship education*. Albany: State University of New York Press.

Ichilov, O. (1991). Political socialization and schooling effects among Israeli adolescents. *Comparative Education Review, 35*(3), 430–446.

Merryfield, M. (1994). Shaping the curriculum in global education: The influence of student characteristics on teacher decision making. *Journal of Curriculum and Supervision, 9*(3), 233–249.

Merryfield, M. (1998). Pedagogy for global perspectives in education: Studies of teachers' thinking and practice. *Theory and Research in Social Education, 26,* 342–379.

Niemi, R.G., & Junn, J. (1998). *Civic education: What makes students learn?* New Haven, CT: Yale University Press.

Niemi, R.G. (2000, June). *Trends in political science as they relate to pre-college curriculum and teaching.* Paper presented at the annual meeting of the Social Science Consortium, Woodshole, MA.

Torney, J.V., Oppenheim, A.N., & Farnen, R.F. (1975). *Civic education in ten countries: An empirical study.* New York: John Wiley & Sons.

Torney-Purta, J., Hahn, C., & Amadeo, J. (2001). Principles of subject-specific instruction in education for citizenship. In J. Brophy (Ed.), *Subject-specific instructional methods and activities* (pp. 371–408). Greenwich, CT: JAI Press.

Torney-Purta, J., Lehmann, R., Oswald, H., & Schulz, W. (2001). *Citizenship and education in twenty-eight countries: Civic knowledge and engagement at age fourteen.* Amsterdam: IEA.

Torney-Purta, J., Schwille, J., & Amadeo, J. (1999). *Civic education across countries: Twenty-four national case studies from the IEA Civic Education Project.* Amsterdam: IEA.

Verba, S., Schlozman, K.L., & Brady, H.E. (1995). *Voice and equality: Civic voluntarism in American politics.* Cambridge, MA: Harvard University Press.

Youniss, J., McLellan, J.A., & Yates, M. (1997). What we know about engendering civic identity. *American Behavioral Scientist, 40,* 620–631.

CHAPTER 10

CLASSROOM ASSESSMENT OF CIVIC DISCOURSE

David E. Harris

INTRODUCTION

The importance of civic discourse has been emphasized in the scholarship of social studies education. In recent years, emphasis has been placed on oral discourse. We have been urged, for example, to dedicate ourselves to "public talk" as an essential element of the curriculum and to assess the quality of oral discourse produced by students (Barber, 1989; Newmann, 1992; Parker, 1989).

The rationale for oral discourse about public issues is manifold. First, it facilitates the learning of social studies content. The effort to produce coherent language in response to a question of public policy puts disciplinary knowledge in a meaningful context, making it more likely to be understood and remembered. Second, dialogue among students reinforces the development of social perspectives considered fundamental to democratic citizenship, especially tolerance or taking the role of another. This kind of reciprocal thinking, the persistent effort to anticipate the perspective of another, fosters more than communication; it is the essence of moral sensitivity. Third, intelligent conversation promotes reflection crucial to the preservation of democratic values such as consent of the governed, individual liberty, equality under law and, more recently, economic prosperity within the world economy. Fourth, when thoughtfully engaged in conversations about public issues, students are building not only substantive knowledge but also higher order thinking abilities. They use complex language to express their ideas. They must speak not in single words or short phrases but in sentences and paragraphs; they share ideas that are not scripted or controlled, as in teacher-led recitation; they must explain themselves, ask questions, and respond directly to comments of previous speakers.

Significant progress has been made in assessing students' persuasive writing on civic issues (Newmann, 1990), but there has been nothing comparable for oral discourse. Resnick and Resnick (1991) conclude that "what is taught and what is tested are intimately related" (p. 58) and that "You get what you assess" (p. 59). If it follows that we do not get what we do not assess, we are unlikely to produce students who can participate constructively in group discussions of public issues without new assessments which gauge their ability to do so.

This chapter presents a guide for evaluating students' performance in small group discussions of public issues. It integrates the knowledge, skill, and valuing goals of social studies, is grounded in the theory and practice of teaching public issues (Oliver & Shaver, 1966/1974), and is designed for convenient use by classroom teachers. Data collected with the tools of this guide could be used for improving instruction, for assessing individual student achievement, or as part of larger scale social studies program evaluations. Field testing of the guide has been conducted with social studies students and teachers in a small number of Michigan middle schools and high schools. Presentation of the guide is followed by an evaluation of the guide itself using standards from the School Restructuring Study (Newmann & Associates, 1996).

PERFORMANCE CRITERIA
FOR DISCUSSION OF A PUBLIC ISSUE

This discussion assessment guide attempts to identify a set of valid criteria for evaluating the performance of individual students during small group discussion of a public issue. These criteria are derived from the tradition of teaching public issues dating back three decades to the Harvard Social Studies Project which emphasized classroom discussion of controversial public issues (Oliver & Newmann, 1967). The goal of discussion in this tradition is to engage students in substantive conversation that enables each of them to make progress toward constructing a thoughtful position on a question of public policy. Although the emphasis of this guide is on scoring the performance of individuals, their scores could be used collectively to assess the performance of groups as well.

An underlying assumption of the scoring scheme presented in this guide is that students have extensive opportunity to practice discussion before being assessed. Practice would consist of both whole-class teacher-led discussions and discussions among small groups of students. In the context of these discussions, students would learn the assessment criteria and work to improve both their individual and group performances. Teachers would model the kinds of statements implied by the criteria and highlight them when demonstrated by students. Eventually, except for its purpose, small group discussion of a public issue as a learning activity would become indistinguishable from a comparable assessment task.

The discussion of a public issue has both substantive and procedural aspects. We want students to know about the issue and to know how to discuss it productively with classmates. A good performance blends the two. The criteria in this guide are therefore divided into two categories. The substantive criteria pertain to students' understanding of the issue, and the procedural criteria pertain to their ability to engage one another in conversation about it. These criteria are listed as performance criteria in Figure 1.

SUBSTANTIVE	PROCEDURAL
• Stating and Identifying Issues • Using Disciplinary Knowledge • Elaborating Statements with Explanations, Reasons, or Evidence • Stipulating Claims or Definitions • Recognizing Values or Value Conflict • Arguing by Analogy	**Positive** • Inviting Contributions from Others • Acknowledging the Statements of Others • Challenging the Accuracy, Logic, Relevance, or Clarity of Statements • Summarizing Points of Agreement and Disagreement **Negative** • Irrelevant Distracting Statements • Obstructive Interruption • Monopolizing • Personal Attack

Figure 1. Assessing discussion of public issues: Performance criteria.

What follows is a brief description of each criterion with an example to illustrate it. The examples are drawn from a hypothetical discussion by high school students of a persisting public policy issue on the national agenda as of this writing: Should homosexuals be allowed to serve in the armed forces of the United States?

Substantive Criteria

Stating and Identifying Issues

To satisfy this criterion, a student must either state an issue not yet raised in the discussion or identify an issue that has been implied. An issue is a matter of dispute or uncertainty posed as an unresolved question. Public issue discussions revolve around a central policy issue which often entails three subordinate types of issues: ethical, definitional, and factual. If the policy issue has been stated prior to the discussion, merely repeating it during the discussion would not satisfy this criterion.

A policy issue is the overarching focus that guides the entire discussion. The main purpose of the discussion is to work collaboratively toward resolution of the policy issue. It is a question about a matter of governance that requires collective decision making in an arena of citizenship and subsequent action to advance the decision. It can be local, regional, national, or international in scope. In our example the policy issue is national: Should homosexuals be allowed to serve in the armed services of the United States?

Discussions of public policy issues usually involve subordinate ethical, factual, and definitional issues. Productive dialogue cannot occur if students jump mindlessly from one issue to another. In the process of resolving the broader policy issue, it is necessary, deliberately and systematically, to consider other issues embedded within it. An ethical issue poses a fairness question or a question of right or wrong. It asks for a value judgment of what ought to be. A definitional issue poses a question about the meaning of a key concept or term. It serves to clarify ambiguity. A factual issue poses an empirical question regarding what is or was. It asks for a claim that can be verified with evidence. The diagram in Figure 2 presents a taxonomy for discussion of public issues.

Classroom Assessment of Civic Discourse

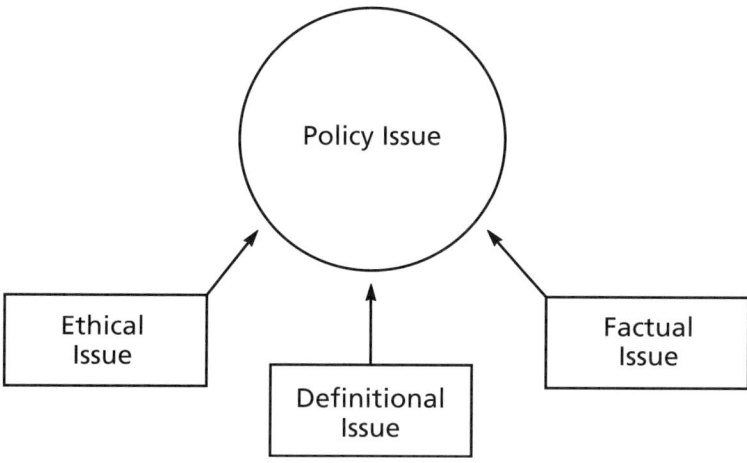

Figure 2. Types of issues.

The three dialogue excerpts below provide examples, respectively, of (1) an ethical, (2) a definitional, and (3) a factual issue:

(1) **Aretha**: People really seem to disagree strongly about whether gays should serve in the military.
 Bob: There have always been gay soldiers and sailors, but most of them have kept quiet about it.
 Cleo: The question is not whether homosexuals have secretly served in the past. That's not at issue. Everyone agrees they have. The question is whether it is fair to exclude someone from military service based on sexual orientation. Do gays have a right to serve their country? (ethical issue)

(2) **Aretha**: Homosexuals might undermine the morale of the fighting force. Their deviant behavior could be upsetting to the majority of those serving.
 Bob: What do you mean by deviant behavior? (definitional issue) Does deviant mean conduct merely different from what most people do, or does it have to be harmful to others?

(3) **Aretha**: Being near people of the same sex with an amorous attraction to you makes many heterosexuals uncomfortable. If homosexuals want to join the armed services, they should first change their behavior.
 Cleo: Can they? I don't know if it's possible. Is sexual orientation learned behavior or is it genetically determined? (factual issue) I think we have to resolve that question

before we can determine what kind of behavior to expect of people.

Using Disciplinary Knowledge

To satisfy this criterion, a student must demonstrate understanding of significant ideas relevant to the issue under discussion; that is, key facts or concepts from pertinent academic disciplines. The understanding expressed would be deep rather than shallow and free of obvious inaccuracies or misconceptions. Each of the three following statements presents an example of using disciplinary knowledge:

(1) **Aretha**: If homosexuals are permitted to serve openly in the armed forces, there will be problems with the Uniform Code of Military Justice which is a separate set of laws that applies only to those in the armed forces. Several parts of the code would have to be adjusted if the ban on gays is lifted, like who you can live with, or what you can do while on duty or wearing a uniform, or who you can claim as dependents.

(2) **Bob**: Not all groups in society are protected under current federal law. Congress intended the civil rights acts to protect people from discrimination based on race, religion, gender, or national origin, but not on sexual orientation.

(3) **Cleo**: Unless heterosexuals are falsely claiming that they are gay in order to get out of the service with an honorable discharge, the current Pentagon policy of "don't ask, don't tell" seems to be driving homosexuals out of the armed forces. The number of military personnel discharged for homosexual activity or for stating they are gay or lesbian rose 17 percent from 1999 to 2000. That is the highest number since 1993 when the new policy went into effect. Since then the rate of expulsion of gay service members has doubled (Sullivan, 2001).

Elaborating Statements With Explanations, Reasons, Or Evidence

To satisfy this criterion, a student would have to make a claim and provide a basis of support for it. The claim might be a position on an issue, or a relevant ethical judgment, or a statement of fact. A position on an issue would be supported with an explanation; an ethical judgment would be supported by reasons; and a factual claim would be verified with evidence. The three dialogue excerpts below provide examples of supporting a claim with (1) an explanation, (2) reasons, and (3) evidence:

(1) **Aretha**: We have been reading and talking about this issue for two days. Is anybody ready to take a stand?

Bob: I think the present policy should continue. Openly gay individuals should be banned from the armed forces. I have been thinking about what was said about equal rights and about the good records of homosexuals who have served with distinction. But, for several reasons I don't think the current ban should be lifted. A majority of those currently serving believe the change would lower morale. Many say they will quit the service if gays are allowed to serve openly. Some prominent military leaders, including prominent Gulf War commander General Norman Schwartzkopf, believe that admitting gays will undermine the primary mission of the armed forces—readiness to fight. And there is also the point about invading the privacy of heterosexuals. (explaining a position on the policy issue)

(2) **Aretha**: Will the presence of homosexuals violate the privacy rights of heterosexuals?

Bob: Not if men and women live in separate barracks.

Cleo: Separating people by gender would not ensure privacy. People are packed very tightly in army barracks and on naval ships. In the shower or in the sleeping quarters of a submarine there is little privacy. Men or women, even if separated by gender, would still be exposed to the unwelcome glances of gays or lesbians.

Aretha: I think admitting homosexuals would violate the privacy rights of heterosexuals. There is no grouping possible to protect privacy—men with men, women with women, men with women, even gays with gays. When you join the military, you are entitled to a reasonable expectation of privacy. No one should be placed in circumstances where they are the unwilling object of someone's sexual attention. (supporting an ethical judgment with reasons)

(3) **Aretha**: If the ban on openly gay service men and women is lifted, there will be more sexual misconduct in the armed forces.

Bob: Do homosexuals commit sexual assaults more than heterosexuals?

Cleo: Not according to a Pentagon study cited in the federal district court decision from California that we read. The rate of such offenses is higher for heterosexuals than homosexuals in the armed services. Furthermore, look at what the Tailhook scandal suggests about male sailors sexually harassing females. The evidence we have does not support the claim that gays in the military will cause an increase in sexual misconduct. (supporting a factual claim with evidence)

Stipulating Claims Or Definitions

To satisfy this criterion, a student must stipulate a resolution to an ethical, definitional or factual issue. Stipulation means offering a tentative answer to be accepted at least temporarily in order to move the discussion forward. Stipulations are usually offered when there is no consensus on an issue and the information necessary for resolution is not readily available. To prevent the discussion from getting bogged down and for the sake of argument, a statement can be stipulated to see where it leads. The three dialogue excerpts below present examples, respectively, of stipulating (1) an ethical claim, (2) the definition of a term, and (3) a factual statement:

(1)   **Aretha**: Several times equal rights have been mentioned. We keep asking whether heterosexuals and homosexuals should have the same rights.

          Bob: Let's assume, for the time being, that people are entitled to be treated equally regardless of sexual orientation. (stipulating an ethical claim)

(2)   **Aretha**: Former President Clinton and others have argued that restrictions on serving in the armed forces should be based on conduct. He says it should be what you do not who you are.

          Bob: What is conduct? Would telling someone you are gay be conduct? Would reading a gay magazine?

          Cleo: This is difficult. I have trouble distinguishing between thought, expression, and conduct.

          Aretha: Let's say that conduct means expressed behavior. It can be spoken or written or other kinds of action, but it can't be merely unexpressed thoughts or feelings. Also, let's agree for our discussion that conduct refers to behavior while on military duty or while off-duty but in uniform. (stipulating a definition)

(3)   **Aretha**: Some people are worried that the military will be overwhelmed by homosexuals, that they will take over and change the culture of the armed services.

          Bob: That fear exaggerates the number of homosexuals in society.

Cleo: How many are there? I keep hearing that 10% of the population is homosexual.
Bob: That figure is based on the Kinsey studies of nearly half a century ago. More recent studies indicate a much lower percentage. *Time* magazine reports that a better estimate is well under 5%. For purposes of our discussion, let's assume that between 2% and 4% of the population is homosexual. (stipulating a fact)
Cleo: O.K., if we use that figure, how does it affect our thinking about the policy issue?

Recognizing Values or Value Conflict

To satisfy this criterion, a student must identify a core democratic value that has emerged in the discussion or a clash between two or more such values. Core democratic values are concepts that represent the ethical beliefs underlying a democratic society, for example: religious liberty, free expression, equality, fair procedure, property rights, respect for diversity, limited government, and majority rule. These values serve as criteria when citizens make judgments about matters of public concern. Although generally held in common, they are sometimes a source of conflict. The main dispute over policy issues often arises from differences in meaning that people attach to these values or from differences in the priority attached to them. The two dialogue excerpts that follow illustrate, respectively, (1) recognition of a democratic value, and (2) identification of a value conflict:

(1)   **Aretha**: Our main purpose for having military forces is to defend the country from enemies. The issue of the ban on gays should be decided according to its effect on this mission. What effect does the ban have on the readiness of the armed forces to fight?
           Bob: You seem to be saying that the deciding factor should be national security. (recognizing a democratic value)
(2)   **Aretha**: This issue requires us to choose between values.
           Bob: Which values?
           Cleo: On the one hand we value equality which means all citizens should have an equal opportunity to serve their country. We also believe in the right to privacy as a basic liberty which means people have a right to control both information they receive and the distribution of information about themselves. These two values seem to clash over the issue of homosexuals in the military. We have to decide which of these values should have priority in this case. (identifying a value conflict)

Arguing by Analogy

To satisfy this criterion, a student must draw a parallel between the issue under discussion and a similar case. An analogy should entail more than a superficial resemblance. The likeness must be deep and logically related. Analogies are often made to establish or challenge the consistency of an ethical argument. The dialogue excerpt below illustrates this type of analogical reasoning:

> **Aretha**: Maybe gays should be banned from the military for their own protection. If they serve openly, they might become the victims of violent attacks from those who are prejudiced against them.
> **Bob**: That sounds like a "heckler's veto" to me. It gives violent bigots control over public policy. Those who threaten to harm the innocent should be excluded, not their victims.
> **Cleo**: That reminds me of President Truman's policy of racial integration of the armed forces. There were many prejudiced Whites who did not want Blacks to serve with them. Some threatened to do them harm. If it's right to ban gays because some dislike their sexual orientation, then it would have been right to segregate Blacks because some despised their race. (analogy)

Positive Procedural Criteria

Inviting Contributions From Others

To satisfy this criterion, a student would have to elicit the thinking of a classmate. The purpose of the invitation would be to draw someone else into the discussion and to broaden participation. The invitation validates the worth of everyone's contribution to the discussion. The following dialogue excerpt illustrates such an invitation to participate:

> **Aretha**: We have been discussing this issue for some time now. I am still trying to make up my mind. I'm not sure yet where I stand. I know that Bob supports keeping the current ban and that Cleo thinks it should be lifted. Both of them have presented their reasons, and they know why they disagree. We haven't heard from you yet, Dawn. Do you agree with Bob or with Cleo? (Invitation)

Acknowledging the Statements of Others

To satisfy this criterion, a student must respond to a statement made by another student in a way that builds a consecutive interchange between them. The reply should be responsive to the statement and indicate that the student understood it and thought about it. The following dialogue excerpt illustrates this type of response:

> **Aretha**: If I were homosexual, I wouldn't want to be part of an organization where I wasn't welcome.
>
> **Bob**: That is your personal attitude, Aretha, but how do you think your feelings about rejection pertain to the policy decision to be made here? (acknowledgment and response)

Challenging the Accuracy, Logic, Relevance, Or Clarity of Statements

To satisfy this criterion, a student must respond to the statement of another student by respectfully suggesting that it is inaccurate, illogical, irrelevant, or unclear. The nature of the challenge should be stated and an invitation to respond to it should be extended. In the example below, the challenge is directed at the logic of a statement:

> **Aretha**: Some people support the ban out of fear of AIDS. Frankly, I am sympathetic. The rate of AIDS among homosexuals is higher than among heterosexuals.
>
> **Bob**: You have a good point. If gays are excluded, AIDS is less likely to spread in the armed forces.
>
> **Cleo**: Yes, but it's possible to protect men and women in the service from AIDS without banning homosexuals. Blood testing would do it. We could exclude those who test HIV positive, whatever their sexual orientation. It doesn't follow that the ban on gays is necessary to prevent the spread of AIDS in the armed forces. Do you agree with my logic? (logical challenge)

Summarizing Points of Agreement and Disagreement

To satisfy this criterion, a student would present at least a partial summary of points discussed and their disposition in the discussion so far. A summary clarifies where the discussion has been and sets the stage for it to move forward. The dialogue excerpt below illustrates this type of summary:

> **Aretha**: This can get very confusing. I'm not sure what I believe any more. There are so many issues and there is so much disagreement.

> **Bob**: For quite a while now we have been grappling with an ethical issue: Is it fair to treat homosexuals differently than heterosexuals? We agreed that it is an issue involving the value of equality. We also agreed that the value of privacy seems to conflict with the value of equality, and that we might have to choose between them to resolve this issue. We also agreed that everyone has an equal right to serve the country. The consensus broke down, however, when Aretha said that national security should take precedence over equal rights, because without it there will be no protection of anyone's rights. We have not yet resolved whether or not gays serving in the military poses a threat to national security. (summary)

Negative Procedural Criteria

Irrelevant Distracting Statements

This criterion would be met if a student made a statement that obviously did not pertain to the issue and tended to derail the discussion. It could be deliberately or inadvertently distracting. The two examples below illustrate such statements:

(1) **Aretha**: The real problem with the military is the volunteer army. Do you think there should be a draft?

(2) **Bob**: Could we talk about something that isn't so boring, like where people are partying after the game?

Obstructive Interruption

This criterion is met when a student cuts off what another student has started to say preventing the statement from being completed and impeding the progress of the discussion. Only obstructive interruptions that rudely seize the floor for oneself apply here. Some interruptions, made congenially, might be attempts to get a person to be more relevant or brief and would be constructive. An obstructive interruption is readily apparent when it occurs, so no example is provided here to illustrate.

Monopolizing

This criterion is met when one student repeatedly dominates the discussion with the effect of preventing others from contributing. It would not be the result of a single statement but rather a pattern of overpowering others by not yielding the floor. It becomes evident when one student does a conspicuously disproportionate share of the talking. Less assertive students consequently withdraw or show reluctance to speak because they have been intimidated by a vocally dominating classmate. No example of monopolizing is provided because it is best detected through direct observation and is difficult to capture in a transcript.

Personal Attack

This criterion is met when a student offensively criticizes another student. This type of personal assault or insult should be distinguished from a legitimate challenge to someone's argument. The personal attack is abusive and is likely to hurt the feelings of the person targeted. Two examples follow:

(1) **Aretha**: Bob, you said you were worried about government promoting a homosexual lifestyle, that it threatens the stability of family life. That's a stupid idea! There is no such thing as a homosexual lifestyle. They have as many different lifestyles as heterosexuals. I'm sick of your stereotypes!

(2) **Bob**: Dawn, you hardly say anything, and when you do, it doesn't make much sense.

ASSESSING STUDENTS' PERFORMANCE

The Assessment Task

The performance criteria elaborated above can be embodied coherently in an assessment task to be performed by students. A format for creating assessment tasks designed for use in Michigan schools is presented here to illustrate how participating in a small group discussion of a public issue might be laid out as an assessment task. Although the format is adopted here for the task of discussing a public issue, it has been designed to be a generic tool for uniform formatting of any assessment task. This format is also used in *Powerful and Authentic Social Studies (PASS): A Professional Development Program for Teachers* (Harris & Yocum, 2000).

The format consists of five components for describing an assessment task. Each of these components is presented below for the task of participating in a small group discussion of a public issue.

Abstract

This task assesses a student's ability to participate constructively and thoughtfully in a discussion of a public issue with 5–6 classmates. The policy issue selected as an example for the task is: Should homosexuals be allowed to serve in the armed forces of the United States? Students inform themselves about the history of the issue and record a videotape of their small group's discussion. The teacher assesses the performance of each student in the discussion using an established set of performance criteria for classroom oral civic discourse.

Prompt

Prior to being assigned this task, students have participated in a whole class discussion of the issue of gays in the military. In preparation for that discussion students were assigned readings selected to present opposing views on the issue. To activate their prior knowledge of the issue and to provide additional information for performance of this assessment task two prompts are provided. The first is the seven-page decision of the U.S. District Court for the Eastern District of New York in a case involving a challenge to the "don't ask, don't tell" policy by a member of the armed forces discharged under the policy: *Able v. United States,* 847 F. Supp. 1038 (E. D. N. Y. 1994). The second prompt is a Stanford University Law School moot court transcript with briefs for petitioner and respondents in the hypothetical appellate case of *Ewing and Sloane v. The United States Department of Defense,* available online under the title "Don't Ask, Don't Tell, Don't Pursue" (http://dont.stanford.edu/moot/moot.htm). This case involves two members of the armed services expelled under the current policy. The teacher might want to select other readings that present opposing views on the issue as prompts for the assessment task.

Directions to Students

"We have been deliberating about the issue of whether homosexuals should be allowed to serve in the armed forces of the United States. You are now going to discuss the issue with five classmates. Your discussion will be videotaped, and I will use the videotape to evaluate your individual performance."

"Check the listing of discussion groups posted in the classroom to identify the members of your small group. Consult with the other members of the group to set a 45-minute block of time for your discussion. Schedule the block of time in the library to use a conference room and video camera. Bring a blank videotape to the discussion. Identify a member of your group to set the camera at a fixed position on its tripod so that it captures the faces of all members of the group and audibly records everything that is said. See the media specialist for help in operating the camera if it is needed. Your group may choose to record the discussion outside of school if appropriate equipment is available and permission is granted."

"Prepare for the discussion in advance. Read the materials from the two cases provided (*Abel v. United States; Ewing and Sloane v. The United States Department of Defense*) to stimulate your thinking about the issue. Also, review the performance criteria for a good discussion of a public issue distributed in class. Your individual performance in the discussion will be evaluated using these performance criteria. See the scoring guide posted for this task for more details about the criteria that will be used to evaluate your discussion performance."

"Remember that this is not a debate. The purpose of the discussion is not to impose your position on others but to clarify the issue and evaluate various positions. Be sure that all members of your discussion group have an opportunity to express their thinking during the discussion. As a result of the discussion you should be better prepared to express your individual position on the issue, and to support it with evidence, democratic values, and logical reasoning."

"Your videotape should be no longer than 30 minutes. It is due in class one week from today."

Procedure

The performance of a student can be evaluated while directly observing a small group discussion or afterward if the discussion is recorded. When direct observation is used, a trained scorer silently observes the discussion and records impressions at the close of the discussion. When the discussion is videotaped, as in this instance, a trained scorer, presumably the teacher, records impressions after viewing the videotape. During the videotaping, the teacher need not be present and the discussion need not take place in the regular classroom. Because students can be trained to record videotapes of their discussions, and the teacher can work with the rest of the class while one or more small group discussions are being recorded, the videotape method might prove more practical than direct observation.

Whether the discussion is directly observed or videotaped, the number of students participating should be small enough to provide sufficient opportunity for all members of the group to express their thinking. A group of 5–6 students is recommended with the discussion lasting up to 30 minutes. The amount of time might be shorter for elementary school students.

Begin the assessment task by preparing and distributing a copy of both prompts to students. Assign each student to a small discussion group of six. Post the names of students in each group in the classroom. Make arrangements with the librarian/media specialist for students to reserve 45-minute blocks of time during or after school to record their discussions in a library conference room.

Arrange for a video camera on a tripod with appropriate microphone to be available in the conference room and for a technician to be available if students need help operating the recording equipment. Read the assessment task directions to students and post a copy in the classroom. Also, post a copy of the scoring rubric. Respond to any questions students have about the assessment task assignment.

Scoring Rubric

The scoring rubric (Figure 3) is used to determine a rating for the performance of each student as a discussion participant. On the scoring sheet (Figure 4), a rater enters a score for each student using the five-point scale presented in the rubric: 1 = Unsatisfactory, 2 = Minimal, 3 = Adequate, 4 = Effective, and 5 = Exemplary. The scoring rubric presented is intended for high school students. The standards of performance could be appropriately lowered for younger students while maintaining both the performance criteria and the five point rating scale.

The overarching consideration in scoring is the degree to which a student's contribution to the conversation clarifies the policy issue being considered and helps the group make progress toward resolution. Three elements of performance focus the assessment: whether or not the student has (a) presented accurate knowledge related to the policy issue, (b) employed skills for stating and pursuing related issues, and (c) engaged others in constructive dialogue. A student's contribution to the conversation receives one of five scores:

UNSATISFACTORY (1)
The student has failed to express any relevant foundational knowledge and has neither stated nor elaborated on any issues.

MINIMAL (2)
The student has stated a relevant factual, ethical, or definitional issue as a question or has accurately expressed relevant foundational knowledge pertaining to an issue raised.

ADEQUATE (3)
The student has accurately expressed relevant foundational knowledge pertaining to an issue raised during the discussion and has pursued an issue by making a statement with an explanation, reasons, or evidence.

EFFECTIVE (4)
The student has accurately expressed relevant foundational knowledge pertaining to an issue raised during the discussion, pursued an issue with at least one elaborated statement and, in a civil manner, has built upon a statement made by someone else or thoughtfully challenged its accuracy, clarity, relevance, or logic.

EXEMPLARY (5)
The student has accurately expressed relevant foundational knowledge pertaining to an issue raised during the discussion, pursued an issue with an elaborated statement, and has used stipulation, valuing, or analogy to advance the discussion. In addition, the student has engaged others in the discussion by inviting their comments or acknowledging their contributions. Further, the student has built upon a statement made by someone else or thoughtfully challenged its accuracy, clarity, relevance, or logic.

Figure 3. Assessing discussion of public issues: Scoring rubric.

> Enter a student's name and then make a check mark (✓) to indicate the student's score.
>
> Student: _____
>
> | UNSATISFACTORY (1) | MINIMAL (2) | ADEQUATE (3) | EFFECTIVE (4) | EXEMPLARY (5) |
> |---|---|---|---|---|
> | | | | | |
>
> Student: _____
>
> | UNSATISFACTORY (1) | MINIMAL (2) | ADEQUATE (3) | EFFECTIVE (4) | EXEMPLARY (5) |
> |---|---|---|---|---|
> | | | | | |

Figure 4. Assessing discussion of public issues: Scoring sheet.

Validity and Reliability of Scoring

Training would be required before a teacher could use the scoring rubric with confidence. The training would begin with an introduction to the performance criteria and their definitions as presented in the preceding section of this chapter. After raters are clear about the meaning of each criterion, they are introduced to the scoring rubric.

Once acquainted with the performance criteria and scoring rubric, teachers being trained are ready to view an actual videotape of a student discussion. Two viewings will be necessary at first, one to get oriented to the discussion topic and the students, and a second to attend carefully to the performance of each student. Following the second viewing, raters record a score for each student on the scoring sheet. When determining their ratings, teachers should appeal to the descriptors for performances characterized as Unsatisfactory, Minimal, Adequate, Effective, or Exemplary as presented in the scoring rubric. When raters disagree about a rating, they should refer to these descriptors again in an effort to resolve the disagreement.

Additional videotapes should be used as needed for teacher trainees to reach agreement in their ratings. To help work toward agreement, one or more videotapes, previously rated by experts, could be used to present prototypical performances for each of the five ratings. As an additional training aid, the generic descriptions for each rating presented in the scoring rubric could be elaborated to include specific statements students might make when discussing a particular policy issue.

Agreement among raters is important for establishing reliability. Are the ratings consistent among scorers? Is the rating given by one teacher the same as that given by another? The answers to these questions must be "yes" if we are to have confidence that the ratings are reliable. Teachers must be able to report to students, parents, school officials, and the public that these ratings are not arbitrary claims based on subjective whims. Scores of various teachers should be periodically compared and the degree of agreement should be examined.

There are various ways to establish reliability. One I recommend is to determine the percentage of agreement among raters simply by calculating the percentage of students who receive the same score from two scorers. The expectation is that they would agree at least three-fourths of the time. Beyond this reliability standard of 75% agreement, we add the requirement that when raters do disagree, most of the time (75%) the disagreement is no more than one point on the five-point rating scale. An alternative reliability standard that could be used is agreement 75% of the time with scores assigned by an expert (with disagreement, when it occurs, no more than one point 75% of the time). Once either of these standards of reliability has been met, the training of teachers as qualified raters is complete.

For larger-scale program assessments, where small groups are sampled from the classes of several different teachers, possibly from different schools, three raters would be desirable to enhance reliability. Each rater scores each student independently. If all three ratings were the same, the common rating would be entered (for example, ratings of 2, 2, and 2 would be scored as 2). If two ratings were the same and the third rating discrepant by only one point, the discrepant rating would be eliminated (for example, ratings of 1, 1, and 2 would be scored as 1). If there were ratings of three consecutive points, the middle rating would be entered (for example, ratings of 2, 3, and 4 would be scored as 3). The only remaining possibility would be three different ratings separated by more than two points. In that case, the midpoint between the highest and lowest rating would be entered.

Standards for Authentic Assessment

One way to gauge the quality of this assessment of classroom civic discourse is to determine whether it meets a set of research-based standards for authentic assessment intended to raise the intellectual quality of teaching and learning. These standards are taken from the national School Restructuring Study (Newmann & Associates, 1996). That study posed a vision of *authentic achievement* which refers to intellectual accomplishments that are worthwhile, significant, and meaningful, such as those demonstrated by accomplished adults in their personal, work, or civic lives.

Authentic achievement in schools involves students (a) in construction of knowledge (b) through disciplined inquiry (c) that has value beyond school. Students construct or produce meaningful knowledge, rather than merely reproduce it. They express this knowledge in written and oral discourse, by making and repairing things, and in performances for audiences. When engaged in disciplined inquiry, students use an established knowledge base, strive for deep understanding of a major concept or problem, and express conclusions through elaborated communication. Authentic student achievements have value beyond school when they have practical impact apart from documenting the competence of the learner, i.e., they are useful beyond being an indicator of success in school.

A set of seven standards for authentic assessment tasks was derived from these three general criteria for authentic achievement. The national study found that when classroom assessment tasks met these standards, the academic achievement of students was raised significantly (Newmann and Associates, 1996). The study also discovered that it is rare for teachers' assessment tasks to meet these standards. A goal of educational reform compellingly implied by the School Restructuring Study is to build teachers' capacity to employ classroom assessment tasks that meet these standards. The assessment task posed in this chapter for assessing civic discourse serves that goal, because it scores relatively high on the seven standards for authentic assessment:

> *Standard 1—Organization of Information.* To meet this standard a task asks students to organize, synthesize, interpret, explain, or evaluate complex information in addressing a concept, problem, or issue. The discussion of public issues assessment task asks students to interpret current policy, to explain its intent and consequences, and to evaluate whether the policy is effective and whether it comports with constitutional values.
>
> *Standard 2—Consideration of Alternatives.* To meet this standard a task asks students to consider alternative solutions, strategies, perspectives, or points of view in addressing a concept, problem, or issue. The assessment task of discussing gays in the military as a public issue asks students to consider opposing views on the issue. In deciding whether to support or oppose the current ban on homosexuals serving openly in the armed forces, students weigh arguments of both proponents and opponents of the policy.

Standard 3—Disciplinary Content. To meet this standard a task asks students to show understanding and/or to use ideas, theories, or perspectives considered central to an academic or professional discipline. The assessment task of engaging in civic discourse about current military personnel policy asks students to consider numerous concepts central to the discipline of political science, for example democratic values and constitutionality.

Standard 4—Disciplinary Process. To meet this standard a task asks students to use methods of inquiry, research, or communication characteristic of an academic or professional discipline. When students analyze court decisions and apply their analyses to taking a stand on the issue, they are engaged in the kind of jurisprudential inquiry characteristic of the study and practice of law. Further, analogical reasoning, a feature of law-related inquiry, is employed by students to express their thinking about the issue.

Standard 5—Elaborated Communication. To meet this standard a task asks students to elaborate on their understanding, explanations, or conclusions through extended writing or speaking. This public issue discussion assessment task asks students to engage each other in thoughtful dialogue. They must speak to one another not in single words or short phrases but in sentences and paragraphs that probe deeply into a controversial public issue. They express their own thinking and invite each other to explain their ideas.

Standard 6—Problem Connected to the World Beyond the Classroom. To meet this standard a task asks students to address a concept, problem, or issue that is similar to one that they have encountered or are likely to encounter in life beyond the classroom. Discussion of public issues is a responsibility for citizens of a democratic society. Students will be called upon to participate in this type of discourse whenever they confront issues of governance, whether for the nation, on a matter of international or multinational policy, on a municipal or state referendum, or for governing a religious community, union, professional association, or other civil society group to which they belong. Moreover, the issue of gays in the military is a real and persisting matter of public concern that all citizens are likely to encounter on the public agenda.

Standard 7—Audience Beyond the School. To meet this standard a task asks students to communicate their knowledge, present a product or performance, or take some action for an audience beyond the teacher, classroom, and school building. The recorded discussion of this civic discourse assessment task does not directly meet this standard. Students' discussions are observed only by students and their teacher. The task does pave the way, however, for students to express their view on a public issue in writing to a public official, possibly a member of Congress. A sequel to the oral discourse assessment might be to have students write a persuasive essay expressing and justifying their position on the issue that could be sent to policy makers.

CONCLUSION

I have presented a guide for evaluating students' performance in small group discussion of public issues and followed that with an evaluation of the guide against standards for authentic assessment that are intended to raise the intellectual quality of teaching and learning in schools. The overarching justification for the guide is to teach students to engage in and make constructive contributions to face-to-face discussions of public controversies. The criteria for assessing student performance presented in the guide have content validity in that they depict what competent citizens actually do when they converse thoughtfully about public issues in a democratic society. The guide also has external validity, because it performs well against standards for assessment tasks that represent authentic intellectual work by accomplished adults. Given its validity, the guide can be used with confidence as an authentic assessment tool to promote robust and civil discussion of public issues by young people.

ACKNOWLEDGMENT

This chapter is a much-revised version of my chapter, "Assessing Discussion of Public Issues," in R. W. Evans & D. W. Saxe (Eds.), *Handbook on Teaching Social Issues* (Washington, DC: National Council for the Social Studies, 1996, pp. 288–297). Adapted with permission of the publisher.

REFERENCES

Barber, B.R. (1989). Public talk and civic action: Education for participation in a strong democracy. *Social Education, 53*, 355–370.
Harris, D., & Yocum, M. (2000). *Powerful and authentic social studies (PASS): A professional development program for teachers.* Washington, DC: National Council for the Social Studies.
Newmann, F.M. (1990). A test of higher order thinking in social studies: Persuasive writing on constitutional issues using the NAEP approach. *Social Education, 54*, 369–373.

Newmann, F.M. (1992). The assessment of discourse in social studies. In A.R. Tom (Ed.), *Toward a new science of educational testing and assessment.* Albany: State University of New York Press.

Newmann, F.M., & Associates. (1996). *Authentic achievement: Restructuring schools for intellectual quality.* San Francisco: Jossey-Bass.

Oliver, D.W., & Newmann F.N. (1967). *Taking a stand: A guide to clear discussion of public issues.* Middletown: Xerox Corporation/American Education Publications.

Oliver, D.W., & Shaver, J.P. (1974). *Teaching public issues in the high school.* Logan: Utah State University Press (original work published 1966).

Parker, W.C. (1989). Participatory citizenship: Civics in the strong sense. *Social Education, 53,* 353–354.

Resnick, L.B., & Resnick, D.P. (1991). Assessing the thinking curriculum: New tools for educational reform. In B.R. Gifford, & M.C. O'Connor (Eds.), *Changing assessments: Alternative views of aptitude, achievement, and instruction* (pp. 37–75). Boston: Kluwer Academic Publishers.

Sullivan, A. (2001, June 17). They also served. *The New York Times Magazine,* 13–14.

CONTRIBUTORS

Patricia G. Avery is Professor of Education at the University of Minnesota, Twin Cities. Her research on political socialization and civic education has been published in numerous journals, including *Social Education, Theory and Research in Social Education, The Social Studies, Theory into Practice,* and *American Educational Research Journal.*

James A. Banks is Russell F. Stark University Professor and Director of the Center for Multicultural Education at the University of Washington, Seattle. His books include *Cultural Diversity and Education: Foundations, Curriculum, and Teaching* (2001), *Teaching Strategies for the Social Studies* (1999), *Educating Citizens in a Multicultural Society* (1997), and *Teaching Strategies for Ethnic Studies* (1997).

John J. Cogan is Professor of Education at the University of Minnesota where he focuses upon citizenship education within a comparative and international education framework. His work has been published in numerous journals, including *Social Education, American Educational Research Journal,* and *Comparative Education Review.* He is the co-editor of *Citizenship for the 21st Century* (1998, 2000) and *Civic Education in the Asia-Pacific Region* (2002).

Elizabeth Frazer is Lecturer in Politics, Department of Politics, University of Oxford, and Official Fellow and Tutor in Politics, New College, Oxford. She is the author of *Problems of Communitarian Politics: Unity and Conflict* (1999), has published a number of articles on political education, and is currently working on the problem of "what politics ought to be."

Carole L. Hahn is Professor of Educational Studies at Emory University in Atlanta where she teaches social studies education and comparative education. Her publications include "Student Views of Democracy: The Good and Bad News," *Social Education* (November/December, 2001), and *Becoming Political: Comparative Perspectives on Citizenship Education* (1998).

David E. Harris, previously the social studies education specialist for the local school districts of Oakland County, Michigan, is currently Professor of Educational Practice at the University of Michigan in Ann Arbor. He is co-author of *Reasoning With Democratic Values* (1985) and *Powerful and Authentic Social Studies—PASS* (2000).

Jennifer L. Hochschild is a Professor of Government at Harvard University, with a joint appointment in the Department of Afro-American Studies. Her books include *Facing Up to the American Dream: Race, Class, and the Soul of the Nation* (1995); *The New American Dilemma: Liberal Democracy and School Desegregation* (1984); and *The American Dream and the Public Schools*, co-authored with Nathan Scovronick (Oxford University Press, 2003).

Akira Ninomiya is Professor of Comparative and International Education at Hiroshima University, Japan, and the Director of the International Students Center. He is the author of *Schools in the World: From A Cross-Cultural Perspective* (1997) and has been involved in the Schooling for Tomorrow project. He is currently working on the internationalization of school curriculum and school education including higher education.

William A. Nixon is a Ph.D. candidate in American legal history at Indiana University, Bloomington. His current work includes an official history of the Court of Appeals of the State of Indiana.

Yoon K. Pak is Assistant Professor of Educational Policy Studies at the University of Illinois at Urbana-Champaign and a core faculty member of the University's Asian American Studies Program. An elaborated version of her chapter appears in Yoon K. Pak, *Wherever I Go, I Will Always Be A Loyal American* (2002).

Walter C. Parker is Professor of Education at the University of Washington, Seattle, where he chairs the Social Studies Education program. His books include *Democracy, Diversity, & Deliberation in Education: From Idiocy to Citizenship* (2002), *Social Studies in Elementary Education* (2001), and *Educating the Democratic Mind* (1996).

John J. Patrick is Professor of Education at Indiana University, where he is Director of the Social Studies Development Center. His recent publications include *The Supreme Court of the United States: A Student Companion* (2001), *The Oxford Guide to the United States Government* (2001), and *The Bill of Rights: A History in Documents* (2002).

Wendy Klandl Richardson is a doctoral candidate in Human Development (Educational Psychology) at the University of Maryland, College Park. She has worked on data from the IEA Civic Education Study in preparation for a dissertation on classroom discussion. She was previously a social studies teacher and has supervised Maryland preservice teachers.

Nathan Scovronick teaches education policy and directs the undergraduate program at the Woodrow Wilson School of Public and International Affairs at Princeton University. He served in several policy positions in the New Jersey state government, including Executive Director of the Treasury Department and Staff Director of the Senate Committee on Education.

Judith Torney-Purta is Professor of Human Development in the College of Education, University of Maryland, College Park. She chaired the International Steering Committee for the IEA Civic Education Study. Her books include *Citizenship and Education in Twenty-eight Countries: Civic Knowledge and Engagement at Age Fourteen* (2001) and *Civic Knowledge and Engagement at Age 17–18 in Sixteen Countries* (2002).

Thomas S. Vontz is Assistant Professor of Education at Rockhurst University in Kansas City, Missouri. He is the author of numerous articles and books on civic education including a research monograph, *Project Citizen and the Civic Development of Adolescent Students in Indiana, Latvia, and Lithuania* (2000).

INDEX

A

Adolescent beliefs about democracy survey study, 185–186, 208–209
  attitudes, 194–196
  engagement, 196–199
  knowledge, 189, 190f–192f, 193
  predicting factors (of knowledge/engagement), 199–200, 201f, 202
    important educational components, 202
  study overview, 187–188
    items in assessment, 188
    student sampling, 188
  and teacher beliefs/practices, 203
    content/objectives for civic education, 203–204, 205f–206f, 207
    instructional methods, 207–208
    sampling of teachers, 203
  see also Civic Education study (IEA)
American attitudes
  American dream, 4, 22n
  citizenship vs. U.K. attitudes, 32
  equitable school funding, 15
  group schooling claims, 11, 19
  preparation for democratic citizenship by schools, 67
  scholarly parochialism, 171–172
  school desegregation, 13
  see also Asian American attitudes
American dream, 4, 6
  and equal opportunity, 8
Aristotle, ix
Asian American attitudes, loyalty toward democracy, 43–44
Assimilationist ideology, xii

B

Benjamin, Harold, 151
Bilingual education, 17
Blunkett, David, 30
Brown v. Board of Education, 8
  see also School desegregation
Bruer, John T., 101

C

Catholic schools, 9
CDI (Civic Development Inventory) instrument, 107
Churchill, Winston, viii
Cicero, on world citizenship, 163
Citizenship education, see also Diversity/unity balance; Multinational curriculum development

Citizenship education/Seattle Public Schools–WW II study, 44
  contemporary concept of race, 52
  loyalty/democracy despite exclusion, 54–56
  progressive democratic citizenship tradition, 44–45
  providing context for students expression, 56–57
  response to Pearl Harbor bombing, 47–49
  Washington School, 49–53
  see also Successful Living
Civic discourse/classroom assessment, 231
  assessment task, 223
    abstract, 223–224
    directions, 224–225
    procedure, 225
    prompt, 224
    scoring rubric, 226, 226f
    scoring validity/reliability, 227–228
    standards, 228–231
  negative procedural criteria
    irrelevant distracting statements, 222
    monopolizing, 222–223
    obstructive interruption, 222
    personal attack, 223
  performance criteria, 212–214, 213f
    arguing by analogy, 220
    disciplinary knowledge application, 216
    statement elaboration (explanations/reasons/evidence), 216–218
    stating/identifying issues, 214–216, 215f
    stipulation of claims/definitions, 218–219
    values/values conflict recognition, 219
  positive procedural criteria
    acknowledging statements of others, 221
    challenging statements, 221
    inviting contributions from others, 220
    summarizing agreement/disagreement, 221–222
  rationale for oral discourse, 211–212
Civic Education study (IEA), xi, xiii, 63, 88–89, 186
  assessments, 85, 87–88
  Domain 1 data sources
    courses, 68–70
    experiences, 74–77
    perspectives, 71–74
    textbooks, 70–71
  Domain 2 data sources
    courses, 78
    perspectives, 79–80
    textbooks, 78–79
  Domain 3 data sources
    courses, 80–81
    perspectives, 81–83
    textbooks, 81
  Domain 4 data sources
    courses, 83–84
    experiences, 85
    perspectives, 84
    textbooks, 84
  domains of investigation, 64
    democracy/political institutions/citizens' rights and responsibilities (Domain 1), 67–68
    economic–political systems connections, 83
    national identity (Domain 2), 77–78
    social cohesion and diversity (Domain 3), 80
  instructional activities, 85–87
  in and out-of-school settings, 64
  overview, 187–188
  research methods, 65

individual interviews, 66
state survey, 65
student/school surveys, 67
student/teacher focus groups, 66
textbook analysis, 65–66
see also Adolescent beliefs about democracy survey study
Civil Liberties Act (1988), 57
Connected Knowledge, 101
Constitution, and teaching structures/functions of government, 35
Content-based civic education, 100–102
and *Project Citizen*, 105–106, 110
Cooper, Frank, 44
Counts, George S., 52
Crick, Bernard, 30
Cromer, Alan, 101

D

Democracy, xivn, 115
collective outcomes from schools, 6
common core of knowledge, 6–7
common core of values, 7
dealing with diversity, 7
providing equal opportunity, 8
teaching democratic practice, 7–8
see also Political tolerance
"Democratic education," 28
Dewey, John, 46
and issue-centered education, 95–96
and "reflective" thinking, 96–97
Diversity/unity balance, 131–132
and changes in citizenship education, 132–133
implications from research, 146
see also Social psychological theory
and cultural communities, 133–134
and effective citizenry, 136–137, 137f
and global identifications, 134–136
Dubois, Rachel Davis, 52

E

Education, 22n
American attitudes toward, 4, 11, 67
curriculum updating, 152
goals and practice interaction, 12
see also Groups/distinctive treatment of; School desegregation; School funding/equitable; Tracking impact on political tolerance, 118–119
literature and composition, 46–47
multiple goals, x
and commitment to democracy, 4, 6–8
key role in American dream, 4, 5–6
responding to claims of particular groups, 4–5, 8–10
practices to implement goals/values, 10–12
as social policy, 3
"social studies" and citizen preparation, 64, 93, 97, 99
see also Citizenship education/Seattle Public Schools–WW II study; Civic discourse/classroom assessment; Diversity/unity balance; Issue-centered education; Middle school education; Multinational curriculum development; Political education (United Kingdom); Political tolerance
Educational authority, and teaching democratic practices, 7–8
Educator goals, democratic citizens formation, ix, 93
Engle, Shirley H., 99
Evans, Ronald W., 99
Evanson, Ella, 45, 51, 58n

F

Franklin, Benjamin, 3, 6
Fundamentalist Christian education, 17

G

Globalization, xiiin, 175
   and curriculum relevance, 153–154
   global community citizenship, 132, 134–136
   theory vs. "global education" theory, 176
   see also Multinational curriculum development
Groups/distinctive treatment of, 4–5, 8–10
   evidence on outcomes, 18–19
   multicultural education, 16–17
   separation by needs, 17–18

H

Held, David, 175
Hertzberg, Hazel Whitman, 99
Hunt, Maurice, 99

I

IEA (International Association for the Evaluation of Educational Achievement), xi, 63, 209n
   see also Adolescent beliefs about democracy survey study; Civic Education study (IEA)
Individual attainment goal
   absolute success, 5
   competitive success, 6
   relative success, 5–6
   see also American Dream
Interpretive mode, 161–162
Issue-centered education, xi, 73, 94, 110
   arguments supporting, 99–100
   criticisms of, 100–102
   and Progressive reform movement, 95
   Socratic heritage, 95
   support by educators, 99
   see also Dewey, John; *Project Citizen*

J

Japanese Americans
   attitudes toward their citizenship, 44
   and Civil Liberties Act (1988), 57
   imprisonment during World War, II, 44
   see also Citizenship education/Seattle Public Schools–WW
Jefferson, Thomas, ix, 64
   "objects of primary education, " 10

K

Kilpatrick, William H., 52
King, Martin Luther Jr., vii

L

Liberal democracy, 3
   assumptions about, viii
      fragility of; viii-ix
      requirement for democrats, ix
   moral superiority, viii
Liberalism, xivn

M

Metcalf, Lawrence E., 99
Middle school education, and development of civic roles, 93
Mortensen, Martha, 48
Multidimensional citizenship, 162–164
Multinational curriculum development, xii, 177–178
   ancillary components, 170–171
   citizen characteristics, 159–160
   consensus trends, 157–159, 158t–159t
   deliberation basis of proposed curriculum, 165–166, 167–168, 173
   educational strategies, 160–161
   ethical considerations, 166–170
   limitations, 173–177
   multinational dimensions of proposed curriculum, 164–165
   purpose/method, 154

analysis and interpretation, 157
data, 154–157
vs. scholarly parochialism, 171–172
see also Globalization; *Multidimensional citizenship*

N

Newmann, Fred M., 99
Niemoeller, Martin, 116
Nisei *see* Japanese Americans

O

Ochoa, Anna S., 99
Oliver, Donald W., 99

P

Peddiwell, J. Abner, 151
Political education (United Kingdom)
anti-political culture, 36, 40–41
and oppositional values as "personal and social education," 38
origins in 1980s, 37–38
rejection of left-right axis, 37
"citizens" vs. "subjects," 32
concerns prompted by constitutional changes, 31–32
controversial topics, 34–35
impact on of obscurity of constitutional principles, 35
lack of consensus on "basic study," 34
lack of consensus on nature of politics, 27
Northern Irish concerns, 30
Promoting Social Competence report, 30
recent government (Labour) policy, 28–30
see also Blunkett, David; Crick, Bernard
scepticism about "teaching democracy," 33
Scottish curriculum, 30–31, 40
values education, x, 28, 39–40

Political tolerance, vii, 50, 113
in adolescents, 127
methods to increase, 123–127
research, 119–121
secondary schools survey, 121–123
education for, xi–xii
and classroom climate, 126–127
Tolerance for Diversity of Belief curriculum unit, 123–124
education as a predictor, 118–119
as a learned behavior, 121
obstacles to teaching, 113–114
reconceptualizations, 117, 118
relationship with democracy, 114–116
research on adults, 116–119
Pring, Richard, 28
Project Citizen, xi, 94, 109
challenges, 103–104
implementation/format, 104–105
suggested enhancements, 109–110
influence of *Report on the Social Studies in Secondary Education*, 98
international evaluation of, 106–107
CDI (Civic Development Inventory) instrument, 107
findings, 108–109
issue-centered program variation, 102, 105
purpose, 103
targeted users, 103

R

"Reflective" thinking, 96–97
Report on the Social Studies in Secondary Education, 97–98
Roosevelt, Franklin D., Executive Order, 9066, 44
Rugg, Harold, 52

S

The Saber-Tooth Curriculum, 151–152
School desegregation, 13–14

School funding, 20
   and competitive success issue, 6
   equitable, 15–16
Sears, Arthur G., 45, 48–49
   on racial tolerance, 52
Shaver, James P., 99
Social psychological theory
   categorization, 138–139
   contact hypothesis, 139–140
      cooperative learning and interracial contact, 140–141
      cross-cutting superordinate groups, 145
      curriculum interventions, 142–145
      implications for teaching/learning, 146
   minimal group paradigm/ social identity theory, 138, 139
   see also Diversity/unity balance and changes in citizenship education

Successful Living, 45–46
   role of composition, 46

T

Tate, Nick, 28
Tracking, 19–21

U

U.K. *see* Political education (United Kingdom)

V

Values education vs. citizenship education, x
   see also Political education (United Kingdom)
Vogt, Paul, 116
Voltaire, vii

W

Wolcott, Harry, 161